National Guide
to
Real Estate

National Guide

to

Real Estate

H. Glenn Mercer

Emeritus, San Francisco City College

Homer C. Davey

Foothill College

PRENTICE-HALL, INC., ENGLEWOOD CLIFFS, N.J.

PRENTICE-HALL SERIES IN REAL ESTATE

HD255
, M37
Copy 2

KBB

© 1972 by
PRENTICE-HALL, INC., Englewood Cliffs, N.J.

13–609263–2
Library of Congress Catalog Card No: 72–169086

Current printing (last digit):
10 9 8 7 6 5 4 3 2 1

PRENTICE-HALL INTERNATIONAL, INC. *London*
PRENTICE-HALL OF AUSTRALIA, PTY LTD., *Sydney*
PRENTICE-HALL OF CANADA, LTD., *Toronto*
PRENTICE-HALL OF INDIA PRIVATE LIMITED, *New Delhi*
PRENTICE-HALL OF JAPAN, INC., *Tokyo*

Printed in the United States of America

Preface

The *National Guide to Real Estate Principles* is an introductory text that presents basic real estate information. The material is organized to provide either the general reader or the beginning real estate student with the fundamentals of real property ownership and transfer, and to guide him toward further studies of real estate law, finance, appraisal, and economics.

The *National Guide* is written in a manner that both practitioner and layman can understand. It will serve as a handbook and guide for the professional real estate executive and as an aid to those who wish to pass a state real estate examination. The general reader will gain a working knowledge of real estate that will enable him to assume a more effective role as consumer or investor. Systematic study of the principles outlined in this text will enable the vocational student of real estate to succeed in his chosen occupation.

The text format follows the cycle of real property through purchase, ownership, and eventual resale. It includes a thorough analysis of real property contracts and other critical subject areas such as the Federal Consumer Protection Act, the Revenue Act of 1969, fair housing laws, financing, and creative financing.

The authors wish to acknowledge their indebtedness to Professor Daniel J. Page, supervisor of the real estate program at the University of Michigan; to Professor Karl G. Pearson, Director of Real Estate Education, University of Michigan; and to George W. Schueler of the Realty and Land Exchange Company, Wanamasso, New Jersey for their expert help in reviewing the *National Guide to Real Estate Principles*.

H. GLENN MERCER
HOMER C. DAVEY

Contents

National Guide
to
Real Estate

1

Introduction

The real estate business embraces a wide variety of fundamental services and offers an opportunity for both personal achievement and a sense of performing work of the highest importance for the community.

The activity of planning, creating, procuring, financing, appraising, and managing human shelter is a broad and complex vocation. Its scope and importance offer a variety of career opportunities and simultaneously open doors to substantial rewards. Besides food and clothing, our essential requirement is shelter. The real estate industry not only shelters the family units, but also provides for commercial and industrial enterprises. Despite the ups and downs of the business cycle, there is in such activity the stability that comes with performing a variety of essential services.

"Under all is the land."[1] Real estate is tangible and meaningful to everyone because it underlies nearly all phases of human endeavor and growth, and is closely allied with economics, law, accounting and finance. Because real estate is destined to play a major role in the future lives of all citizens, it is important to understand its part in the American economy.

Economic analysis

Economics, according to Webster's Dictionary, is ". . . the science that investigates the conditions and law as affecting the production, distribu-

---

[1]*Reference Book*, (Sacramento, Ca.: State of California, Department of Real Estate, 70 ed.) p. 35.

1

tion, and consumption of wealth or *the material means of satisfying human desires."* This definition is easy to apply to real estate when we realize that people have a desire to own real estate—a material thing—and will expend money to satisfy this human desire. Because the amount of money or economic goods a person will pay or exchange depends upon many factors, we must be aware of various economic and sociologic factors and the effect they have or will have on a given parcel of real estate. There are many forces—physical, economic, political, and social—constantly acting on all property to influence value; the effect of these forces can most logically be measured by making a study of the most dynamic.

NATIONAL ECONOMY

The state of the union is of paramount importance for the value of any private property. There will be few economically healthy regional, city, and neighborhood areas unless the United States economy as a whole is generally healthy. There can, however, sometimes be economically deprived regions within an otherwise vibrant, healthy national economy.

Of particular importance to real estate activity is the availability of money on a national level at reasonable interest rates. Most real estate ventures, whether they be the construction of homes, apartment houses, commercial shopping centers or industrial parks, rely heavily on the availability of low-cost financing. Since two-thirds of the wealth in the United States consists of real estate, and the largest single monetary investment that most American people make is a home, the importance of financing and its relationship to a healthy national economy is apparent.

A major control over the availability of money is the Federal Reserve Banking System, which was established by the Federal Reserve Act in 1913. The principal function of the Federal Reserve is to regulate the flow of both money and credit. The Federal Reserve Bank controls the available supply of money by setting the discount interest rate—the rate of interest that member banks must pay when they borrow from the Federal Reserve System. This discount rate, in turn, determines what interest rate the member banks charge borrowers, and the result is a loosening or a tightening of available funds throughout the country to forestall a recession or curb an inflation.

To be fully aware of the health of the national economy we must also ask, What is the availability of mortgage funds? Are we in a period of recession or inflation? What will be the short range future of the economy? These are but a few of the questions which are evaluated to help us make knowledgeable judgments of the influence of various national trends on real property values.

REGIONAL ECONOMY

A study of the regional economy is a second consideration in the economic analysis of a parcel of real property and of the availability of outside revenue. The value of all real estate in a particular region depends on certain factors.

The economic base of greatest importance is the *availability of steady jobs*. The impact of regional employment variations on property values cannot be overemphasized. This can best be illustrated by what has happened in many parts of the United States when a major employer in aeronautics, because of changeover to aerospace and missiles, laid off several thousand people at one time. The effect was almost disastrous on those employees who were forced to sell their homes to relocate in other areas. Many homeowners forced to sell took as much as 30 percent loss on their homes. The major reason the impact was so great was that this particular layoff represented a large proportion of the total regional work force.

The *increased mobility of people*, made possible by the extensive use of the automobile, the expanding job market, and the diversity of employment opportunities, has also played an important role in the establishment of local property values. People will now buy a home that may very well be 30 to 50 miles from their place of employment. The value of property is thus measured, in part, by good employment, adequate roads, desirable climate and similar factors. This is true not only of people interested in single family residential properties, but of those concerned with multiple residential, commercial, and industrial properties as well. An economic "mutual dependence" enters into this consideration. The developer of a large shopping center, for example, is very conscious of regional economic aspects of an area, since the success of his development will depend on the availability and attraction of large numbers of people with the ability to buy goods; these people will in turn locate most readily in a desirable area.

The major source of outside revenue rests with *basic industries*, that is, those industries that draw in money from outside the region, including automotive and aircraft manufacturing, electronics or computer equipment, aerospace development, or a thriving agricultural enterprise. These industries are all essential components of a healthy economic base of a region, and each region will, of course, vary in basic industries. Some areas rely almost entirely on an especially pleasant climate, or beautiful scenery, or the chance for visitors and residents to engage in their favorite sports to attract people willing to spend money; thus, these natural resources and conditions have become the *basic industries* of the area. They not only add to the desirable living conditions but also bring in wealth contributing to economic prosperity. Good examples of this type of regional natural resource attraction include the climate of Florida and California in the winter; ski areas, desert spas, and water resorts throughout the country; and forest and mountain areas in the West, Northwest and East. Whatever the attraction, the practitioner of real estate professions must be able to gauge the influence that these industries will have on regional property values.

Another value to a region is the proximity to many *institutions of higher learning*. Major universities within one hour's driving time and community colleges with their many community services available to area residents are a measurable plus value.

Politically, many separate jurisdictional seats of government in the area affect and reflect the type of community. All types of land may be used: minimum single-family residential lots or lots of one acre size. They are the result of a planned community and of *zoning regulations*—another important factor in maintaining property values. It is the responsibility of these area governments, within their jurisdictional control, to solve such regional problems as air or water pollution, treatment and disposal of waste, and preservation of natural resources.

To sum up, then, a thorough appraisal of the economic, physical and political makeup of the region is important to real estate value measurement. Regional factors include tangible social forces which also influence value measurement: the interrelationships of people and their attitudes toward one another. Elaboration of some of these social considerations will be made later in this chapter.

In review, an effective regional analysis should include the following considerations at least:

Physical or environmental considerations

1. Climate
2. Air and water pollution control
3. Adequacy of fresh water sources
4. Adequacy of waste disposal facilities
5. Existence and protection of natural scenic beauty
6. Adequacy of public transportation facilities
7. Availability of open spaces
8. Availability of utilities
9. Natural harbors or waterways
10. Adequacy of airports
11. Adequate noise abatement and control
12. Adequate freeways and roadways
13. Adequacy of commercial centers and shopping facilities
14. Availability of community centers and higher education

Political considerations

1. Adequacy of regional governmental controls
2. Adequacy of cooperation between government units in solving inter-city and interregional problems and concerns

Social concerns and considerations

1. Public attitudes toward law and order
2. Attitudes toward responsibilities of the individual
3. Attitudes toward and provision for welfare programs
4. Community improvement programs and schedules
5. Mixtures of the several racial, ethnic, cultural, social, economic and religious groups and philosophies into harmonious interrelationships

CITY ANALYSIS

The closer we move geographically to a parcel of real property, the more profound the effect of the reactive forces upon value within this smaller geographic area. As we go from regional analysis to city analysis, the physical size of the area of study is reduced to precise boundaries. We have reduced the study not only as to physical boundaries, but also as to the *economic* ranges, *social* attitudes, and in many cases political ideologies or philosophies. Often similar forces are acting upon city values and regional values, so some of the earlier considerations will be reapplied in our analysis of the city.

Physical and environmental considerations in a city analysis would include adequacy of waste disposal, of public transportation facilities, of playgrounds and parks, of public utilities, of flood control, of essential roads and highways and public works, of medical facilities, of educational institutions, of cultural centers and churches, of shopping centers and all types of housing.

In analyzing a city from an *economic* aspect, one must keep in mind that when cities were completely separate communities, job opportunities in a city were of primary importance. With the trend toward more urban and suburban development, cities and communities tend to overlap, with the result that people often live in one community and work in another. We, therefore, cannot consider *city* job opportunity without considering the region.

There are two additional basic economic considerations in a city analysis. These are (1) a sufficient tax base to provide necessary governmental services and (2) sufficient individual incomes to support the tax base and to maintain property values at a maximum.

Just as with a regional analysis, certain *political* considerations are necessary in city analysis. As cities enlarge and become more crowded and individual property rights become more important, a primary concern to a person seeking to buy a single-family residence is the proposed master plan of the city and the degree of control by the planning department in zoning matters. These two factors are of special importance as they impinge upon establishing and maintaining maximum values. Strict and effective zoning laws in construction and architectural standards may make a community known for its aesthetic appeal. Adequate governmental services in a city area are particularly important; we must evaluate how they complement or expand those services of other governmental units, such as the county and state. For a variety of valid reasons, the real estate consumers as well as practitioners are thoughtfully aware of the importance of a city council or board of aldermen responsive to the needs of the community.

Of immense and increasing importance in maintaining values of single-family residential real property are the *social* attitudes of the residents: (1) civic and community pride, (2) community improvement programs, (3) law, order and responsible citizenship and a respect for governmental agencies, and (4) the interrelationships between the several racial, ethnic, cultural, social, and economic groups that make up the area.

Civic pride, or its absence, is evident almost immediately to a stranger, since it shows in so many physical ways. The quality of construction and maintenance of homes, the existence of parks, playgrounds, and cultural or community centers are immediate indications. The design and care of streets is another, and the absence or abundance of landscaping throughout the city—including homes, office buildings, government buildings, schools, parks and streets—is still another.

NEIGHBORHOOD ANALYSIS

A further study in an economic analysis of single-family residential property must include an analysis of *adjacent properties* which surround and attend each other, exerting an influence on *values*. A single property cannot be separated from its neighborhood, for the value of all property is influenced not only by its own physical makeup but also by the physical, economic and social makeup of the property and residents of those properties which surround it. This is, obviously, more important in residential properties than in many other types; it would not necessarily be the case in real property from which oil or mineral deposits were to be extracted. In such cases the physical makeup of neighboring properties would have little or no influence providing proper access and legal authority could be acquired to extract the deposits.

A *neighborhood*, defined by Webster, is "a district or section, especially with reference to the condition or type of its inhabitants." When relating the word to a residential area we might say a neighborhood is a community in which homes exhibit a certain degree of homogeneity in their physical makeup and the occupants a certain degree of homogeneity in their social and economic composition. In earlier times people gathered together in small groups or communities for many reasons, principally for protection; usually these people had quite similar economic and social interests, and held similar political views and religious beliefs. Today the political and religious beliefs might be quite divergent, yet there are still homogeneous features, the most prominent being economic and social.

The neighborhood exerts a greater influence on the value of single family residential property than on multiple family property. A person might rent an apartment in a neighborhood in which he would not consider buying, or one with physical arrangements or construction not entirely to his liking, since it usually is a temporary residence, does not require a sizable down payment, and offers no problem of selling, should he desire to move. Those who plan to buy a home, on the other hand, buy with a view to permanence, and neighborhood is often a deciding factor in the purchase.

All improved real property experiences basic stages in its "life cycle" and contributes to what is known as *changing neighborhood complexion*. As it experiences its own youth, maturity and old age, a neighborhood in which homes are located is subject to change not only from wear and tear of physical construction, but also from the character and attitudes of the inhabitants. Many times as the years go by, families of lower socioeconomic level move into neighborhoods where once lived only families of high socio-economic status and ability. This is especially true in large urban areas, where often the succeeding families are larger than, and further down the economic scale from, the original families. In some areas, as the neighborhood reaches old age and decay, a new use for the land is generated by a more intensified demand for space, and the land is zoned for multiple residential units. Whenever change takes place, there must be an awareness of how the changes reflect upon the value of property.

It is important not to overlook the fact that a neighborhood partially reflects the attitudes of the residents and that, whatever the socioeconomic level of the people, value is influenced a great deal by these attitudes; for example, many neighborhoods of moderately-priced homes exhibit a high degree of pride in ownership, evidenced by care, maintenance and attitude, which serves to maintain maximum values within the neighborhood individually and collectively.

That which determines the *boundary* of a neighborhood is influenced by a variety of factors. Some residential neighborhoods are a square mile or more, while others may be only one or two blocks. At times it is major traffic ways, whether they be freeways or city streets, which determine the boundary of a neighborhood; at other times the boundaries will be such natural landfalls as streams, creekbeds, hills, or forested areas. Most often, however, the boundaries are simply a different quality or style of home and a different character of inhabitants. The boundaries which describe a neighborhood are not limited, of course, to physical, social, or economic determinants but might be established as a result of political subdivisions, school districts, or other government-imposed entities such as wards or precincts. Whatever the boundaries, they can usually be determined by the experienced and practiced real estate professional.

One purpose of these highlights of the impact of economic conditions and factors is to remind the reader that the present value, the future benefits, and an appraisal of the period over which a property can be expected to yield a return on investment can only be projected by a careful analysis of the economic factors which influence property values both now and in the future.

Career opportunities in real estate

A career in real estate offers many rewards for the right person. The real estate salesman or broker works with people as well as with property ownership and transfer. He has a great deal of freedom as he schedules his appointments; therefore, he must be able to organize his time for maximum benefit to his client and to himself.

The real estate salesman and broker handles a product that everyone needs, and, since everyone is a potential customer, a good living can be made in real estate. He must be willing to learn and to work hard. Most salesmen are not paid a fixed salary but work on a commission based on the actual sale and transfer of property. Success in this field depends upon talent and work, but hard work and application to the job can result in a higher income than is possible on a fixed salary.

The agent must learn a great deal about real estate before he can begin to work. To make sure that he is well trained, most states require that he pass a *real estate license test* before he may act as agent in real property transactions.

The opportunity to counsel with and provide a service to homeowners is important, as six out of ten persons own their own homes. The equity in his home and his life insurance may represent the entire estate of the individual. In order to serve the needs of these homeowners, the person in real estate should possess the following qualities:

1. He must be an energetic person who enjoys work.
2. He must be a person who is not interested in being chained to a desk.
3. He must be interested in studying and gaining knowledge of the community in which he is working.
4. He must be enthusiastic about his job.
5. He must have a knowledge of contracts, financing, and appraising of property value, and he must avail himself of every opportunity to know his product.
6. He must like people and enjoy helping them to solve their problems.

No other field of endeavor offers rewards commensurate with those of real estate in personal satisfaction and income potential. It should be pointed out that not all people have salesmanship abilities. The objective of education and training in this field is not limited to making property sales, and it is appropriate at this time to point out the areas of specialization possible in this complex industry. Another objective is the trend toward upgrading the real estate industry as a profession. Degree programs with majors in real estate have been introduced by some universities and colleges, and others include real estate courses as a part of the business administration program.

AREAS OF SPECIALIZATION

Areas of specialization include real estate brokerage, property management, appraisal, land development, industrial brokerage, mortgage lending, farm brokerage, investment counseling, and research.

Brokerage. The real estate brokerage business is concerned with the selling and leasing of property. A broker or salesman works on a commission basis. His activities include: (1) selling or offering to sell, (2) buying or offering to buy, (3) listing or soliciting for prospective purchasers, (4) negotiating the purchase, sale, or exchange of real property, (5) negotiating loans or soliciting borrowers for lenders, (6) leasing or offering to lease real property, (7) negotiating the sale, purchase, or exchange of a lease, (8) renting, placing for rent, or collecting rents, (9) selling, buying, and negotiating promissory notes and mortgages, and (10) assisting persons wishing to file and purchase, lease, or locate state or federal land.

A large segment of the brokerage firms deal in residential housing. Although his activities may be principally concerned with soliciting listings and selling homes, the broker should have a knowledge of available real estate financing, local zoning laws, and the highest and best use for property. He should also take every opportunity to serve the needs of his community.

Property Management. A professional property manager is a custodian of another's property. He normally earns 5 to 6 percent of the gross income from the property. The property manager (1) serves as an interpreter of financial statements, and (2) acts for the property owner in the management and maintenance of his property, whether it be single or multiple units, office buildings, industrial buildings, or commercial shopping centers.

The professional property manager devotes his entire time to the management of properties. He must be aware of current real estate trends in the community and economic conditions in the state and nation. He is an expert in the preparation of rental schedules and income and expense analyses for the buildings that he manages. He knows what the average expenses are for similar buildings in the nation, state, and community in which the property is located. Frequently, new real estate brokerage firms will include a property management department.

Appraisal. The professional real estate appraiser is valued for his opinion and judgment of the value of property. He is an expert in the appraisal of residential, commercial, industrial, and special purpose property. Members of the American Institute of Real Estate Appraisers (and those who are privileged to use the designation M.A.I.) are perhaps the most respected members of the real estate industry. The appraiser is looked to as an expert in condemnation proceedings. He may work on an hourly or fee basis.

Opportunities for employment in the appraisal field exist through savings and loan institutions, commercial banks, and through an apprenticeship with full-time appraisers.

Land Development. Land development is a highly specialized field. The developer is a creator of residential subdivisions, industrial parks, commercial shopping centers, and office complexes, among others.

The land developer must keep abreast of local, state and national economic trends and conditions. He will build and hold an inventory of land for as long as six months in advance of a large land development. The developer understands trends of community growth and zoning. A residential subdivision located in the wrong area within a community might mean disaster to the developer while creating a blight on the community itself.

Industrial Brokerage. The industrial broker is alert to community needs and objectives, and assists industry in locating in his community. He knows the assets of his community and has first-hand information on transportation facilities, schools, churches, the tax base of the community, and so on. The industrial developer may be a creator of industrial parks, a growing trend in many communities. He knows how to merchandise industrial property and present it attractively to the industrialist. He understands industrial financing and knows what money is available for smaller industries wishing to locate in the community.

Mortgage Lending. The mortgage lending phase of the industry offers opportunities for the young college student and others wishing to enter real estate. Opportunities exist as loan officers in savings and loan institutions, commercial banks, and mortgage banking firms. The loan officer will work on a salary or fee basis (perhaps one percent of the loan). The loan officer solicits and processes loans for borrowers. The mortgage banking firm may act as a loan correspondent for savings and loan institutions, commercial banks, insurance companies, mutual banking institutions, and so on.

The loan officer should be familiar with current money market conditions in the state, nation, and his community. He has a thorough knowledge of FHA-insured loans, Veterans Administration loans, and conventional loans. He is familiar with the mortgage money market and understands its relationship to other types of investments such as stocks, bonds, and mutual funds.

Farm Brokerage. Farm brokerage is indeed a specialized field. The successful farm broker is familiar with crops and soil conditions in the area in which he operates. He has a knowledge of farming methods and is familiar with farm equipment and other chattels which may be transferred with the sale of real property. He is aware of community growth trends and alert to changes in the highest and best use for the property of owners whom he represents.

Investment Counseling. The real estate investment counselor has wide experience in the investment field, and his education should include a bachelor's or master's degree. He should divorce himself from the usual real estate activities in order to provide the best possible impartial advice. The investment counselor usually works on a fee basis. Counselors are employed by buyers, sellers, investors, and developers in the field. The counselor may solve the problems of the investor by providing advice and counsel on the most opportune time to sell or lease property. The counselor's success will naturally depend on the success of the follow-through on his suggestions to his clientele. A counselor may make a feasibility study to advise a developer as to whether or not land is suitable for development. He may perform a service as an advisor to industry wishing to locate in the community.

Research. Many private concerns, universities, and colleges provide research facilities. Many graduate students at state colleges and universities may research valuable real estate projects.

2

The Nature of Real Estate

Before the student can understand the principles of real estate and prepare himself to enter one of the many phases of the real estate industry, it is necessary that he have a clear understanding of what "property" is and, more particularly, the distinctions between "real" and "personal" property.

Property may be defined as "the thing of which there may be ownership." There may be ownership of both real and personal property.

Real estate or real property

Real estate or real property consists of the following: (1) land; (2) anything affixed to the land; (3) that which is appurtenant to the land; and (4) that which is immovable by law.

"Land" is the solid material of the earth whether it be soil, rock, or other substance. The common law broadens this concept to include not only the surface of the land or earth but also the space beneath it to the very center of the earth and to the sky above.

In theory, since the owner of a parcel of land owns to the center of the earth, he ordinarily owns the minerals therein. If he sells his land, he sells not only the surface but the minerals, unless he specifically reserves them in the deed unto himself. We see that two ownerships may exist in real property: (1) the fee in the land itself, and (2) the fee in the mineral, oil and gas rights. The various estates and interests in land will be discussed in Chapter 3.

A few states—Kansas, Ohio, and Pennsylvania among others—called *ownership states*, permit absolute ownership of oil and gas. Other states, such as California and Louisiana, do not allow absolute ownership until reduced to personal possession. In these states, an owner of real property who also owns the mineral, oil, and gas rights, may drill for same providing he has not conveyed them to another. He must, however, drill straight down on his property and not slant drill on the land of his neighbor.

Water rights have also been the subject of litigation in many states. While the law may vary in different states, the doctrines set forth in the following paragraphs will usually apply:

Percolating water, underground water not confined to any well-known channel or bed beneath the surface of the earth, is governed by the doctrine of correlative user: The owner of land has a right in common with other adjoining land owners to use his fair share, but he must not waste the water.

Water beneath the surface of the earth confined to a well-known channel or stream is governed substantially by the same rules of law which are applied to surface streams and lakes. The owner of property whose land adjoins a lake or outer courses on the surface of the land enjoys what are known as *riparian rights* to the use of the water. Riparian rights mean that he has no absolute ownership of the waters, but has a right in common with adjoining landowners to a fair share of the water. Owners of property on a navigable stream own to the low water mark of the stream. An owner whose property adjoins a nonnavigable stream owns to the center of the stream. The boundary of an owner's land on a seacoast is the high water mark.

Flood waters are considered a common enemy. The owner may use any reasonable means to keep them off his land and run them to somebody else's property.

Property owners who own land not abutting on a watercourse or stream may usually arrange to bring water to their property by applying to the State Water Commission in the state in which the property is located or to a similar state commission.

Anything attached or affixed to the land may be regarded as a part of the land itself. A legal description may describe only a ten-acre parcel of land, and yet include all buildings, fences, and other pieces of permanently attached property on the land. For example, a building on a foundation is real property. If rollers are placed beneath the building and it is moved off the foundation, it becomes personal property. Fence posts and fences may be considered as personal property. Once the fence posts are placed in the ground, and fencing on the posts, they become real property.

Property is *affixed* to land when it is attached by roots as in the case of trees, vines, or shrubs, embedded in it as in the case of walls, permanently resting upon it as in the case of buildings, or permanently attached to what is thus permanent by means of cement, plaster, nails, bolts, or screws.

The courts have used five general tests to determine whether a piece of property is a fixture and should be considered real property:

1. The intention of the person affixing the personal property to the land
2. The method used in affixing the personal property
3. The adaptability of the personal property so attached for ordinary use in connection with the land
4. The existence of an agreement between the parties
5. The relationship between the parties involved

Who gets a fixture if it is not mentioned in the deed? While courts have not been in full agreement, between buyer and seller the buyer is usually given the benefit of the doubt. Between landlord and tenant the tenant is usually given the benefit of the doubt.

Trade fixtures, fixtures used in conducting a business, are considered an exception to the rule. If a tenant installs trade fixtures for use in his business, he may remove them from the premises providing the property is returned in the same condition in which he found it, normal wear and tear excepted.

That which is incidental or appurtenant to the land may be considered real property. Exceptions to this rule include industrial growing crops and things attached to or forming a part of the land which are to be severed under the contract of sale. The disposal of such goods will be governed by the provisions of the U.S. Uniform Commercial Code in absence of a state statute.

Personal property

Anything that is not real property is considered *personal property.* Personal property is movable. Items of tangible property (called *choses in possession,* also *chattels*) include clothing, furniture, automobiles, and so on. Items of intangible personal property (called *choses in action*) include stocks, bonds, contracts, and trust deeds.

Contracts are personal property. A lease is a contract to use the land of another and is a personal interest therein. In real estate a lease is called a *chattel real.*

Other distinctions should be made between real and personal property. All contracts dealing with sales of real property must normally be in writing and signed by the party whose title is charged. Sales of personal property, however, need not be in writing if the price is less than $500, although they should be. The acquisition and transfer of land is governed exclusively by the laws of the state in which the property is located, and some personal contracts may also be recorded. Personal property is governed by the laws of the state of the domicile of the individual owner. Tax laws between real and personal property have significant differences. The real estate broker and investor should consult his CPA concerning tax regulations and laws. Personal property when sold is transferred by sale using a bill of sale. Real property is transferred by a conveyance, commonly called a *deed*.

Methods of land description

Every parcel of land sold, mortgaged, or leased must be properly described or identified. Legal descriptions are usually based upon the field notes of a civil engineer or a surveyor. When dealing with property, such legal descriptions can usually be obtained from tax receipts, title insurance policies, abstracts, deeds, or mortgages. The real estate broker or salesman should exercise care when writing such a description.

Real estate may be described by three general methods: (1) metes and bounds; (2) U.S. Government section and township system; and (3) recorded tracts, maps, or lot and block systems. A combination of these three may be used in some descriptions.

METES AND BOUNDS DESCRIPTIONS

Metes and bounds mean measurements and boundaries. Older descriptions include references to objects such as sycamore trees, stones, rivers, farms, and other markers which over the years may have been erased. Such an older description may have referred to the southerly line of the "White Farm."

Metes and bounds descriptions are further complicated in that they include angles and measured distances from stakes or other objects which are not always permanent. They further include language not common to most students of real estate, and can only be understood by the civil engineer or surveyor.

U.S. GOVERNMENT SECTION AND TOWNSHIP SYSTEM

The United States Surveyor General has jurisdiction over the surveys of all public lands in the United States. Base lines and meridians have been established throughout the country with descriptive names in order to locate and describe lands. From these base lines and meridians we may accurately describe property. A map showing all of the principal base lines and meridians appears on the next two pages.

PRINCIPAL MERIDIANS
OF RECTANGULAR

16

OF THE FEDERAL SYSTEM
SURVEYS

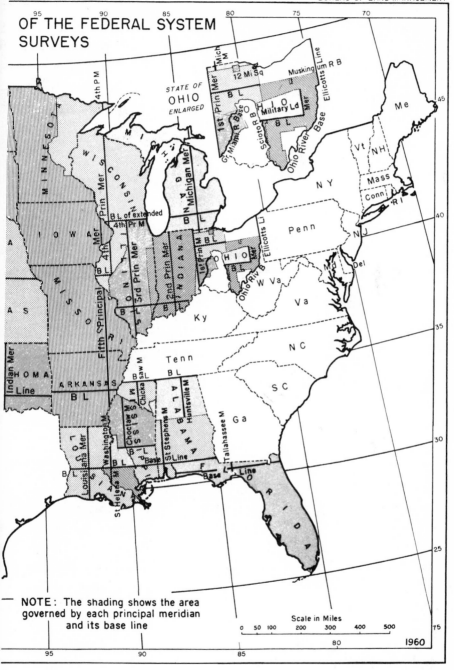

STATE OF
OHIO
ENLARGED

NOTE: The shading shows the area
governed by each principal meridian
and its base line

Scale in Miles

0 50 100   200   300   400   500

1960

17

Meridians which run north and south are divided into lines six miles apart called "ranges"; those which run east and west into lines, also six miles apart, called "townships." The areas or squares between the intersections of these ranges and townships are called "townships." A township is six miles square and contains 36 sections and 36 square miles. A township plat showing the numbering of the 36 sections is shown in Fig. 1.

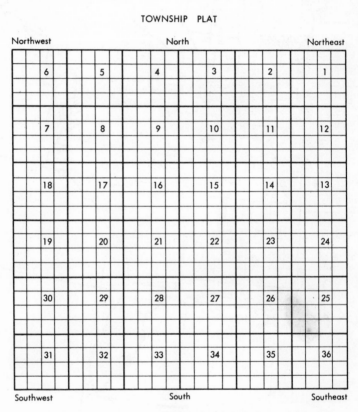

TOWNSHIP PLAT

Northwest   North   Northeast

6	5	4	3	2	1
7	8	9	10	11	12
18	17	16	15	14	13
19	20	21	22	23	24
30	29	28	27	26	25
31	32	33	34	35	36

Southwest   South   Southeast

Figure 1

A section may be further divided, for a more particular and specific legal description, into quarter-sections and fractional parts of quarter-sections.

In the examples that follow, trace the legal description in Figs. 2 and 3.

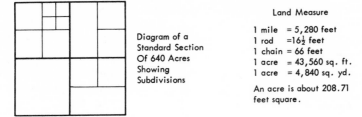

Diagram of a
Standard Section
Of 640 Acres
Showing
Subdivisions

Land Measure

1 mile = 5,280 feet
1 rod   =16½ feet
1 chain = 66 feet
1 acre = 43,560 sq. ft.
1 acre = 4,840 sq. yd.

An acre is about 208.71
feet square.

Figure 2

1. The NW¼ of section 4. Since this is ¼ of a section that contains 640 acres, this description contains 160 acres.

2. Starting at the NW corner of section 17; thence in a southeasterly direction to the southeast corner of the NE¼; thence in a southeasterly direction to the southeast corner of the SW¼ of the SW¼ of section 16; thence due west to the SW corner of section 17; thence back to the point of beginning (520 acres).

3. The E½ of the NE¼ and the N½ of the SE¼ of section 15; the W½ of the W½, the SE¼ of the NW¼, the SW¼ of the NE¼, the NW¼ of the SE¼, and the NE¼ of the SW¼ of section 14 (480 acres).

4. The NW¼ excepting therefrom the NW¼, the NE¼ and the SE¼ excepting therefrom the SW¼ of section 29 (400 acres).

A land description is read backwards. In 1, note that we first find the section and then go to the NW¼ of that section.

In 2, we start with the first semicolon or section 17, locating the northwest corner. Starting with the next semicolon, we find the NE¼, take the SE corner of the portion of the section, and draw a line connecting the two points. The next semicolon starts with section 16, in which we locate the SW¼, and again the SW¼ of the portion, putting a dot at the SE corner. In the next portion of the description, we again locate section 17, place a dot at the SW corner, and draw a line between the two points. Now proceed to the point of beginning.

In practice, however, such description would include the township and range numbers, such as:

The E½ of the NE¼ of the SW + pf section 36 TIN, R2 E, 3rd principal baseline and meridian.

The baseline and meridian are the location, the section number, and then the appropriate part of that section.

LOT, BLOCK, AND TRACT DESCRIPTION

Subdivisions are discussed in Chapter 19. When a developer subdivides property, a subdivision map must be filed with the appropriate govern-

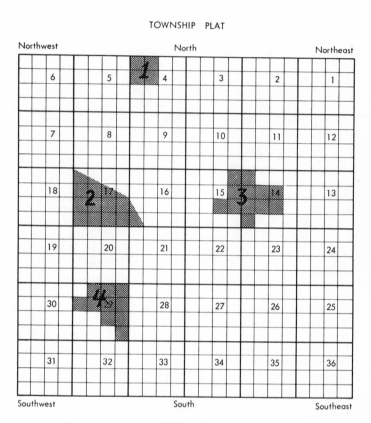

Figure 3

ment agency. Once this map is recorded, all future conveyances of lots may refer to this map. Such a description might state: Lot 4, Block 10, tract 1245 as per maps recorded November 5, 1969, page 75, Book 123, Official Records, County of Lyon, City of Emporia, State of Kansas.

Review questions

1. Define real property and personal property. Why is the distinction of such importance?
2. The courts have used five general tests to determine whether a piece of property is a fixture and should be considered real property. What are these tests? Which party would the law favor in the following situations? (a) Vendee or vendor? (b) Tenant or landlord? (c) Mortgagor or mortgagee?

TOWNSHIP PLAT

Northwest		North			Northeast
6	5	4	3	2	1
7	8	9	10	11	12
18	17	16	15	14	13
19	20	21	22	23	24
30	29	28	27	26	25
31	32	33	34	35	36
Southwest		South			Southeast

Figure 4

3. On the following township plat, shade in the following legal description: (A proper description must include a baseline and meridian.) The North ½ of the Northwest ¼ of Section 22, Township 2 North, Range 3 West; How many acres is it?
4. Define the following: (a) riparian rights, (b) doctrine of correlative user, (c) appurtenant to the land.
5. Distinguish between *choses in action* and *choses in possession*.

Multiple-choice questions

1. Base lines run: (a) east and west, (b) north and south, (c) south and west, (d) north and east, (e) not at all.
2. Which of the following would have no bearing on whether an item is considered personal property? (a) the relationship between the two people involved in a dispute, (b) the manner of attachment or whether the item is a

"fixture", (c) any agreement between buyer and seller concerning the item, (d) the cost of the item, (e) the adaptability of the personal property so attached.

3. A riparian owner: (a) possesses all water adjacent to his property, (b) would have his rights protected by the public record, (c) could always be identified by a search of the public record, (d) all of the foregoing, (e) none of the foregoing.

4. An item of personal property may be called: (a) a tenure, (b) a chattel, (c) a *chose in action*, (d) all of the foregoing, (e) none of the foregoing.

5. Personal property is: (a) immovable, (b) appurtenant, (c) anything affixed to the land, (d) other than real property, (e) none of the foregoing.

6. A township is: (a) one square mile, (b) six miles square, (c) one mile square, (d) six square miles, (e) none of the foregoing.

7. A Texas resident who owned real property in Florida died. His heirs go to court. Who would have jurisdiction over the probate, as far as the real property is concerned? (a) Texas, (b) Florida, (c) the District of Columbia, (d) the Federal Courts, (e) the widow.

8. One-fourth of one-fourth of a section of land contains how many acres? (a) 320, (b) 160, (c) 40, (d) 640, (e) 180.

9. Which of the following would best describe real property? (a) fixtures and buildings, (b) buildings, appurtenances, and fixtures; (c) fixtures and appurtenances, (d) land, fixtures, and appurtenances; (e) none of the foregoing.

10. Sales of personal property need not be in writing if the price is: (a) less than $500, (b) more than $500, (c) $500 and upwards, (d) less than $1,000, (e) more than $50.

3
Ownership and Classification of Property Rights

All land has an owner, whether it is an individual, a state, or the federal government.

The right to own property is the right to use and possess it to the exclusion of others. Bowman describes the ownership of property as a "bundle of rights." This "bundle of rights," he states, "is the exclusive right of a person to own, possess, use, enjoy, and dispose of a determinate thing, either real property or personal property, consistent with the law."[1]

Estates

Ownership and tenancy interests may be divided into two major classifications of estates:

1. Freehold estates which are not fixed or ascertained for a specified period of time
2. Less-than-freehold estates, which are for a fixed period of time

FREEHOLD ESTATES

Freehold estates are classified into two major categories:

1. Estates in fee, or fee simple (also known as estates of inheritance or perpetual estates)
2. Life estates

---

[1] Arthur G. Bowman, *Real Estate Law in California*, 3rd ed. (Englewood Cliffs, N.J., Prentice-Hall, Inc., 1970), pp. 22 and 23.

An *estate in fee* or a *fee simple estate* is the largest estate known to our law. It does not matter that there are one, two, or even three mortgages against the property, as mortgages are only liens. An estate in fee is for an indefinite period of time, and the owner may dispose of it during his lifetime or he may will the property. If the owner dies without a will, the laws of intestate succession will provide for the disposition of the property. The presumption in our law is that a fee simple estate is being conveyed in every grant of real property unless the grant indicates a lesser estate was intended.

Estates in fee may be either absolute or qualified. An absolute fee simple estate is one without any qualifications or restrictions. A qualified estate, on the other hand, is one that carries a condition or a limitation. For example, Alice's parents grant her all of their real property as long as she does not marry until she is 21 years of age. Should she marry before she is 21, the estate may revert to the original grantors. As another example, suppose a condition is put on the property that no cattle shall be brought upon it during the first ten years after the grant is made. The grantee brings cattle, in fact, five years after date of purchase. Under such conditions, the property may revert to the original grantors. Such reversions to the grantor are not necessarily automatic and a quiet title action in court may be necessary to reestablish the grantor's title to the property. A *fee simple qualified estate* may also be called a *fee simple determinable*.

An *estate on condition* may be a *condition precedent* or a *condition subsequent*. An *estate on condition precedent* is one that will commence upon the happening of a certain contingency. An *estate on condition subsequent* is one that will terminate upon the happening of a certain contingency.

The second major classification of freehold estates is that of a life estate, technically known as a life estate *pur autre vie*. Suppose that Adam and Barbara, husband and wife, wish to give their property to their daughter Carol during their lifetime, yet would like to reserve the right to live on the property until their deaths. They can grant Carol their real property, reserving for themselves a life estate, and may place any restrictions they wish against the property. The grant of the life estate may provide that Carol shall not marry until the age of 21. If Carol should marry before she is 21, the life estate would be terminated and legal title to the property would revert to Adam and Barbara. If Carol were to attempt to sell the property, the life estate would immediately terminate and the fee simple title would revert to Adam and Barbara.

Suppose Jane, a daughter, grants to her mother and father a life estate in her home. Since the life estate reads "for the lives of Adam and

Barbara," should Adam die, Barbara would still have a life estate in the property. If Barbara should then die, Jane would again obtain title to the property as a remainderman or woman, unless otherwise stated. Donald, (the husband), may create a life estate for the lives of Adam and Barbara, and upon the deaths of Adam and Barbara, the property would go to Jane, Jane also having a life estate. Upon the death of Jane, the property will revert to Donald or to his heirs. This would be referred to as a *reversion in fee.*

LESS-THAN-FREEHOLD ESTATE

The second major classification of estates is that of less-than-freehold estates. Less-than-freehold estates consist of four main categories:

1. Estates for years
2. Estates from period to period
3. Estates at will
4. Estates at sufferance

Such estates are sometimes referred to as *leasehold estates.*

An *estate for years* is for a definite period of time, fixed in advance by agreement by the lessor and lessee or landlord and tenant. The time fixed may be for six months, one year, or two years.

An *estate from period to period* is one which continues from one period to another period, as designated by the lessor and lessee in their agreement. For example, it may be from month to month, from quarter to quarter, or from year to year.

An *estate at will* is one that may be terminated at the will of either the lessor or lessee. By statute in some states, either party must give the other notice, usually 30 days.

An *estate at sufferance* is one in which the lessee, who rightfully has possession of the land, retains possession after the expiration of his term of lease. He is there, as the name implies, at sufferance of the landlord.

Methods of acquisition of real property

There are five principal ways in which a person may acquire title to property:

1. Will
2. Succession
3. Accession
4. Occupancy
5. Transfer

OWNERSHIP ACQUIRED BY WILL

A person may acquire property by will. Property acquired by will is dependent upon death. A deed cannot be used in place of a will with instructions for a third party to deliver it to the grantee upon death, because it will be void and lack proper delivery. For example, Adam draws a grant deed in favor of Brown. He gives instructions to Cole to deliver the grant deed to Brown upon his death. Such a deed would be void because it lacks proper delivery. Also, deeds are void where a husband and wife execute a deed of their separate property in favor of the other with instructions to the other to record upon the death of either. There has been no valid delivery in this case and, hence, no transfer of title. In each of the above cases, the property should have been disposed of by will. The intention to transfer title must be present.

Three types of wills are generally recognized:

1. Formal or witness will
2. Holographic will
3. Noncupative will

A *formal or witness* will is a will made by a licensed attorney. Usually two witnesses are required for validity of such a will. A person moving from one state to another should take care to see that his will conforms to the statutes of that state. Furthermore, all wills should be reviewed by legal counsel periodically. When an amendment to a will is made a codicil is used and executed in the same way as the will.

A *holographic will* is one written entirely in the testator's handwriting. It is written, dated, and signed by him, and no witnesses are required. An inherent danger may exist in the holographic will, however, in case the heirs should question the soundness of mind of the testator.

A *noncupative will* requires no writing or formalities, but can only be made in anticipation of death under special circumstances. Such a will is rarely used. For example, Adam is hit by an automobile on the freeway; thinking that he is dying, Adam gives his last will and testament orally to Brown and Cole. If Adam dies, such a will is a noncupative will, and may be given and witnessed by Brown and Cole. Should Adam, however, go into the hospital and live, but die one month later, such a will would not be good, because it would not then be in contemplation of death. Statutes of the various states should be checked. Such a will usually has limited use. In California, for example, it is limited to personal property not to exceed $1,000. It must be reduced to writing by the witness within 30 days and offered for probate within six months.

The male named by a decedent in his will to carry out the provisions of the will is called the *executor*, and the woman is the *executrix*, When the decedent dies intestate, the court takes charge of the estate and appoints an administrator or administratrix.

PROPERTY ACQUIRED BY SUCCESSION

If a person dies intestate (without leaving a will), the probate code of each state will provide for the disposition of his property upon death. This is called *intestate succession*. Such probate laws are definite regarding the rights of next of kin.

PROPERTY ACQUIRED BY ACCESSION

Accession, meaning addition to, may come in *three* ways. First, accession may be by accretion (the increase or expansion of land by action of natural forces such as a river). Accretion may occur by *alluvion*, where the soil and the sand are washed upon the banks of a river to form firm ground, or by *reliction*, where the river, lake, or sea recedes permanently below the water mark.

Second, accession of property may be by *avulsion*, when part of the bank of a river or stream is carried away by some sudden violence to another part of the same river bank. The owner of property so carried away may reclaim it within one year after the new owner takes possession of it in most states.

Third, property may be acquired through the addition of *fixtures*. Fixtures added become a part of the real property itself. Improvements need not, however, become a part of the real property. Generally, the law will not permit a person to take advantage of another in such a case. Law may permit a person who affixed improvements to the land of another in "good faith," believing the land to be his, to remove such improvements. The owner of such improvements must, however, put the property of the real owner back in its original condition or pay damages.

PROPERTY ACQUIRED BY OCCUPANCY

If a lessee abandons his lease, the landlord may take possession and exercise full control of the premises. Leases will be discussed in Chapter 9.

Property acquired by *occupancy through adverse possession* is defined as the gaining of ownership of another person's property against his will. Five requirements must be present to acquire such title:

1. The possession must be actual occupancy, open and notorious.
2. It must be hostile to the true owner's title.
3. It must be under a claim of right or color of title.
4. The possession must be continuous and uninterrupted for a period of five years.
5. The claimant must have paid all real property taxes assessed on the property for five years continuously.

Possession of all the land claimed need not be actual if it is sufficient to constitute "constructive possession"; neither must occupation be by the adverse claimant himself. The claimant may rent or lease a portion or all of the land so claimed to another. This is referred to as "tacking on."

There are certain limitations on the doctrine of adverse possession. An owner under disability, such as a minor or an insane person, is protected under most state statutes. Federal and state-owned lands are also protected against such claims.

Easements may be obtained in a similar manner by prescription. An *easement by prescription* is one that is acquired through the right to use another's land against his will. All of the requirements for adverse possession must be present except the last, the assessment and payment of taxes. To prevent such a right from being obtained by another, the owner should block any pathway over his property for at least 48 hours during any one calendar year.

PROPERTY ACQUIRED BY TRANSFER

This is the usual method known by grantors and grantees through the sale of property. Deeds will be discussed in Chapter 10.

Real property classified as to title

As stated earlier in the chapter, all property is owned. That which is not owned by the state or the federal government is owned by the individual. Ownership is classified in several different ways.

SEVERALTY OWNERSHIP

A person may own property in severalty, or have separate ownership in real property, simply by owning it himself. Only his signature is required under such circumstances for a transfer. A husband and wife may keep separate property during marriage.

TENANCY IN COMMON

Property may be owned under a *tenancy in common*. A person owns property as a tenant in common if he owns an undivided interest with others in the same property. Such tenants need not take title of property at the same time. For example, Adam, Brown, Cole, and Donald own property as tenants in common. Brown sells his interest in the property to Smith. Smith now becomes a tenant in common with Adam, Cole, and Donald. Assume that Adam dies. His property, in the event that he died intestate, will go to his heirs. Adam, however, may will his property if this is his desire, and the heirs of Adam will become tenants in common with the other tenants.

All tenants in common have a right to share in the profits of the property, and all must share in the necessary expenditures on the property. Such sharing will usually be in proportion to their investment; however, if proportions are not stated, all will share equally. In case each invested $10,000 originally, each will share proportionally. However, if Adam invested $5,000, Brown invested $10,000, Cole invested $15,000, and Donald invested $20,000, Adam must pay one-tenth of the expenses, and by the same token is entitled to receive one-tenth of the profits. Brown is entitled to one-fifth of the profits, and so on.

All tenants in common have an equal right to possession of property. Assume that Adam, Brown, and Cole exclude Donald from possession of the property. Donald's right, if he cannot regain possession peaceably, is secured through a partition action in which he asks the court to partition the property. In the event that such a partition is not practicable, the court may force a sale of such property, in which case the proceeds of the property will be equally or proportionally divided among the tenants in common.

JOINT TENANCY

Property held in joint tenancy by more than one person requires that all owners are joint, equal, and of undivided interest in specified real or personal property. Four unities must be present: unity of interest, unity of title, unity of time, and unity of possession. Thus, under a joint tenancy, owners have an equal interest, have the same quality of title, take title at the same time, and have an equal right to possession.

There must be an intent on the part of the parties to create a joint tenancy. That is, the grant must read "as joint tenants" or "in joint tenancy" (for example, "Adam and his wife Barbara, joint tenants"). In

California, owners may redeed property to themselves, thus creating a joint tenancy.

Joint tenancy carries the right of survivorship, which is the principal reason for its creation. For example: Adam, Brown, and Cole own property "as joint tenants." Adam dies, and the title now vests in Brown and Cole. When Brown dies, Cole owns the property in severalty. The survivors further take the property free of all debts of the deceased joint tenant unless liens have been placed against the property prior to the joint tenant's death. For example, Adam's creditors move against Adam as one of the above joint tenants, but, before a lien is filed and an attachment levied, Adam dies. The survivors take the property free of such liens.

A joint tenant may sell his interest in the joint tenancy. In the above illustration, assume that Adam sells his interest in the joint tenancy to Smith. Smith now becomes a tenant in common with Brown and Cole; however, Brown and Cole are, and may remain, joint tenants.

In some other states, community property laws exist. Basically, community property consists of all the property acquired by the husband and wife during a valid marriage.

The husband has management of the community real and personal property if he exercises it, but the wife has practically equal rights otherwise. The husband and wife must join together in the conveyance of community real property. The husband, however, may lease community property for a year or less without the consent of the wife.

Each spouse may will his half of the community property. If one fails to do so, and dies intestate succession, such property will go to the surviving spouse.

Community property is liable for the debts of the husband, whether the debts were contracted as a part of the community real property or not. The wife's earnings are not liable for the debts of the husband, unless contracted by the husband for the necessities of life or for the necessities of the wife while they are living together. The earnings of the husband after marriage may not be liable for the debts of his wife before their marriage, but the other community property may be liable.

When the husband turns over the management of community real and personal property to the wife, he may be estopped to deny otherwise in future litigation.

If either the husband or wife had property before marriage, it may remain their *separate property* and each may dispose of it as he or she wishes.

Both husband and wife may inherit property or receive it as a gift, and it may remain their separate property. It should be pointed out that all rents, issues, and profits of such property, where commingled with community funds, may become community property.

If separate property is sold by one of the spouses, and the profits are used to buy new property, such property may still remain separate. For example, the husband owned an apartment house before marriage, on which he maintained separate records of all income and expense. If he sells the apartment house and buys securities with the profits, these securities may still be separate property. A portion of property may be both community and separate property. When the husband owns an apartment house before marriage and after marriage uses community funds to make payments on this property, the ownership of the portion after marriage will be considered community property, while the portion obtained before marriage remains separate property.

Community property laws favor the wife where separate property is concerned. The *burden of proof* is always with the husband to prove that the property in the wife's name is not her separate property; the point of proof still rests with the husband to prove that property in his name is not community property. When community funds are used to purchase property and title is taken in the wife's name alone, the law presumes a gift of such property on the part of the husband to his spouse.

Tenants in partnerships

A *partnership* is an association of two or more individuals joined together as co-owners to operate a business for profit. These partners own such property as tenants in partnership. All partners must join in the conveyance of property. Unless otherwise agreed, all partners share equally in the profits and expenses of business operations. This may be true even though their investments are not equal. The articles of partnership should state how the partners are to share the profits and expenses.

Each partner has an equal right to possession of property while it is in the name of the partnership. If a partner dies, his interest in the partnership will pass to the surviving partners. The heirs do have a right in the partnership interest as such, but not in specific property. The partnership property cannot be seized or sold to pay the debts of a partner's individual creditors, but his share of the profits may be obtained.

Recording and constructive notices

All states have adopted a *recording system* which will more fully inform those purchasing or investing in real property of the ownerships and conditions of title. A system of recording was started with the American colonies.

The basic purpose of a recording system is to protect against secret conveyances of land and to provide a system whereby parties might be informed of the conditions of title by inspection of the records. The reader should remember that, under this system, recording is allowed but not usually required.

Generally an *instrument* may be recorded after it has been properly acknowledged or verified. An instrument affecting title to real property is recorded in the county in which the property is situated. Where property lies in more than one county, it should be recorded in both counties. When an instrument is properly recorded, it gives constructive notice to all purchasers or encumbrancers of the conveyance of the property. All persons are deemed to have knowledge of everything existing on the county records; therefore, anyone dealing with property for which an instrument has been recorded would have notice. This would be true even if he had not availed himself of the opportunity to inspect the records and had no actual notice of the conveyance.

A distinction should be made at this time between *constructive notice*, which is imputed by law, and *actual notice*, which consists of express information of fact. Thus, if a person records a valid instrument or document with the county recorder, constructive notice is given. For actual notice, he must go to the individual concerned and give such notice.

Recordation of an instrument does not necessarily validate it. It may be void or ineffective before such recording. Examples of such instruments would be undelivered deeds or forgotten instruments.

Let us examine the effect of recording by means of an example. Adam, the owner of a parcel of land, conveys it to Brown by a deed. Brown, trusting Adam and not wishing to go to a great deal of work, accepts the grant deed but fails to record it with the county recorder. Adam, an unscrupulous individual, resells the same parcel of land to Cole. Cole, having no knowledge of the prior conveyance, records his deed in the county in which the property is situated. Cole's deed will prevail over the deed of Brown. Brown will now have to look to Adam for damages suffered. Had Cole knowledge of the prior conveyance, then Brown's deed would prevail, because if the person receiving the second conveyance has any knowledge whatsoever of a prior conveyance, his title will not stand, though recorded.

When an instrument has been deposited with the county recorder and properly acknowledged, it is marked "filed for record" and at this time it is deemed recorded. When a deed is filed, it is cross-indexed under the names of both grantor and grantee; therefore, anyone who knows one of these names may learn the other by inspecting the records.

What instruments are entitled to be recorded? All instruments other than those not authorized by law may be recorded; therefore, if an instrument is not authorized by law and it is recorded by mistake, no constructive notice to third parties is given. The student of law should consult the state statutes as to the instruments that may or may not be recorded.

All instruments, documents, or judgments affecting the title to real property may be recorded. Such documents would include mortgages, deeds of trust, contracts of sale, leases, and written agreements between property owners. Certain documents must be recorded if they are to be effective. These include a verification of a power of attorney where it is to convey or execute instruments that affect community property, declaration of homestead, and declarations of abandonment of homestead. Involuntary liens such as mechanic's liens or judgment liens will not be effective until they are recorded, but a mechanic's lien will date back to the start of the project as long as it is recorded within the time period prescribed by statute.

It is to be remembered that recording protects a bona fide purchaser or an encumbrancer, but a personal investigation of the property should be made to determine what unrecorded interests exist. For example, unrecorded interests in properties might include a contract of sale or a lease. Assume that Adam sells his property to Brown under a contract of sale and that contract of sale is not recorded. Adam, holding the legal title to the property, may sell his fee in the property subject to the existing contract of sale, which is an unrecorded instrument. If Adam now sells the fee title to Cole, Cole must then respect the rights of Brown in the property, and when Brown has discharged the conditions of his contract, Cole will be compelled to convey the property to Brown.

Other unrecorded instruments affecting the title to property might include an easement, a sewer line, a fence, or a wall. In modern financing and second deeds of trust or developments, "subordination agreements" are sometimes used. Under such agreements, some persons waive their rights in favor of others. For example, such instruments are in purchase money deeds of trust. Thus, when Adam sells his 60 acres of land and agrees to subordinate it to Brown, a developer, for the construction of single family residences, it amounts to nothing more than a second mortgage. Brown, because of the subordination agreement, may now negotiate for a first mortgage in order to develop the property.

Buying and selling your home

    I. How to Buy a Home

        A. First, decide what you can pay. Everyone who starts acquiring property reads the want ads. It should be remembered that most of the ads carry "puffed up" information.

            1. How much cash can you put in? Your broker or salesman will leave this financing situation up to you, but you should al-

ways leave enough cash in the reserve. "If you buy in inspiration, you pay in perspiration, and sell in desperation."

2. What monthly payments can you soundly afford? Schedule of payment books are available at the bank and are helpful in telling you what your principal and interest payments will be on the loan amount for a given time.

3. Consult with the mortgage loan manager of your nearest financial institution. In every institution there are people who will tell you about loans that can be obtained. You should always inquire about taxes in an area before you decide to look there. The timing of buying your home is important in many cases. You may not have a choice, but money is a commodity on the open market and interest rates will vary according to the seasons of the year. Practically all financial institutions have more money in the first two quarters than the last two of the year. Your payments are governed by: length of the loan, interest factor, and down payment. Home loans are usually for 25–30 years. In applying for a loan, you should consider your age, your present and probable future income, and your monthly expenses. According to FHA, if your monthly income is four to five times your monthly payment on the home selected, you are in a good financial position to buy.

II. Pick Your Neighborhood

A. Does it appeal to you and your family? Is it apt to maintain its present desirability, or deteriorate?

Everyone is concerned about the selection of the neighborhood; therefore, you should consider all the things that appeal to the rest of the family: schools, shopping centers, churches, theatres, playgrounds, and parks. The breadwinner should have the first choice in making a selection, since transportation is very important to him. Adequate fire protection is essential; otherwise, you will be subject to a higher rate of fire insurance. Essential, too, is the supply of utilities available to you. The rights of ingress and egress are the property owner's responsibility. When buying subdivided property, read the restrictions. Check into easements, rights of entry, dominant easements, servient easements, and so on.

B. Distances of home from essential services and business, and other important considerations.

Traffic and noise affect the value of property. You should never pay top price on property that has undesirable factors. Neighborhood maintenance should be considered. Age is not always the important factor with property; usually the class of people in the neighborhood and the way that they maintain their property should be deciding factors.

III. Selection of Location for Your Site or Lot

A. The lot value

This should be discussed with a broker who is fully informed of land value.

B. The soil

The soil must be compacted properly and the house must be built on a pad. The manner in which the soil will compact depends upon the way the pad is prepared.

C. Filled ground or natural site

A soils engineer is the only person who should be relied upon to find how the land is filled and compacted.

D. Drainage

Be sure to investigate the drainage of water; you may be liable for a suit if you change the course of water from your property onto someone else's land.

E. Size of lot

There should be room for expansion, privacy, air, and setback restrictions.

F. Orientation of Lot

There should be some open exposure for the house for a good balance of heat and light.

IV. Selection of Your Home

A. Size and arrangement

American people are still pushing up the sizes of their dwellings, so your selection should be one with adequate space for the present and future. There should be closets available for everything—linens, clothes, coats, bath necessities.

B. Type of house

1. Most modern houses today have both a formal living area and an informal living area. This, naturally, depends on your financial situation. The utilities of the house must be considered, such as those in the kitchen. Most of the electric gadgets and equipment in today's kitchen can be financed by FHA if they are attached to the house.

2. The house should have eye appeal as well as functional appeal. The colonial house has been accepted for over 150 years and is still accepted. Don't forget to consider the furniture and its location—reasonable wall space must remain after all furniture is in place.

C. Equipment

1. Plumbing should have an inspection. The buyer should know whether it is suitable for operation.

2. Heating should also have an inspection if it looks worn; it is very important to the home.

3. Wiring should be investigated to find the type of wiring with which the home is equipped. You should check to see that you have adequate circuits to carry the load required for your electrical fixtures. In almost every old house, the circuits are inadequate.

D. Construction

1. Foundation. If the foundation is cracked and slippage has started on the house, this should be investigated. Because ter-

mites will build a stack right up through the cracks to the wood structure, remove all wood from soil contact. Good ventilation of the foundation makes it dry, and poor ventilation makes it damp. Don't overlook the ventilation of the house.

2. The roof is built to go with a certain type of architecture. Don't hesitate to contact someone who is familiar with roofing if it looks as if it may leak. The light spaces between the shingles don't mean that the roof is no good—this is normal air ventilation. Roofs are usually good for 15–20 years.

3. How can you tell the age of a house? The meter box usually has a date stamped on the building permit, and the toilet usually has a date stamped on the water bowl; however, chronological age doesn't always make a big difference. It is the maintenance of the house that counts.

4. FHA requires hardwood floors, and it is generally a good idea to have them because the carpet will eventually wear out. This is an individual choice. Check all fireplaces—when you burn wood in the fireplace, it may black up the entire room if it is poorly ventilated. If the house is properly insulated, it keeps heat in during cold weather. Proper insulation is economical.

V. Final Word

Whether you hope to build, to buy, or to improve your present home—immediately or in the future—it's a good idea to start discussing your plans with your broker, loan agent, and builder.

Points to check before you buy

Shopping facilities
Chuches and amusements
Community pride
Neighbors
Police and fire protection
Schools
Playgrounds
Trash and garbage disposal
Street layout
Transportation
Growth trend
Lay of the land
Trees
Water
Sewerage
Protection against encroachment
Traffic
Hazards
Privacy
Nuisances

These 20 points are to be considered about any neighborhood. To compare houses, rate them on the above as good, fair, and poor.

Selling your home

The price of real estate has gone up in value almost constantly. Real estate is something you buy, use, and, when you no longer need it, sell.

The average homeowner in many areas sells his property after six or seven years. At this time, you should have a realtor to assist you. He not only has the legal ability to deal in property but also has the moral obligation to support the Real Estate Code. You can feel confident when you see the term "realtor" because he must follow a code of ethics or be subject to the revoking of his local board, state and national membership.

In order to get the highest price possible for a home, the owner should do the following:

1. Avoid rushing into a sale.
2. Allow enough time to be sure that as many people as possible who might buy the property are contacted.
3. Be sure the price of the home is right.
4. Prepare for sale—show the home only when it looks its best.
5. Plan a sales program—including financing.

Types of loans and lenders will be discussed in Chapters 7 and 8. If a new loan is to be obtained, the purchaser should protect himself by a proper recital in the contract. For example:

Purchasers to obtain new loan in the minimum amount of $25,000 for a minimum period of 25 years with interest not to exceed 7¾ percent per annum.

Further, the purchaser may wish to specify the lender, type of loan, and the real estate points he is willing to pay for said loan.

Some people sell their homes without professional help. However, most homes are sold with the help of professional real estate people. The help of a licensed real estate broker is desirable when a home is to be sold because of the following:

1. He has a great deal more knowledge about fair prices, possible buyers, and legal requirements than most homeowners.
2. He is licensed and examined by a state real estate commission.
3. If permitted to use the title *realtor*, he belongs to an organization that maintains a strict code of ethics. He must live up to his code to use this title.

Real estate brokers charge a fee based on the selling price of the property. The real estate agent will secure a better selling price, as a rule, (including his commission), than will the owner—this fact has been proven by a survey of sales records. The realtor must use diligent efforts and do everything that is necessary to sell the property. A reasonable amount of property showing is essential. If the realtor fails to do this, the seller should go to his board and report this, cancel his agency agreement, and be assigned to another agent. Your property will sell faster, at a better price, if you follow these helpful suggestions:

1. Have your property looking its best at all times.
2. Keep the yard neat and clean. Have the shrubs trimmed and the lawn cut. Make the prospect want to come inside. The first impression is extremely important.
3. Dress up the windows. They are the "eyes" of the house.
4. Keep the house tidy—not as a furniture store display window, but as a comfortable home in which to live.
5. Have the garage clean and neat. Broken window panes or loose door knobs make an unfavorable impression.
6. Make all minor repairs such as sticking doors, leaky plumbing, broken light switches, and so on. Little things like these make a house hard to show, and often kill a sale.
7. If you have a dog, keep him out of the house and under control. Many buyers are afraid of a house dog.
8. Shut off or tune down the radio or television set; they are distracting.
9. Let plenty of light into your rooms. Nothing adds to cheerful atmosphere more effectively than light.
10. A moderate amount of heat adds a feeling of coziness in cold weather. Fresh air is equally desirable on hot days.
11. Never apologize for the appearance of the house. It only emphasizes the faults.
12. If redecorating is needed, do it, if possible. Properly done, it creates appeal. Some decorators will do a limited amount of work and take their fee out of the sale.
13. Be prepared at all times to show your property. The prospect you turn away might be the logical buyer.
14. If the prospect asks questions about the house and neighborhood, answer directly and honestly. Questions about the transaction should be referred to the agent.
15. Leave the showing of the house to the salesman. Interrupting his sales presentation may lose a sale.
16. Please feel free to discuss frankly with your realtor any problems that may arise relative to the marketing of your property.

The selling of property, especially a home, involves a certain amount of inconvenience to the occupant. All real estate salesmen are aware of this and will be as considerate as possible. With the owner's cooperation, they will work energetically to find a buyer—and the possibilities of a sale will be enhanced if the property bears a marketable price tag.

Review questions

1. Distinguish between ownership and tenancy interests as classified under estates and freehold estates.
2. List and explain five principal ways in which a person may acquire title to real property.
3. Name and discuss the three types of wills commonly recognized in most states by which a person may acquire property.
4. Distinguish between severalty ownership, tenancy in common, and joint tenancy. Discuss the merits of each.
5. State the basic purpose of a recording system and distinguish between actual and constructive notice.

Multiple-choice questions

1. The owner of a life estate may *not*: (a) allow rent-free possession by relatives during his life, (b) lease the property for any period, (c) possess it exclusively during his life, (d) leave the property by will, (e) do any of the foregoing.
2. Ownership loss under adverse possession is: (a) a voluntary alienation, (b) an involuntary alienation, (c) condemnation or eminent domain, (d) not an alienation of property rights, (e) none of the foregoing.
3. One of the joint tenants dies. His interest: (a) goes to his heirs, (b) goes to a third party remainderman, (c) goes to the surviving owners, (d) goes to the surviving spouse, (e) goes to the federal government.
4. A broker leases property from Mrs. Smith for five years. Mrs. Smith dies before the lease expires. It is learned after her death that she had only a life estate. The property reverted to heirs, and the heirs told the lessee to vacate. The lease was: (a) valid until end of the lease, (b) valid only during life of Mrs. Smith, (c) never valid because it was for more than one year, (d) valid and may be enforced by the new owner, (e) valid and may be enforced by the lessee.
5. A will which is written, dated, and signed in the handwriting of the testator is: (a) a manugraphic will, (b) a holographic will, (c) a noncupative will, (d) a formal or witness will, (e) none of the foregoing.
6. With what type of estate would the phrase "of indefinite duration" most usually be associated? (a) estate for years, (b) estate from period to period, (c) estate of inheritance, (d) less-than-freehold estate, (e) none of the foregoing
7. Which of the following would be considered a freehold estate? (a) mortgage, (b) lease, (c) fee simple, (d) estate for years, (e) none of the foregoing.
8. Which of the following would be a less-than-freehold estate? (a) fee simple defeasible, (b) fee simple absolute, (c) leasehold estate, (d) life estate, (e) none of the foregoing.
9. If a brother and sister purchased a piece of property, how could they take

title? (a) in joint tenancy, (b) in tenancy in common, (c) in fee simple, (d) any of the foregoing, (e) none of the foregoing.

10. In most states, when a deed, lease, or a conditional sales contract is recorded, the instrument must be: (a) acknowledged, (b) verified, (c) approved, (d) signed by the grantee, lessee, or vendee; (e) signed by the grantor, lessor, or vendor with the signature acknowledged by a proper official.

4

Liens and Encumbrances

An *encumbrance*, broadly defined, is any claim, interest, or right in property possessed by another which may diminish the true owner's rights or value in the estate. It does not, however, necessarily prevent him from transferring the fee or an interest therein. Encumbrances may be divided into two categories: (1) liens (encumbrances that affect title), and (2) encumbrances that restrict the use or affect the physical condition of the property. These will be discussed separately.

Liens

Liens are defined as forms of encumbrance that make the debtor's property security for the payment of a debt or discharge of an obligation. Typical examples of liens are trust deeds, mortgages, mechanic's liens, taxes, special assessments, attachments, and judgments. Trust deeds and mortgages are more properly considered in the chapter on Real Estate Finance and therefore will be omitted here.

Real property liens may be classified as *specific liens* and *general liens.* The specific lien affects a specified parcel or parcels of real property while the general lien affects all parcels of the debtor's property. An example of the latter would be a general judgment rendered by a court of proper jurisdiction. Examples of specific liens would include mortgages, mechanic's liens, property taxes, and special assessments against a specific parcel of property.

Liens may be further classified as *statutory liens* and *equitable liens.* A statutory lien is one created by statute such as the mechanic's lien.

Equitable liens are liens which the court of equity will enforce mainly because under the circumstances, justice would seem to require such action. For example: A orally agrees to sell his land to B. The statute of frauds requires that this contract be in writing. Under the oral agreement, B enters upon the property and constructs valuable improvements thereon. A refuses to follow through with the conveyance. B sues A and A refuses to convey property. In most states the court would require a conveyance by A. To do otherwise would permit an unjust enrichment at the expense of B. An equitable lien would also arise if an owner entered into a written contract to borrow money on his land.

Mechanic's liens

The *mechanic's lien* is created solely by statute and is based upon the theory that all persons who bestow their labor or furnish materials should be paid. In most states this is true, even if the property upon which these persons worked or furnished materials must be sold. It does not matter that the owner of the property has paid the contractor in full; if the contractor has not paid his employees, these employees may file a lien upon the property in question for the amount due them. Thus, if Jones, a homeowner, employs Smith, a carpenter, to put a new roof on his house, and Smith performs under the contract, Smith is entitled to file a lien upon Jones's property if Jones does not pay him as stated in the contract. Assume that Jones pays Smith, but Smith fails to pay his employees. These workers, too, have bestowed their labor, and therefore have the right to be paid. They may file a lien against Jones's property. In this case, if Jones has already paid Smith, Jones would have to file for money damages against Smith, the contractor. This same right extends generally to materialmen, architects, contractors, builders, and all persons of every category who provide labor, services, materials, or equipment that contributes to the improvements of the real property.

Laws dealing with mechanic's liens vary among the states. Some states have contract statutes wherein the lienor must show that he made certain improvements to property at the request of the owner. In these states, someone other than the owner, such as a lessee (tenant), may not have improvements completed with a consequent lien filed against the owner's property.

Other states may have consent statutes wherein it suffices to show that the owner or his agent consented to improvements. In these states, if a tenant or lessee has improvements made, a proper mechanic's lien may be filed against the owner's property. In those states having consent statutes, it is usually necessary for the owner to protect himself by filing a document known as a *notice of nonresponsibility*. This filing gives all persons concerned clear notice that the owner will not be held responsible for the work being done. This is usually accomplished by filing a verified copy of a notice of nonresponsibility with the county recorder in the county in which the property is located, and by posting a copy of it in a conspicuous place on the property. Assume that Adam, the owner of a duplex, notices that one of his tenants is having painting done by a contractor on the interior of his apartment. Adam, not wanting to be responsible, immediately files a verified copy of a notice of nonresponsibility with the county recorder, and another is posted on a conspicuous part of the property. This gives constructive notice that Adam, owner of the property, will not be responsible for improvements being done, and the contractor or material men must now look to the tenants for their compensation. Legal advice should be sought by the property owner to verify that all code requirements are met.

FILING OF MECHANIC'S LIEN

The statutes of each state will provide time limits for filing the *notice of mechanic's lien* or mechanic's lien. A few states require that a separate notice be filed within a certain period of time, usually 20 or 30 days before the work commences. This prior notice tells the owner that the work being done may constitute a mechanic's lien.

If the original contractor, his employees, or his subcontractors have not been paid within the time specified by statute, (usually three to four months after completion of the job), then each has a right to file a mechanic's lien.

When does the mechanic's lien begin? In some states the lien attaches upon commencement of the project. In others, the priority of lien will be fixed according to the time of recording. In the latter case, when the lien reaches the recorder's office, the date and time of recording are stamped on the document, and a note that states the actual time of recording is generally appended. This will establish the priority.

Care should be taken to conform to the statutes in filing a mechanic's lien. Certain information must usually be present in the document. The general information that must be present includes:

1. The full name and address of the lienor
2. The name and address of the owner
3. The name and address of the person with whom the contract was made, when there is a subcontractor or an employee of the contractor
4. Legal description of the property
5. Dates on which the work was done

TIME LIMIT OF MECHANIC'S LIEN

Statutes will provide not only the time limit by which a mechanic must file his lien, but also a time limit by which the lienor must move in order to enforce his lien. The mere filing of the lien itself does not automatically entitle the lienor to his money. The time limit before which he must file his complaint and start foreclosure proceedings varies from 90 days after the filing of the mechanic's lien to three years. The foreclosure proceedings are normally handled in the same manner as the foreclosure of the mortgage. The latter type of foreclosure action is discussed in Chapter 7.

NOTICE OF COMPLETION

Some states require that a *notice of completion* be filed. Where the statutes require such notice, it is usually crucial that the owner establish the exact time, to the day, at which the improvement is completed. The owner may do so by filing a notice of completion with the county recorder in the county in which the property is located. Such a document shows the owner's name and address, the date of completion, the owner's interest or estate in the property, a legal description, and the contractor's name, if any. Such notice usually must be verified, rather than acknowledged, by the owner or his agent.

What constitutes the completion of a structure? The completion of an improvement might be any of the following:

1. The formal acceptance by the owner or his agent of the work of improvement
2. The occupation of the improvement, or its use, by the property owner or his agent, and cessation of labor
3. Cessation of labor for a certain number of days and the owner's filing of a notice of cessation with the county recorder

LIS PENDENS

When a *lis pendens* is filed, it is constructive notice to all that an action is pending which may involve a certain parcel of property. Such notice would give all prospective purchasers of said property proper notice. The filing of a lis pendens usually prevents lapsing of the time period on the mechanic's lien.

COMPLETION BOND

The owner of property may also protect himself by having the contractor file a completion bond. In the event mechanics are not paid, any lien will be filed against the bond and not the property of the owner.

PROGRESS PAYMENTS

Often, lenders making a construction loan will make payments to the contractor as work progresses. The amount of work completed and the payment will be set forth in the contract. Payments may be made in thirds or quarters, for example: A contract may provide that one-fourth of the contract will be paid when the basement, subfloor, and house are framed. It will also provide for an inspection by certain authorities. The final payment on the contract will be held until after the lien filing period has passed. An owner paying cash for construction, without obtaining a loan, may follow the same procedure.

WAIVER OF MECHANIC'S LIEN

The owner of property, prior to the commencement of the project, or after it is completed and prior to final payment, may execute an instrument with the contractor in which the contractor waives his right to file a lien. In the event such an instrument is executed, the contractor will be bound by the terms of the instrument. The contractor may, however, be able to obtain a personal judgment against the owner.

RELEASE OF MECHANIC'S LIEN

A mechanic's lien may be released by a document entitled *mechanic's lien release*. The form required may vary among states, and may also be entitled *satisfaction* of *mechanic's lien*.

FEDERAL TAX LIENS

If not paid on the date due, all internal revenue taxes, including the federal income tax, become a lien on all property of the individual concerned and the rights thereto. Such a lien is valid against any trustee, mortgagee, purchaser, or creditor. Notice is filed with the United States District Court Clerk in the district in which the property is situated. Federal or state taxes on the gross estate of the descendent are a lien for the ten years following the passage of property into possession of the purchaser. This lien does not include the proper charges and expenses of administration allowed by the court under the proper jurisdiction.

STATE TAX LIENS

State tax liens may include, but are not limited to: (a) inheritance tax (b) corporation franchise tax, (c) property taxes, real and personal; (d) income tax, and (e) special assessments.

An *inheritance tax* is imposed against the net estate of a deceased person. Some states will have inheritance tax appraisers, appointed by the governor or another designated individual, whose job is to appraise the estate of the deceased. The amount of tax will be a lien against said estate.

Corporation franchise tax is imposed by some states against a corporation for the right to do business in that state. It is usually based upon the income of the corporation with a minimum set fee that may be $25 to $50.

Municipal and state governments usually secure money for their operation in the form of personal and real property taxes. When a person does not own real property, the personal property taxes are referred to as *unsecured*.

If taxes are not paid within the designated time, as provided by statute, the property will be sold to the state. Many states provide an equity of redemption period during which the delinquent tax payer may redeem his property. After this period, the state may sell the property at a "tax sale," giving a *tax deed* or a *quitclaim deed*.

Property taxes take priority over most other liens, including mortgages, so it is a common practice for lenders to set up "impound accounts" or "loan trust fund" accounts. In theory, one-twelfth of the taxes are collected with each payment, and when the taxes fall due the lenders will pay them, protecting their loan. When such accounts are not established, lenders employ a tax servicing agency to check the records and inform them when certain taxes are delinquent on their loans.

SPECIAL ASSESSMENTS

Special assessments for roads, sewers, construction of schools, and so on, may be levied by the appropriate government agencies. Such assessments may be paid by the property owner over a period of years or, in some cases, the property owner may make one cash payment. Such assessments are liens against real property.

ATTACHMENTS AND JUDGMENTS

An *attachment* is a process by which a plaintiff, by court action against a defendant, may have the defendant's real or personal property seized and retained in custody of the law for satisfaction of a judgment. Such a lien is obtained prior to the entry of a judgment so that assurances will be given to the plaintiff that the property will be available to sustain his judgment, assuming that judgment will be in favor of the plaintiff. Such an attachment on real property will remain for the period of time designated by statute, and may usually be renewed for an additional period of time.

Attachments may sometimes be made in an action for unlawful detainer to recover past due rents, in action by the state, county, or city for collection of taxes, or in action for money on an unsecured contract.

An attachment is released in any one of the following ways: (1) dismissal of the action by the court, (2) dismissal by the sheriff after the debtor settles his claim, (3) recording of the abstract of judgment obtained in the judgment, or (4) the debtor's claiming legitimate exemption of certain property.

It should also be noted that an attachment may be issued in a suit for commission due when the exact amount is known.

All of the property (both real and personal) of an individual is subject to attachment, except that which the law specifically exempts. This is all-inclusive, and includes property of record as well as property not of record owned by the debtor.

Property exempted might include earnings of the judgment debtor or defendant up to a certain amount, homesteads, and property in the custody of the law under receivership or bankruptcy.

A *judgment* is the final determination by a court of competent jurisdiction concerning the rights of the parties involved. The final decree is always subject to appeal to a higher court that may reverse, amend, or affirm the decision of the lower court. After the time period for such appeals has passed, the judgment becomes final. Once the decree of any court is recorded with the county recorder in the county or counties where the nonexempt property of the judgment debtor is located, the judgment becomes a lien. The document recorded is the certified abstract of the judgment or decree. Such a lien will normally remain a lien for the period of time specified by statute.

Judgment creditors enforce an attachment by obtaining a *writ of execution* issued in the name of the people and subscribed to by a judge or a clerk of the court. Such a writ directs the sheriff to seize and sell all nonexempt property of the judgment debtor.

Encumbrances

The term *encumbrance* is a generic term which includes liens. A lien is a particular type of encumbrance. An encumbrance affects the title, use, or physical condition of property. A lien arises from a debt.

Easements

An *easement* is an interest that one has in the land of another that entitles him to a limited use of the land. Easements are of two classes: (1) easements appurtenant, and (2) easements in gross.

EASEMENTS APPURTENANT

An *easement appurtenant* is said to "run with the land." Such an easement is created for the benefit of another and belongs to a particular tract of land; therefore, two tenements exist: (1) the dominant tenement, and (2) the servient tenement. The dominant tenement has the benefit of the easement, and the servient tenement is burdened with the easement (see Fig. 5).

Mutual stock in a water company is considered appurtenant to the land, as are water courses and easements. For example, Adam is the owner of White Acre; Brown, the owner of Black Acre. Brown grants Adam an easement over the east 20 feet of his lot for road purposes. Brown has the servient tenement, and Adam has the dominant tenement.

Adam now transfers his property to Smith. The easement that Adam acquired is transferred to Smith and is said to "run with the land." It

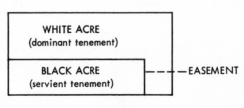

WHITE ACRE
(dominant tenement)

BLACK ACRE
(servient tenement)

— — — —EASEMENT

Figure 5

does not matter that the easement is not mentioned in the grant that Adam gives. The fact that Adam gives a grant deed to Smith means that Smith automatically gains the easement that Adam has in the property, and Smith acquires any water rights that Adam had. Such rights would include stock in a mutual water company, or riparian rights of Adam.

EASEMENT IN GROSS

An *easement in gross* is a personal right in the land of another with no dominant tenement. Such a right does not attach to the land owned by the easement holder; therefore, easements in gross must be expressly transferred. Examples of easements in gross include easements held by utility companies, or the telephone company. Although easements may be created in a number of different ways, they are usually created by express grant, express reservation, operation of law, prescription, dedication, or condemnation. We shall concern ourselves in the text only with easements created by express grant, express reservation, operation of law, or prescription. Easements may also be created by agreement between owners of adjoining land, but they are usually created by deeds.

Because easements by express grant or express reservation are usually created by deeds, all of the essentials of a deed must be present. Such elements include:

1. Proper description of the parties
2. Granting clause or operative words of a conveyance
3. Sufficient description of the easement for it to be easily located
4. Execution of the instrument by the grantor
5. Proper delivery

A deed conveying fee simple title to a parcel of land may be void where the description is indefinite, but a deed to an unlocated easement might be valid. For example, a 20-foot easement "over lot 23" would be valid, although the exact location might not be specified. Such a location could be determined by agreement of the parties, or subsequently by use.

An *easement created by reservation* might be made when a land owner sells a portion of his land and desires to reserve for himself an easement over a portion of the property. Such a description might read as follows:

> The North ½ of the Northeast ¼ of section 17, Township 1 South, Range 2 East, Mt. Diablo Baseline and Meridian. Grantors reserve for themselves, their heirs and assigns an easement appurtenant over the west 30 feet of said parcel of land for ingress and egress.

An *easement by operation of law or necessity* is created where a grantor sells or conveys a portion of his land and such portion is without access to a road. For example, Adam sells Brown the north ten acres of a 20-acre parcel. The parcel so conveyed has no access to a roadway. In such cases, the courts have held that implied easement or way of necessity passes to the grantees as an appurtenance to the land conveyed. To effect such an implied easement, there must be a strict necessity. For example, if Brown has access to any other road, such an easement need not be given.

An *easement by prescription* may be acquired by adverse use. Certain essential elements are necessary, however, to establish such an easement in most states:

1. There must be open and notorious use of each easement.
2. Its use must be uninterrupted for a period of five years.
3. It must be hostile to the true owner's wishes.
4. The person so claiming must claim some right of use.

To prevent such easements from being created, the property owner should periodically put up road blocks for a period of 48 to 72 hours. An easement that has been created by prescription may also be cancelled by nonuse after a certain number of years.

Title insurance companies will not insure an easement obtained by prescription unless the claimant establishes his right through a quiet title action.

Easements may also be terminated in a number of other ways, the more important of which include:

1. *Express release*, usually by a quitclaim deed from the holder of the dominant tenement to the holder of the servient tenement
2. *Merger of the estates*, whereby the holder of the dominant tenement becomes the owner of the servient tenement
3. *Adverse possession*, whereby the easement is destroyed by the use of a servient tenement in an adverse manner continuously for five years

Restrictions

Restrictions are usually of two kinds, *private deed* and *zoning*. Private deed restrictions are placed on property for the protection of all lots in the tract by subdividers or developers. Zoning restrictions are created by governmental agencies such as cities and counties in their adoption of zoning ordinances.

Private deed restrictions are usually recorded in a separate document; thus, all deeds to parcels of land within a given tract will contain a reference to the recorded declaration of restrictions. The recording of the declaration of restrictions gives constructive notice to all of their existence.

Today modern subdividers and developers usually draft their general plan restrictions in the form of covenants and conditions that are enforceable by the grantor and by the purchasers of lots in the subdivisions.

SINGLE PLAN RESTRICTIONS

A distinction should be made between *general plan restrictions* and *single plan restrictions*. Single plan restrictions are in favor of the grantor alone, his successors, or assignee, and are not necessarily for the benefit of other lot owners.

If a subdivider or developer intends the general plan restrictions to be for the benefit of all the lots in a designated area, the restrictions must so state. Otherwise, difficulties may be encountered in enforcing such restrictions.

A set of valid building restrictions within any given subdivision is enforceable between the land owners if they act in time to enforce such restrictions. Restrictions must be uniformly enforced against all lot owners without discrimination. Thus, if Adam, the owner of lot 10, does not comply with the restrictions, and Cole later fails to comply, the other lot owners may be estopped to deny that the restrictions are to remain in force.

If restrictions state "for residential purposes only," this embraces all types of family residences, including single family dwellings, duplexes, triplexes, apartment units, and so on.

As a rule, restrictions usually do not prohibit the owner from building a private garage on the property, even though it is not attached to the main residence. Also, where restrictions state that outbuildings must be a certain distance from the rear portion of the property, this does not prevent the lot owner from building an attached garage to his house, if it is constructed as an integral part of the residence.

Restrictions in a modern subdivision sometimes provide that all plans and architectural designs shall be approved by a planning committee composed of property owners within said subdivision. Such restrictions are valid as long as refusals are made in good faith by such committee. When such provisions prevail and the planning committee no longer functions, the approval of plans will generally not violate the building restrictions, providing the improvements remain in harmony with the rest of the subdivision.

TERMINATION OF DEED RESTRICTIONS

Restrictions may be terminated in several ways:

1. Termination of the prescribed period of restrictions
2. Agreement of the grantors and owners of lots within the subdivision
3. Merging of ownership
4. Operation of law

Usually the person creating the deed restrictions will provide for a date of termination, but a date is not essential to the validity of such restrictions. When no date is given, restrictions will remain in effect for a reasonable period of time. Two rights exist in the enforcement of restrictions. First is the right of the grantor to enforce the restrictions against all grantees in the tract. The grantor in this case usually reserves the right to reenter if there is a breach of the conditions. The second right is a mutual right of various lot owners within the tracts to enforce the restrictions in favor of themselves. The grantor in the subdivision is the only one entitled to the condition reserving the right to reenter the property and divest the grantee of title. Individual lot owners may ask for an injunction or may sue for money damages suffered.

A restriction, whether in the form of a covenant or condition, may be changed, waived, or released by agreement of the parties. This may be done by having the party entitled to enforce the restriction execute a quitclaim deed. The same purpose may be accomplished by an agreement signed by the proper parties.

When ownership of property is merged into a single fee simple estate, the restrictions will be terminated. Should certain portions of the property be sold later, new restrictions must be created if it is the wish of the grantor.

If restrictions prove to be inequitable to the property owners involved, courts will sometimes deny the enforcement of these restrictions, as in a case where hardships would result to the owners.

ZONING RESTRICTIONS

Zoning may be defined as the right of government agencies to regulate the use of buildings and land. The constitutions of the various states provide that any county, city, town, or township may make and enforce (within its scope) zoning regulations pertaining to the use of land. The planning commission, whether city or county, is charged with the responsibility of zoning. Its power, however, is limited to recommendations. Final approval of its action rests with the city council or county board of supervisors, whichever applies. Zoning will be discussed more fully in a later chapter of this text.

Encroachment

An *encroachment* may be defined as the wrongful projection of a building, wall, or fence of one property onto that of another. Such encroachment may be from the air as well as from the ground.

If the encroachment (in the case of a building) is resting upon the land of another, it is a permanent trespass. Actions against trespass on this type of encroachment must be brought before the court during the time period specified by statute. Usually the action requested is for the removal of the encroachment and for damages suffered.

Encroachments from the air constitute a nuisance, rather than a trespass, and actions against these usually have no time limit. When such encroachments remain, they are considered a continuing trespass and are actionable until the nuisance is abated.

When the encroachment is intentional, an injunction will usually be granted by the court and even though the damage may appear slight and the cost of removal of the encroachment great, the court will usually require the nuisance to be abated.

Homesteads

Most constitutions or statutes of the various states provide for a homestead. This consists of a family dwelling, together with all outbuildings and the land upon which they rest. The purpose of such homesteads is to provide a roof over the debtor's head should a financial crisis develop. As a rule the debtor may usually have only one valid homestead which protects him against creditors up to a certain cash value. The homestead does not affect voluntary liens placed on the property such as mortgages or deeds of trust, mechanic's liens, and so on. The declaration of homestead is only valid if it is filed with the county recorder in the county where the property is located. Legal counsel should be consulted to make sure that such a declaration meets all statutory requirements. Usually selling the property or filing a declaration of abandonment will terminate the homestead.

Review questions

1. Define the two categories of encumbrances that affect title to real property.
2. Distinguish between the specific lien and the general lien.
3. Discuss the full implication of the mechanic's lien and its affect on the owner's title to real property in your state.
4. What constitutes the completion of a building or structure and how may an owner protect himself against mechanic's liens after the final construction contract payment?
5. In what way does the easement appurtenant differ from the easement in gross?
6. What is meant by deed restrictions and how may they be removed?

Multiple-choice questions

1. An easement appurtenant is terminated by merger: (a) when the person holding the easement becomes the owner of the land subject to the easement, (b) when the owner of the easement does not use it for a specified term of years as is determined by state statute, (c) when the owner of the easement gives it to the owner of the land, (d) in any of the above cases, (e) in none of the above cases.
2. Two adjoining land parcels have an easement between them with one owner holding a dominant tenement and the other a servient tenement. Under these circumstances: (a) the holder of the dominant tenement cannot use the easement for ingress and egress, regardless of the type held; (b) the burdened property is owned by the holder of the dominant tenement, (c) the easement can be eliminated by merging the two properties under one owner, (d) this type of easement can only be created by prescription, (e) none of the foregoing are correct.
3. An easement: (a) is a general lien on real property, (b) is a specific lien on real property, (c) is an encumbrance on real property, (d) is an equitable restriction on real property, (e) is neither an encumbrance nor a lien.
4. A mechanic's lien is recorded for the benefit of: (a) mechanics, (b) contractors and subcontractors, (c) materials men, (d) all of these, (e) none of these.
5. The seizure of a defendant's property to satisfy an anticipated judgment is accomplished by: (a) attachment, (b) writ of execution, (c) lien, (d) lis pendens, (e) notice of responsibility.
6. Which of the following would not be classified as a lien against real property? (a) unpaid real property taxes, (b) an easement appurtenant, (c) installment payment on an assessment bond, (d) recorded abstract of judgment, (e) mortgage.
7. Prescription most nearly means gaining title by: (a) warranty deed, (b) duress, (c) death of a relative, (d) open and notorious use for a specified period of time, (e) progress payments.

8. Zoning regulations permit use of the real property. The deed contains limits on construction and restrictions. In this case, which will prevail? (a) deed restrictions, (b) zone variance, (c) master zoning law, (d) building code, (e) the decision would be left to the property owners.
9. Of the following, which may be homesteaded in most states? (a) one-half of a duplex, (b) a home including several acres of farm land, (c) a home in a city, including an adjoining lot for gardening, (d) all of these, (e) none of these.
10. The Great Eastern Telephone Company has an easement on real property being sold by Broker Jones. The easement is not mentioned in the deed. The easement is: (a) a specific lien, (b) a general lien, (c) an encumbrance, (d) an attachment, (e) none of the foregoing.

5

Law of Contracts (General)

Introduction

Every day each of us enters into some contract, whether it be expressed or implied, and nothing is more important to the student of real estate than an understanding of the law of contracts. Emphasis will be given in this chapter to contracts as they pertain to the real estate industry.

The salesman in his everyday business activities will encounter many types of real estate contracts. These contracts include the listing agreement or authorization to sell, deposit receipt, exchange agreement, lease, trust deed, mortgage, title insurance policy, and escrow instructions. The student will note a diversity of forms in certain contracts. For example, listing agreements include the open listing, exclusive authorization and right to sell, exclusive agency, net listing, and multiple listing. Some contracts will be identified under several names; for example, the contract of sale is also called an agreement to purchase, an installment sales contract, or a land contract.

Definition of contract

In general, a *contract* is a promise or exchange of promises by two or more persons to commit or not a particular act, for the breach of which the law will give a remedy or the performance of which the law will recognize a duty. More simply put, a contract is an agreement to do or not to do a certain thing. In substance, a contract is a mutual agreement between parties capable of contracting for a lawful object, and for a sufficient consideration.

56

CLASSIFICATION OF CONTRACTS

Contracts, when created, may be *expressed* or *implied*. In an express contract, the parties declare the terms and manifest their intentions in words, either orally or in writing. For example, Adam goes to a car agency and decides to buy an automobile. The contract is made out, and signed by both the representative of the automobile agency and Adam. Such a contract is an expressed one. An implied contract, on the other hand, is one that is shown by the acts and conduct of the parties rather than in words. For example, Adam makes an appointment with his attorney and goes to see him concerning a legal problem. Adam implies by his very presence in the attorney's office that he will pay a legal fee. The attorney, in accepting Adam into his office, implies that he will give legal counsel to Adam.

Contracts may also be classified as *bilateral* and *unilateral*. A contract is said to be bilateral where a promise is made for a promise. For example, Adam tells Brown, "I will give you $1,000 if you will reshingle my house." Brown so promises, and a contract is formed. Adam has promised to pay Brown, and Brown has promised to shingle Adam's house for $1,000. Such a contract is also an expressed one, since the parties have declared the terms and their intentions in completing the contract. A contract is unilateral when a promise is given by one party and such promise is intended to induce some performance on the part of the other party. If one of the parties acts, the other is obligated. In the above illustration, Adam tells Brown, "I will pay you $1,000 if you will shingle my house." Brown says nothing, but returns one week later and shingles the house. Adam is obligated to pay Brown $1,000. This contract may also be called an implied contract.

Contracts may also be classified by performance. An *executed contract* is one in which both parties have performed. In the above illustration, when Brown finishes shingling Adam's house and Adam pays Brown $1,000, the contract is said to be executed. A contract is executory when something remains to be done by one or both of the parties. In the same illustration, before either Adam or Brown fulfills his obligation the contract is executory in nature. Brown completes the shingling of Adam's house. The contract is still executory because Adam has not paid Brown $1,000. As soon as Adam pays Brown $1,000, the contract is executed.

DEFINITION OF TERMS

In our study of contracts we should start by making a clear distinction among four terms. These are: void, voidable, unenforceable, and valid.

A *void* contract has no legal effect. Examples of such contracts include those made to commit crimes or to sell real property to a minor under the age of 18.

A *voidable* contract is valid and enforceable on its face, but may be rejected by one of the parties. For example, a minor between the ages of 18 and 21 buys an automobile. Such a contract is enforceable toward the automobile agency, but may be disaffirmed by the minor when he reaches majority. Other voidable contracts are those induced by fraud or duress.

An *unenforceable* contract is valid on its face but, for some reason, cannot be proved or sued upon by either party. Contracts outlawed by the statute of limitations would be examples of this type of contract.

A *valid* contract is one that is binding and enforceable on both parties, and contains all essential elements of a contract.

Essential elements of contracts

According to Witkin, there are four essential elements to every contract:

1. Parties capable of contracting
2. Their consent
3. A lawful object
4. A sufficient cause or consideration[1]

In addition, all contracts for the conveyance of real estate are required to be in writing.

Parties capable of contracting

Parties must be *competent* to enter into a contract. Virtually all persons, with certain exceptions, are considered competent. These exceptions include minors, persons of unsound mind, and persons deprived of their civil rights. Minors are persons under the age of 21. In general, all contracts by minors under the age of 21 are voidable. Real estate licensees and others making contracts with minors should deal only through guardians appointed by the court. In some jurisdictions, statutes may provide that a woman ceases to be a minor upon attaining her 18th birthday. A few statutes, including California law, provide that minors who are married, and 18 years of age and older, may enter into valid and binding contracts including contracts to purchase or sell real estate. If the minor later divorces, this does not change his status.

---

[1]B. E. Witkin, *Summary of California Law*, 7th ed. (San Francisco: Bender-Moss, 1960), I: 13.

Regardless of his age, a minor is deemed incapable of appointing an agent; hence, a minor who attempts to appoint an agent by power of attorney will find such delegations of authority void.

A minor is responsible for the necessities of life for which he negotiates. Necessities of minors may, of course, vary according to their standard of living. For example, where the father of a minor child makes $25,000 per year and another minor's father makes $10,000 a year, the two standards of living are quite different. That which would constitute a necessity in one case might not always constitute a necessity in another.

Ordinarily, money loaned to a minor is not considered a necessity even though the minor may purchase necessities with it. However, when the loan is made and the lender makes certain that the money is used for expressed necessities, an exception to the rule is made.

A minor may not recover what he has lost when an innocent purchaser of the goods is affected. For example, Adam, a minor, sells Brown certain goods. Brown buys these goods believing in good faith that Adam is of majority. Brown now resells these goods to Cole, an innocent purchaser. Adam, the minor, will not in such cases be allowed to disaffirm the contract. The U.S. Uniform Commercial Code, section 2-403(1) does not provide for protecting minors under such circumstances.

Valid contracts of the minor

1. *Veterans.* Several states have enacted legislation giving the veteran the right to execute certain types of contracts, notably real property contracts.

2. *Business or employment contracts.* Some states by statute, and others by court decision, provide that a minor may not shield himself from liability under a contract of employment or business under which he operates as a person having full legal capacity.

3. *Contracts approved by the court.* In many jurisdictions permission may be obtained from the court for the minor to execute a contract. Thus, a minor could execute a contract for professional performances on stage and screen.

4. *Commercial bank accounts.* Some states have enacted legislation providing that a minor may open a bank account in his own name. In such cases the minor is strictly held accountable for his account.

INSANE PERSONS

Persons judicially declared *unsound of mind* may not make valid contracts. All such contracts are void.

Contracts are voidable when the court has not officially declared a person unsound of mind, and such contracts may be disaffirmed during periods of competency. In order to fall within the rule of insanity, a person's mind must be so disarranged that he does not understand that he is making a contract or the consequences thereof. Exceptions to the rule of liability are generally the same as those for minors.

Statutes vary from state to state concerning felons or persons deprived of their civil rights. In some states a valid transfer of property may be made, but in other states permission must be obtained from the state parole board to enter into valid contracts. Generally, disability of the felon holds only during the time of imprisonment.

Under common law, all contracts of the married woman were void, but this limitation has been removed in most states.

Consent

For a contract to have *mutual assent*, there must be a meeting of the minds. Normally, this is evidenced by an offer of a contract and its acceptance. In case of litigation, the court will try to decide what reasonable people would have done under the circumstances.

In order that there be true mutual assent, an acceptance of the contract must be made in the *exact terms* of the offer. For example, Adam offers to sell his home for $75,000. Brown offers to purchase the property for $65,000. Brown agrees to assume a first deed of trust or mortgage in the amount of $46,000, and that possession is to be given at the close of escrow. There has been no mutual assent, since Brown's acceptance was not on exact terms of the listing contract. Adam then agrees to Brown's offer at a price of $70,000. When Adam's qualified acceptance of Brown's offer is made, Brown is released from his original offer because there is no mutual assent; Brown's acceptance under Adam's terms constitutes acceptance of a counter offer.

An offer must be communicated in the method specified. In the event that a method is not specified in the offer, any usual method of acceptance may be used. When mail is specified as the manner of communication, the offer is deemed accepted when the contract is put in the mail box.

When may an offeror withdraw his offer? He may do so at any time before it is accepted by the other party, or by the time specified in the agreement. In some circumstances, death or insanity will also terminate it. An exception is made in the case of an option.

An *option* is a contract to make a contract. A consideration is paid by the optionee for the right to buy the property under the terms and conditions set out in the option agreement.

In order for mutual assent to be present in any contract, there must be no *fraud* or concealment of material facts. It is an old rule of common law that if a person speaks, he must speak the whole truth.

A mistake in a contract does not necessarily invalidate it. Adam offers to sell Brown his 92-acre ranch for $1,000 an acre. A survey of the property is made while in escrow, and it is discovered that there are only 89 acres in the parcel of land. In such a case, an adjustment is normally made in the price. Modern contracts for the sale of real property will state "for the total purchase price of $92,000," in order to eliminate such discrepancies.

Generally, no mutual assent occurs where there has been a *mistake of law*. For example, Adam buys a parcel of land from Brown believing it to be C-1 zoning. It is in fact zoned R-4. There has been no mutual assent and, therefore, no contract.

A contract is voidable when it is entered into under pressure of *duress*, *menace*, or *undue influence*. The law permits a person under such pressure to void the contract. The offended party may also have other legal remedies available to him. *Duress* is the use of force; *menace* constitutes a threat to commit duress. Menace would include threats of detention or of violent injury to the person. Undue influence may occur when one party takes unfair advantage of another's weakness of mind, necessity, or distress. Examples include the undue influence of the husband over the wife, the parent over the child, or the broker over the principal.

Lawful object

Contracts must have a legal purpose or a *lawful object*. In most states, any contract which is contrary to statute, public policy, or good morals does not have such an object. For example, in a state having a maximum interest rate of 12 percent, any contract bearing an interest rate above this amount would be considered an usurious contract and, therefore, would not be considered to have a legal purpose or a lawful object.

Some contracts provide for *liquidated damages*. These are provisions that fix damages in anticipation of a breach of the contract. Such provisions may be valid when actual damages would be impossible or difficult to determine.

An *exculpatory clause* is a clause in a contract whereby one of the parties attempts to exempt himself from liability of damages resulting from his own negligence or that of his employees. As a general rule, however, when the party so trying to exempt himself has contributed through his own negligence to the injury, he may be held liable.

Contracts offering for sale the property of another person come within the state license laws. In most states, to engage in the sale of property, a broker's or salesman's license is required. Such contracts do not have legal purpose or lawful object. Any person acting as an unlicensed agent may be subject to a fine, to imprisonment in the county jail, or both.

Statute of frauds

The Statute of Frauds was made a part of the English law in 1677. All of the states have adopted similar statutes. The purpose of a statute of frauds is to prevent perjury, forgery, and dishonest conduct in verifying the existence and terms of certain types of contracts.

The statute of frauds in most states will provide that certain contracts are invalid unless some note or memorandum is in writing and signed by the parties to be charged or their agents.

The state civil codes usually require that certain contracts be in writing. They further provide that these contracts are invalid unless some note or memorandum is in writing and signed by the party to be charged or his agent. These include:

1. An agreement that will not be executed within one year from the date of its making

2. A special promise to answer for the debt or default of another (exceptions to this rule are cases in which the promisor receives a consideration for his promise)

3. A contract for marriage based upon a consideration other than mutual promises to marry

4. A lease agreement for more than one year or the sale of any interest therein (an agency agreement, in dealing with said property, must be in writing and signed by the parties sought to be charged)

5. An agreement authorizing the purchase or sale of real estate for compensation, or a commission by an agent or real estate broker

6. An agreement that cannot be performed within the lifetime of the promisor, such as an agreement to devise or bequeath property or to make provisions in a will for any person

7. Any agreement whereby the purchaser of real property is to pay the mortgage or deed of trust on property purchased by him (an exception is made when the agreement specifically provides for the assumption of the indebtedness in the conveyance of property)

8. Contracts for the sale of personal property in the amount of $500 or more, unless the buyer gives earnest money, makes a partial payment, accepts, and actually receives a portion of the goods (an exception to this rule is made in the case of custom manufactured goods made especially for the buyer)

Contracts in writing will supersede all oral agreements. For example, Adam and Brown agree orally to do certain things in a contract. One week later the contract is put in writing. The contract in writing will supersede the oral agreement.

Parties to a contract may agree to alter or change the contract by mutual assent. There must be an intention to alter or change the contract if this is done. This act may be by a new contract or an executed oral agreement.

A sufficient cause or consideration

Contracts, to be valid, must have a consideration. In general, two types of consideration are recognized, *a good consideration* and a *valuable consideration*. A good consideration is one of love and affection. A valuable consideration, on the other hand, is one of money, property, labor bestowed, the giving up of some right, and so on. The usual consideration in the conveyance of real property is one of money, as when Adam deeds Brown his house for $30,000.

The contract should bear a sufficient consideration. Adam jestingly tells Brown, "I will sell you my new Cadillac for $500." Brown accepts. There is no contract because the consideration is grossly inadequate. If, on the other hand, Adam tells Brown, "I will sell you my new Cadillac for $6,000," and Brown accepts, the consideration would be a sufficient one.

In the absence of fraud or other misconduct such as duress or undue influence, the courts normally will not interfere with the sufficiency of the consideration. When an attempt is made by a debtor to convey property to his relatives or others in order to defraud creditors, such a conveyance will normally be set aside by the court.

It is sometimes asked whether pledges made for *charitable purposes*, such as pledges to a church, have sufficient consideration. When the charitable institution has incurred obligations based upon such pledges, these pledges are enforceable.

An exception is sometimes made for consideration in an *agency agreement*. To illustrate: The clothesline post of Brown, a widow, has fallen to the ground. Adam, a next door neighbor, offers to reinstall the post, and in so doing, he drops the post on a child's foot. Adam, in trying to avoid his responsibility for the injury, could not use a defense of no consideration. In this case, the consideration was a gratuitous one.

Parol evidence rule

This rule refers to prior written or oral agreements between the parties of the contract. When the contract is incomplete, oral evidence may be allowed to complete it. When a contract seems complete and the final expression of the parties is stated in the agreement, parol evidence will not be allowed to alter the agreement by a court of law.

Performance, discharge, and breach of contracts

PERFORMANCE OF CONTRACTS

Both parties to a contract have certain rights and duties to perform. These rights and duties, however, may be assigned unless the contract calls for some personal quality of the promisor and unless the contract forbids assignment. These cases will be discussed later in this chapter.

A contract may be performed by *novation*. Novation refers to the substitution of a new agreement or contract for an existing obligation. The intent of the parties must be to extinguish the old obligation. The substitution of the new agreement is usually between the parties to the original contract. It can, however, be with a new party whether he be the debtor or creditor. Since a new contract has been substituted for an old one, it requires an additional consideration and all of the essential elements for a valid contract. No particular form is necessary.

When no time is specified for the completion of a contract, a reasonable time suffices. The definition of "a reasonable time" will depend upon the circumstances involved. For example, Adam contracts with Brown to build a house; the contract might be for three months. Assume the contract is signed in November. Weather conditions might hold up performance of the contract for from four to five months. When litigation enters into performance under the contract, the court must decide what would have been a reasonable time under the circumstances.

When a date for completion of a contract is specified, both parties should adhere to it. Assume that Adam leases an apartment to Brown. It is specified in the lease agreement that Brown is to pay his rent on or before the 15th of each month. Brown pays his rent and continues to do so for the next three months as follows: One month, Brown pays his rent on the 20th, the following month, on the 30th, and the following month, on the tenth. Unless Adam asserts his rights to collect such rents when they are due, he may not deny that he did in fact give Brown permission to pay his rent late.

When a contract calls for completion on a specified date or within a specified period of time, and such time falls on a nonbusiness day or a holiday, the time for completion will be the next business day. Assume that a contract or an obligation is to be paid and the due date falls on a Saturday or Sunday. The following business day will be considered the due date, as in the case of tax payments. On business contracts, interest will be due until payment on the next business day. In making contracts, attention should be given to the due date in order to avoid extra interest payments, or in order to prepay before any due date falling on a Saturday or Sunday.

DISCHARGE OF CONTRACTS

Contracts may be *discharged* by (1) partial performance, (2) substantial performance, (3) impossibility of performance, (4) agreement between the parties, (5) operation of law, (6) release, or (7) acceptance of a breach of contract.

Contracts may be discharged by partial performance either before or after a breach when such breach is expressly accepted by the creditor in writing. When a claim or debt is in dispute, an acceptance of part performance must be by an expressed agreement in writing.

When the contractor gives a substantial performance and yet, for some reason, the contract is not completed in detail or to exact specifications, the contractor may be entitled to the contract consideration with allowances made to cover damages suffered by the second party to the contract. In order to collect, the contractor must show that he acted in good faith in substantially performing the contract.

A contract may be discharged where there is a possibility of performance for one of the parties. These cases may occur by some act of a creditor or by operation of law. This would be true even though the contract states that this shall not be an excuse. The inability of one of the parties to perform would not be an excuse. It must somehow be in the nature of the thing to be done. Assume that Adam and Brown enter into a valid contract to sell property. Adam dies after entering into the contract and his heirs claim impossibility of performance. This would not be a valid defense because the contract would be binding upon the estate.

There may be mutual agreement between the parties to discharge a contract at any time. This may be done by novation, wherein a new contract is substituted for an old one as in the discussion of performance of contracts. Adam and Brown, parties to a contract, may wish to admit a third party to the agreement, and would substitute a new agreement for the old one. They may also agree to rescind the contract and restore each to his original position. They may enter into a contract and stipulate that the agreement or contract will have no further effect upon Brown's termination of employment with a certain company.

Contracts may be discharged by operation of law. When contracts are signed in blank and later filled in, this constitutes fraud and causes the contract to become voidable.

When one of the parties to the contract alters, cancels, or destroys the subject matter of the contract to the detriment of the other party, this action is considered to release the latter from his obligations under the contract. If a contract is executed in duplicate and a second copy still exists, this rule would not apply. Assume Adam and Brown enter into a valid contract which is executed in duplicate, and Brown then makes material alterations to the contract. Adam, having a duplicate copy of the contract, may enforce it. Under these circumstances, one party may render himself liable to the other party for damages.

Contracts may also be discharged when one of the parties involved makes a breach of contract after acceptance by the other party. In this event, if damages are suffered by the innocent party, he may sue for money damages.

EXCUSES FOR NONPERFORMANCE OF CONTRACTS

Certain excuses or defenses may be used for the nonperformance of contracts, such as (1) violation of governmental laws, (2) loss of personal quality of one party, (3) total destruction of subject matter, (4) commercial frustration, and (5) total destruction of means of performance.

A contract cannot be performed when such performance would mean violation of governmental laws or regulations. Assume that a contract agrees to construct an eight-story building on a certain lot. Ordinances provide that no building shall be higher than four stories. Such a contract cannot be performed. Certain regulations in time of war might also prevent the fulfillment of a contract.

When the contract calls for some personal quality of one of the parties and death occurs to such party, the contract may be discharged. In such instances, it would be impossible for an administrator or executor of an estate to perform under the contract.

When there is total destruction of the subject matter of a contract, the parties thereto are released from fulfillment of such contract. Adam and Brown enter into a two-year lease agreement for Adam's house. At the end of six months, the house is totally destroyed by fire. The parties to the contract are released from performance. Rent paid in advance to the lessor normally may not be recovered, however. A partial loss of the property would not necessarily release the lessee from performance. Timely action by the lessor in restoring the property to its original condition would continue the contract and the lessee would be required to complete his part.

Commercial frustration may be an excuse for nonperformance of a contract. Assume a tavern operator has a five-year lease on a building and a new law is passed by the legislature prohibiting the sale of liquor. Or, assume a lease exists on a building whose lessee sells tires. War occurs and tires are no longer available for sale. These would be examples of valid excuses for nonperformance.

The parties may be released from their obligations when there is total destruction of the means of performance. Adam and Brown enter into a contract to manufacture a certain item that is unique to Adam's business. This operation requires special patented machinery. If such machinery is totally destroyed, Adam may be excused for nonperformance.

The injured party of a breach of contract may sue for specific performance or, if damage is nominal, may elect to sue to recover for foreseeable loss from this act by the contracting party. Usually, minors or incompetents may rescind a contract, except for necessities of life. Contracts are void if made by court-adjudged incompetents. In such cases of unilateral rescission, the party so aggrieved is relieved from his responsibilities under the contract by restoring to the other party anything of value that he received thereunder.

Action for money damages may be obtained when the victim under the contract has suffered some detriment or loss. The victim is entitled in some states to the legal rate of interest on the obligation from the day the right to recover is vested in him. When the contract in question states a legal rate of interest, such rate remains chargeable after the breach as before, or until a subsequent verdict or other new obligation is created. The wronged party must have suffered damages and these must be reasonable. The measure of damages is usually based upon the amount that would compensate the party for all detriments. When no damages have been suffered by the plaintiff, the court will allow only nominal damages. Nominal damages might be only $5.

When the contract conveys an interest in real property, the damages suffered include the purchase price plus expenses incurred in the transaction. Adam agrees to sell his house to Brown for $25,000 and Brown accepts the contract. If Adam should later breach the contract, the damages suffered would include the purchase price of $25,000 plus any expenses in-volved. Such expenses might include the title examination report and escrow cancellation charge.

If Brown, the purchaser, breaches the contract, the damages suffered by Adam would be the excess, if any, of the amount he actually received under a subsequent contract. In the above example, assume that Adam sold the house to Cole for $22,500. Damages suffered by Adam would be the difference between these two figures, or $2,500, plus any other ex-penses that were incurred by Adam in the original transaction.

Liquidated damages are those set in advance of and in anticipation of a breach by the parties to a contract prior to the signing thereof. Adam sells his house to Brown for $30,000. Brown deposits $3,000 to show good faith in the transaction. The sales agreement may provide that if the buyer should withdraw through no fault of the seller, the deposit may be kept by the seller at his option, as liquidated damages.

Remedies for breach of contract

When one of the parties to a contract fails to perform, it is a *breach*. Certain remedies are available to the party not wishing to accept such breach; for example:

1. He may sue for specific performance of the contract to compel pay-ment and acceptance of a deed.
2. He may stand upon the terms of the contract, offer to perform, and sue for damages.
3. He may agree with the purchaser for mutual abandonment and rescission, in which case he is entitled to payments made on contract.
4. He may waive his security and sue for the balance of the contract.
5. He may bring action to require the vendee to pay monies due, or foreclose his rights.
6. He may bring an action to quiet title against the vendee, or he may declare a forfeiture pursuant to the terms of the contract.

When one of the parties enters into a contract under fraud, mistake, duress, or undue influence, such party may rescind it. Adam enters into a contract relying upon material representations made by Brown. Adam later finds out that such representations are not true. He may rescind the contract.

SPECIFIC PERFORMANCE

When money cannot compensate the aggrieved person, the court may call upon the defendant for *specific performance* under the contract. Such action is of particular importance in the real estate business because each parcel of land is unique. When specific performance is granted, the aggrieved party must have offered to perform his obligations under the contract. Also, when specific performance is allowed, it must be just and reasonable to both parties of the contract. Specific performance will not be allowed when a party to a contract has been induced to sign through fraud, concealment, undue influence, menace, or duress.

The remedy of specific performance is available only to the seller or purchaser of property. A real estate broker as an agent may not sue for specific performance on a contract.

STATUTE OF LIMITATIONS

The *statute of limitations* limits the time during which lawsuits may be brought to enforce certain rights or claims of parties to a contract. Unless civil actions are commenced within the time periods prescribed by the particular state statute, the plaintiff may find himself barred from relief. When a person "sleeps on his rights" for an unreasonable length of time and fails to assert his claims, he cannot look to the courts for relief.

Rights of third parties in contracts

Persons not parties to a contract may acquire certain rights therein. This may occur when the third party is a *beneficiary* or an *assignee* of the contract involved.

BENEFICIARIES OF CONTRACTS

When a person is not a party to a contract that is intended to confer some benefits to him, he may enforce the contract to obtain these benefits. Adam agrees to convey certain real property to Brown providing Brown will pay a certain sum to Cole. Thus, Cole is a third party beneficiary and may enforce the contract against Brown.

ASSIGNMENT OF CONTRACTS

Both parties to a contract have certain rights and duties, which may be assigned to others unless the contract specifically forbids it or unless the nature of the contract requires some personal qualities of one of the individuals thereto. Many contracts forbid assignment without the consent of the other party. Suppose Adam leases a commercial building to Brown and the lease agreement forbids assignment without the written consent of the lessor. Under these conditions, Brown may assign the contract only upon securing the written consent of Adam. To assign is to transfer all rights and interests of the assignor but not necessarily the legal burdens. Brown remains secondarily liable on the contract.

Fire insurance policies are personal contracts and cannot be assigned without the consent of the fire insurance underwriter.

If the contract calls for some personal qualities of one of the individuals thereto, it is incapable of assignment.

Review questions

1. Review the definition of a contract and distinguish between an expressed and an implied contract.
2. List the elements of a contract and give examples of the use of each type.
3. How does an option differ from a regular contract of sale? Give one illustration of the use of an option contract.
4. Give five examples of items that must be in writing and signed by the party or his agent to consummate a valid contract.
5. What is meant by the parol evidence rule, and when will the court admit its use for evidence to a contract?
6. Name five ways in which a contract obligation may be discharged.
7. What remedies are available to one party to a contract if the other party does not perform and a breach of contract occurs?
8. Discuss specific performance as a means to enforce a contract. What are the limitations of its use?
9. What rights and duties to a contract may generally be assigned?
10. Make clear distinctions among these contract terms—void, voidable, unenforceable, and valid.

Multiple-choice questions

1. Minors and insane persons may generally be held liable for their contracts in connection with: (a) any personal property under $500, (b) automobiles, (c) necessities of life, (d) construction of a building, (e) no legally enforceable circumstances.
2. For legal purposes a written contract: (a) usually prevails over an oral agreement, (b) never prevails over an oral agreement, (c) rarely prevails over an oral agreement, (d) always prevails over an oral agreement, (e) must always be typewritten.
3. Consideration of a contract may be: (a) a promise to perform some act, (b) the payment of money, (c) a promise to refrain from doing something; (d) a promise of money, (e) all of the foregoing.

4. A mistake of fact or a mistake of law: (a) may make a contract voidable, (b) always makes a contract voidable, (c) may make a contract void, (d) always makes a contract void, (e) still binds the parties to the contract.

5. An executed contract is a: (a) contract completed and fully performed by both parties, (b) contract under the jurisdiction of the probate court, (c) contract signed, notarized, and recorded; (d) contract to be rewritten, (e) contract not fully performed.

6. A voidable contract can normally be rescinded by: (a) a party which has used duress to obtain consent, (b) either party, (c) only the innocent party, (d) only by both parties mutually, (e) undue influence.

7. The law which bars legal claims beyond certain time limits is the: (a) statute of frauds, (b) statute of limitations; (c) probate code, (d) Internal Revenue Code, (e) none of the foregoing.

8. The following contracts are not usually assignable: (a) personal service, (b) fire insurance, (c) consent of parties, (d) without consent of parties, (e) lease agreement.

9. Which of the following statements is generally true? An option is: (a) valid without consideration, (b) valid if the consideration is $25 but is not delivered, (c) valid if the consideration is delivered, even if it is less than $25; (d) not valid if the delivered consideration is less than $100, (e) valid only in connection with real property.

10. The term "rescind" in real estate contracts most nearly means: (a) rejected, (b) reworded, (c) terminated, (d) rewritten, (e) none of the foregoing.

6
Law of Contracts
(Real Property)

In Chapter 5 the general law of contracts was covered. This chapter will deal solely with contracts for the sale or exchange of real property.

Although each real estate transaction is different, the sequence of steps is generally the same. The listing of a property with a real estate broker is the first step in a real estate transaction. The property owner should use care in the selection of a broker. The selection may be based upon the recommendation of a friend or upon previous service of the brokerage firm.

The broker, who has a valid listing agreement, is expected to perform under his agency contract. He advertises the property and shows it to prospective buyers. These prospective buyers may not be in a position to pay cash, so it may be necessary for the broker to arrange adequate financing on the property. He may do this by going to various lenders and securing conditional loan commitments from them for amounts they would lend on the property should a sale occur.

Once a buyer is found ready, willing, and able to purchase the property, the broker will make out a sales agreement incorporating the terms under which the buyer offers to purchase the property. The broker has the responsibility to make certain that all terms under which the buyer is willing to buy the property are set forth clearly and concisely in this instrument. In a few states, the law requires that such sales agreements be filled out by an attorney.

The sales agreement is now presented to the seller for his acceptance. If the seller accepts all the terms as set forth in the sales agreement, it will constitute a binding agreement between the buyer and the seller. If either party withdraws, he will be liable to the other for breach of contract. If the seller does not accept all of the terms of the agreement, he may counter offer to the buyer on those conditions which are not acceptable to him. In this case, it becomes necessary for the broker to return to the buyer for his approval of the new terms in the sales agreement. In the sale of large parcels of property, it is not uncommon for several counter offers to be made before a binding agreement is in effect.

Once the sales agreement has been finally accepted and signed by both the buyer and the seller, and the acceptance has been transmitted to all parties, they are ready to take the necessary steps for closing the transaction.

The subject of "closing" will be covered in Chapter 12 of this text.

Listing agreements

A listing agreement creates an agency; therefore, a broker holding a listing agreement is the agent of his principal.

Brokers may collect a commission on the sale of real property only if the listing agreement is in writing. Contracts for the conveyance of real property are required to be in writing; thus, the listing contracts creating the authorization to sell must also be in writing. A listing agreement need not be in any particular form, but many standard forms are available today. Normally, in order for the broker to assure that a commission will be paid, the listing agreement must be signed by the property owner. When the property is in a community property state, the listing agreement should be signed by both the husband and wife. However, the husband alone may sign a valid listing agreement and commit the community property to a real estate commission. Should the wife refuse to convey the property, the broker would still have a valid suit for payment of commission.

If a broker sells a piece of property upon which he does not have a valid listing agreement, the recovery of a commission may not be impossible. When signed escrow instructions provide for a commission of a certain sum in dollars to be paid to the real estate broker, and the deal is consummated, the broker is entitled to his commission, even though a valid listing agreement was not in effect. When the sales agreement is properly signed by the sellers and it provides for a commission to be paid to the broker, he may enforce its payment.

TYPES OF LISTING AGREEMENTS

Open listing. An open listing gives several brokers an opportunity to procure customers for a property. If the property is sold by a broker, the owners need not give formal notice of the sale to the other brokers. The open listing says that if the broker furnishes a buyer willing, ready, and able to purchase the property under the agreed terms and conditions, he will be paid a commission as provided for in the agreement. However, if the owner sells his own property, he does not have to pay a commission to the brokers. Contractors or builders will use this type of listing on occasion.

The broker, under the terms of an open listing agreement, normally cannot afford to spend a great deal of time or money on the sale of the property. Also, if the property owner quotes a price different from that quoted by the broker, difficulties may arise.

Net listing. In a net listing, the broker retains anything received above the sale amount set by the property owner. For example, A, a property owner, lists his property with B, a broker, for $120,000 net to A. If B sells the property for $130,000 he may retain the difference of $10,000, excluding any expenses in connection with the sale. The agent must disclose the amount of his compensation prior to or at the time at which the principal binds himself to the transaction. The broker as a fiduciary agent must act in good faith toward his principal. The question may arise, "Did he advise his principal as to the true value of the property?" In the example given, assume that the broker sold the property for $140,-000. The burden of proof is upon the broker to show that he did act in good faith; otherwise, his license might be in jeopardy.

Exclusive agency listing. Under an exclusive agreement, the property owner appoints one broker to sell the property as his exclusive agent. Since the owner is not an agent, he reserves the right to sell his own property. If anyone other than the exclusive agent sells the property, a commission must be paid to the exclusive agency broker. Under most state statutes, such agreements must have a definite date of termination. If they do not, the broker's license can be suspended or revoked if he attempts to collect a commission. Assume that B, a broker, secures an exclusive agency agreement to sell A's house. The listing agreement is dated and signed by the property owner and provides that the listing agreement shall remain in effect until cancelled by him. This is in violation of the statutes in a majority of states because the agreement does not have a definite termination date.

Exclusive right-to-sell listing. The exclusive right-to-sell agreement gives the listing broker the exclusive and *irrevocable* right to sell property. If, during the time the agreement is in effect, anyone else makes the sale, whether it is another agent or the property owner, the listing broker is entitled to his commission. As with the exclusive agency agreement, most state statutes prescribe that the exclusive right-to-sell agreement must have a definite date of termination. Any deviation is in direct violation of most state statutes and the broker's license may be suspended or revoked.

Under the exclusive right-to-sell listing agreement, the broker owes a high duty to his principal. He must advertise, and diligently try to procure a purchaser for the property. He must keep his principal informed at all times concerning the progress he is making, and inform him of all material facts.

The state officials charged with enforcing the laws regulating real estate receive complaints from time to time that some brokers have not been diligent in this, with the result that the property has been tied up for a long period of time. Generally, all such written complaints must be investigated. In some cases, the broker may have expended time and effort toward procuring a purchaser for the property, and yet have failed to inform the property owner of his progress throughout the listing period. If he has *serviced* the listing properly and kept the principal informed, but has not been successful in selling the property, it may be possible for him to get such a listing renewed. It is usually considered inadvisable for a broker to take in large numbers of listings unless he feels that he can expend a reasonable sum for advertising and believes in good faith that the properties can be sold.

Multiple listing. Multiple listing associations are conducted by a group of real estate brokers organized to present a service to property owners. Most multiple listing associations are a part of the board of realtors within a given community. Multiple listing agreements are drawn up using the exclusive right-to-sell form. These agreements are sent to a central multiple listing office and copies are distributed to all members of the association. Commissions are split between the listing office and the selling broker's office, with a small percentage going to the multiple listing association to cover costs of operation. When the listing office also sells its own listing, it may retain the entire commission by paying the association its fee. Such listing agreements and such associations have the advantage of exposing the property to a wide group of buyers, increasing the probability of a quick property sale.

Option listing. The option listing agreement can also take the form of any of the listing agreements described above, including the net listing. The option listing does have the added clause that gives the broker the right to purchase the property at the price specified in the contract. In a majority of jurisdictions, the broker must, within a specified period, make a full disclosure of his profit on the transaction. He must further obtain his principal's agreement, in writing, to said amount of profit.

An *option* is a contract to make a contract in the future under specified terms and conditions. To be enforceable, it must be supported by a valid consideration. The broker may wish to use such an agreement in land development. By optioning the property and paying a valid consideration, the broker may agree to buy the property under certain terms and conditions. *Note*: As a principal in the transaction, the licensee must inform the property owner that he is a real estate broker, in order to permit the owner of the property to deal accordingly with him.

In land development, the option agreement will give the developer time to do the engineering work necessary to comply with the various laws for developing the property. Once this work is completed, the developer may exercise his option and proceed with the subdivision. An option agreement is included in the Appendix.

It is not usually necessary that paid consideration be represented by cash. The developer may option a 20-acre parcel of land, pay the property owner $10 in cash, and agree to expend reasonable effort, engineering costs, and so on, in the development of the property. Before the option expires, he may exercise his option to purchase the property under the terms therein.

While listing agreements may vary from state to state, an expanded analysis is given below of the most common clauses included in exclusive right-to-sell listing agreements. This analysis should aid the student in his interpretations.

> 1. *I hereby employ Broker, exclusively and irrevocably, for a period beginning* <u>January 2, 1972,</u> *and ending at midnight* <u>March 1, 1972</u> . . .

The wording "exclusively and irrevocably" means that one broker and one broker alone is employed to sell said property. Under the terms of this listing, if the property owner sells the property, he must pay the broker a commission based upon the selling price. The student's attention is also called to the definite date of termination. If this listing agreement did not bear a definite date of termination, the broker's or salesman's license might be suspended or revoked in many states.

> 2. . . . *and to accept a deposit thereon.*

In listing agreements, a broker is employed to find a buyer willing, able, and ready to purchase the property. Unless a listing agreement provides for such, the broker is not authorized to accept a deposit from a prospective buyer; if he does so, he must act as agent for the buyer and not for the seller. Most listing agreements do provide for the broker to accept a deposit.

> 3. Terms.

The broker or salesman should take sufficient time with the property owner to secure all terms and details of the transaction that might be pertinent. The organization of the terms is important. The minimum amount of cash desired should first be set forth; then, the amounts and conditions of mortgages involved in the sale of the property. Can the first or second mortgage be assumed by the buyer or must he secure his own loan? What assets are being transferred with the real property? Are there items within the household that might be considered real property that the owner wishes to reserve? Assume the property owner wishes to take the draperies from the living room with him when he moves. These should be reserved in the listing agreement; otherwise they are expected to remain with the property. Personal property should be transferred with a bill of sale.

    4. Agreement to pay Broker's commission.

Commission is not fixed by law, but is, rather, a matter of custom in the area. If the broker is to receive a 6 percent commission on the sale of property, this should be stated. The amount need not be given in dollars since the sales price of the property may be different from the listing price.

    5. Legal description of property.

In listing improved real property, it is usually sufficient to give the street address. The legal description is necessary for unimproved land. In the case of land the legal description of which may be two or three pages in length (metes and bounds), such description may be attached as Exhibit A.

    6. . . . . *If a sale, lease, transfer, or exchange of the above described property is made or effected directly or indirectly by me, the undersigned owner, or through any agent or through any other source during the term hereof or any extension thereof, I (we) agree to pay Broker said percent of the above listed price.*

This is an exclusive and irrevocable listing agreement, valid for the stated dates. If the property owner sells, transfers, or leases the property during the term of the listing or any extension of the listing, either through another broker or by himself, or if the property is withdrawn from sale, he is obligated to pay the broker the percentage agreed upon.

    7. *If a sale, lease or other transfer of the above described property made within six (6) months after this authorization (or any extension thereof) terminates to parties with whom Broker negotiated during the term hereof, or any extension thereof, and said Broker notifies me in writing of such negotiations, personally or by mail, during the term of this authorization or any extension thereof, then I agree to pay said commission to Broker.*

This paragraph is often referred to as a "safety clause." Previous to the expiration of the listing, the broker should provide the property owner in writing with a list of all prospective buyers for his property, with whom the broker has had serious negotiations. If he fails to do this, and the owner should consummate a sale to one of these prospective buyers, the broker is not necessarily entitled to a commission. Notification to the property owner may be accomplished in one of several ways. If the owner does not wish to renew the listing agreement, the broker may send a letter to him, previous to the expiration of the listing, reading somewhat as follows: "Dear Mr. Jones: We are sorry we did not have the opportunity to sell your property during the term of the listing agreement. However, during this period of time we have had the pleasure of working with: (Here are stated the names and addresses of the customers with whom the broker worked)."

> 8. Seller's provision for closing in the event a sale is made.

Customs and laws for closing transactions in the various states differ. These differences will be discussed in Chapter 12.

> 9. Liquidating damages. . . . *If deposits or amounts paid on account of the purchase price are forfeited, one-half thereof may be retained by Broker and the balance shall be paid to me provided, however, that the amount paid to Broker shall not exceed the amount of commission.*

This paragraph provides for liquidated damages if the buyer should cancel out through no fault of the seller. If, however, one-half of the amount of the deposit amounts to more than the amount of the stipulated commission, the broker would not be entitled to keep the excess. For example, if the deposit on the property amounted to $5,000, and the broker was entitled to $2,000 based upon the selling price of the property, he could retain $2,000 with the balance of $3,000 going to the seller.

> 10. Acknowledgment and receipt of a copy of the agreement by principal. *I hereby acknowledge receipt of a copy hereof. . . .*

When the prospective seller signs the listing agreement, he is entitled to a copy thereof. Should the broker fail to give him a copy, his license may be suspended or revoked. The burden of proof is always upon the broker. The fact that the seller acknowledges receipt of a copy of the listing contract does not matter. The broker would be required to submit proof in litigation that he did give a copy of the listing agreement to the seller.

The signatures of all owners of the property should be obtained on the listing agreement.

> 11. *In consideration of the foregoing listing and authorization, the undersigned, Broker, agrees to exercise diligence in procuring a purchaser.*

This phrase makes the contract or listing agreement a bilateral one. The property owner promises to sell his property under the terms thereon, and the broker agrees to use diligence in procuring a purchaser. While courts in the various states are not at all in agreement, unilateral contracts as they pertain to listing agreements may not be enforceable.

General contracts of sale

Real estate brokers should be able to prepare all form instruments either incidental to or an important part of the real estate industry. The broker should have these form agreements readily available, but he should be careful not to encroach upon the province of the attorney. Article 7, Code of Ethics of the National Association of Real Estate Boards states:

> The Realtor should not engage in activities that constitute the practice of law, and should recommend that title be examined and legal counsel be obtained when the interest of either party requires it.

Form contracts of sale will vary throughout the states in content and in headings (deposit receipt; real estate purchase contract and receipt for deposit; real estate sale contract; earnest money receipt; offer to purchase; sales agreement; and so on).

It is important that each party to a contract read and understand it before affixing his signature. He should seek legal counsel for explanation if necessary. Below is an expanded analysis of some common clauses in form contracts.

> 1. Deposit of earnest money. *Received from* John Doe and Mary Doe, his wife, *hereinafter referred to as the* Purchaser(s), *the sum of* xxxxxxxxxx Five Hundred and no/100 - - - ($500.00) - - - *Dollars as earnest money. . . .*

A deposit should be large enough to protect the seller in case the purchaser defaults through no fault of the seller. A deposit may take a form other than cash but if so, it should be properly described in the instrument. The earnest money deposit might include cash, a personal check, a cashier's check, a promissory note, or items of personal property such as an automobile or a mink stole.

> 2. Legal description. . . . *for the purchase of property situated in the* City of Detroit, *County of* Wayne, *State of* Michigan, *described as follows:*

Here the legal description should be inserted; however, in conveying improved property it is usually sufficient to give the street address. The legal description is generally necessary for unimproved land. In the case of land the legal description of which may be two or three pages in length, such description may be attached as Exhibit A. It is prudent to include the current vesting of title with the property description.

> 3. Terms of sale. . . . *for the total sum of* <u>Twenty-eight Thousand and no/100 - - - - - - ($28,000.00) - - - Dollars to be paid as follows: The sum of $7,000.00 cash which shall include the above earnest money ($500.00) herein receipted for upon delivery of deed. This offer to purchase is conditioned upon purchasers obtaining a new conventional loan in the minimum amount of $21,000.00 for a minimum term of 25 years, payable at approximately $176.30 per month, including interest at 9 percent per annum. Purchasers shall have 30 days from date of acceptance within which to obtain such loan commitment or waive this condition. Loan fee shall not exceed one (1) percent.*

All terms and conditions of sale should be set forth in a clear and concise manner for the protection of all parties concerned. This includes all contingencies to which the offer to purchase may be subject to.

> 4. Title conditions. *The property to be conveyed by a good and sufficient deed to purchasers shall be free and clear of all liens, encumbrances, easements, restrictions, rights, and conditions of record, or known to the seller, other than the following:*
> (a) *Covenants and restrictions of record, if any.*
> (b) ....
> (c) ....

The above clause may be worded to make the contract of sale subject to covenants, conditions, and restrictions of record only—referred to as CC & R's. If the wording above is used, all liens, encumbrances, easements, restrictions, rights and conditions of record, or known to the seller, should be set forth.

> 5. Items to be apportioned. *Seller and purchaser herein agree to prorate the property taxes which become due and payable for the current fiscal year on a fiscal year basis. Rents, interests, and premiums for existing insurance shall be prorated on a calendar year basis. Adjustments are to be made as of the date of the consummation of sale herein, or delivery of possession, whichever occurs first.*

Other items to be prorated might include special assessments, fuel, and so on.

> 6. Marketable title. *It is agreed that if the title to the said premises is not marketable, or cannot be made marketable within 30 days after notice of such defects to the seller, the earnest money herein receipted for shall be refunded to purchasers upon demand.*
> 7. Purchaser's default. *If the purchaser fails to complete said purchase as herein provided by reason of any default of purchaser, the seller*

shall be released from his obligation to sell the property to the purchaser and may proceed against the purchaser upon any claim or
remedy in law or equity.
Or . . . Upon default by the purchaser in the performance of any
of the conditions contained herein, the earnest money shall be forfeited as liquidated damages, and all rights of the respective parties
shall be at an end.

8. Seller's default. *In the event that the seller is unable to convey title
in accordance with the terms of this contract, the sole liability of
the seller will be to refund to the purchaser the amount paid on account of the purchase price, and to pay the net cost of examining
the title, which cost is not to exceed the charges fixed by_____,
and upon such refund and payment being made, this contract shall
be considered cancelled.*

Note: While the above clause seems to limit the liability of the seller,
the purchasers may have other remedies as outlined in Chapter 5 of this
text.

9. Risk of loss. *If the improvements on the property are destroyed or
materially damaged prior to delivery of the deed, the risk of loss is
assumed by the seller and any earnest money paid by the purchaser
shall be returned to him and this agreement shall become null and
void.*

Note: The "intent" of the parties to the contract may be an important
factor, as far as risk of loss is concerned. If the purchaser takes possession
of the property prior to the closing of the transaction or delivery of deed
and no provision is made for payment of rent, he may, in some cases, become obligated to complete the transaction if the property is destroyed
by fire or materially damaged. If a landlord–tenant relationship is established, the situation is quite different.

10. Closing. *The deed shall be delivered upon the receipt of the required payments at the office of_____, Esq., attorney
for the seller,____(street address)____,____city & state____, at ten
o'clock on the morning of* <u>April 10, 1972.</u>

Customs and laws for closing transactions in the various states differ.
These differences will be discussed in Chapter 12 (Title Search, Examination, and Escrows).

11. Vesting of title. *Unless otherwise designated in the instructions of
the purchaser, title shall vest as follows. . . .*

The manner of taking title may have significant legal and tax consequences; therefore, this matter should be given serious consideration. If
the purchasers are in doubt as to the manner of taking title, legal counsel should be consulted.

12. Time for performance. *Time is of the essence in this contract.*

This clause may have little value. A few agreements contain language permitting the broker to extend time—*Time is of the essence in this contract but the broker may, without notice, extend (for a period of not to exceed one month) the time for the performance of any act hereunder, except the time for the acceptance hereof by the seller and the date of possession.* There are many cases where the right to enforce the contract may be waived. Either party, for example, may waive strict performance by the other's failing to insist on it. At best, the clause seems to permit a party to insist on the contract date and, after timely tender and notice, to reject belated attempts at performance by the other.

13. Binding effect. *The stipulations in this contract are to apply to and bind the heirs, executors, administrators, successors, and assigns of the respective parties.*

The general rule is that death terminates a contract. The effect of the above clause is to make it binding after the death of an individual.

14. Enforcement of contract. *In any suit or action brought on this contract, the prevailing party shall be entitled to recover reasonable attorney's fees to be fixed by the court, and if an appeal is taken from any judgment or decree entered therein, the prevailing party shall be entitled to recover such sum as the appellate court shall adjudge as reasonable attorney's fees.*

15. Possession of premises. *Possession of said premises is to be delivered to purchaser on or before ——————— 19——— .*

Unless otherwise agreed, possession of property usually passes at the close of the transaction or delivery of the deed.

16. Time for acceptance by seller. *Purchaser's signature hereon constitutes an offer to seller to purchase the real estate described herein. Unless acceptance hereof is signed by seller and the signed copy delivered to purchaser, either in person or by mail to the address of the purchaser within———— days hereof, this offer shall be deemed revoked and the deposit shall be returned to purchaser.*

The general rule is that an offer may be withdrawn before its acceptance. The time period specified is placed against the seller and since the buyer has not received consideration for keeping the offer to purchase open, he would not be obligated to do so. If the seller accepts the offer on the day after expiration of said agreement, it would be of no effect unless agreed to by the purchaser.

17. Purchaser's signature. *The undersigned purchaser offers and agrees to buy the above described property on the terms and conditions above stated and acknowledges receipt of a copy hereof.*

Signatures

The purchaser, in signing this agreement, should make sure that all terms and conditions to which he agreed can be met. The purchaser further acknowledges receipt of a copy of this agreement. Most state statutes require that an agent deliver a copy of an agreement to the party at the time he affixes his signature thereto.

> 18. Acceptance by seller and broker's commission. *The undersigned seller accepts the foregoing offer and agrees to sell the property described thereon on the terms and conditions therein set forth. The undersigned seller has employed the brokerage firm of*__XYZ Realty Company__ , ___street address___ , ___city and state___ , *and for broker's services agrees to pay broker, as a commission, the sum of* __One thousand six hundred and eighty__ *Dollars payable as follows:*

_____

_____

Signatures

In most form contracts, when the buyer defaults after the signing of the contract through no fault of the seller or the broker, the earnest money deposit collected is retained as liquidated damages, one-half going to the broker and one-half to the seller. The broker's one-half may not exceed the full amount of his commission. Provisions for liquidating damages must be included in the contract. The broker further has the responsibility to give the seller a copy of the agreement at the time he affixes his signature thereto.

Agreements of sale

Under the agreement of sale, title does not pass to the buyer until the terms and conditions of said contract have been met. The seller holds legal title and the buyer has an equitable interest in the property.

Agreements of sale are also known as *land contracts, installment contracts, contracts of sale,* and so on. Agreements of sale may be recorded in a county recorder's office if the seller's signature is acknowledged thereto. This is not the general practice because it would create a lien of record against the property and, in the event of default, it would be necessary for the sellers to clear their title through a quiet title action. Under the agreement of sale, the seller is referred to as the *vendor* and the purchaser the *vendee.*

The agreement of sale or land contract is frequently used in low-priced developments in which most buyers could not qualify, under institutional lenders' standards, for the amount of downpayment or credit rating. Closing fees and title charges are deferred until title passes, usually for several years, thus reducing the customary closing costs required at the time of the sale.

The seller may wish to use the agreement of sale (installment sales contract) as a tax savings device. The real estate transaction may qualify as an installment sale, if in the year of sale, either no payments are received by the seller, or the payments in that year in cash or property do not exceed 30 percent of the selling price. At least two payments in at least two taxable years are needed to meet the requirement. Under the agreement of sale, the vendor retains legal title to the property and a transfer of title is made after all or part of the selling price is paid. A mortgage may also be used as the security device, which would allow the transfer of title immediately to the new owner. If the taxpayer elects the installment method, he must set forth in his income tax return for the year of the sale or other disposition the computation of the gross profit on the sale or other disposition under the installment method. The subject of taxation is a complete subject in itself and questions concerning taxes should be turned over to a tax expert.

EXCHANGE AGREEMENTS

The trained broker will invariably come upon many opportunities to trade or exchange equities in property. If he is prepared to recognize opportunities for trading real estate, the licensee may increase his efficiency in the business as much as 10 to 30 percent. The majority of brokers, however, depend upon straight cash sales for their commissions.

An exchange of property, rather than a cash sale, may also benefit the principal. Such an exchange may qualify as a *tax-free exchange*. In order to qualify as a tax-free exchange, the real property must be held for productive use in trade, business, or investment. It is rare to find a case in which both properties are clear of encumbrances or are of equal value. When "boot" (cash given in addition to the exchange of properties) accompanies the exchange, the amount of boot must be recognized as taxable income (see Fig. 6).

Review questions

1. Name six types of listing contracts and describe each briefly.
2. Discuss the sequence of steps in the normal real estate transaction.
3. How does the multiple listing differ from the ordinary type of listing of property for sale?
4. Broker Jones obtains a listing on a parcel of land and the sales price is $30,-000. The agreement made no reference to an earnest money deposit. Jones secures an offer to purchase from Smith supported by an earnest money deposit of $2,000. The owner (seller) accepts the deal and demands the earnest money. Discuss the position of each party.

CONTRACT FOR EXCHANGE OF REAL PROPERTY
BETWEEN OWNERS

THIS AGREEMENT, executed and entered into this .... day of .... , 19 .... , by and between

(Owner of property of greater value in the exchange) ....

.... hereinafter called the first party, and

....

.... hereinafter called the second party,

WITNESSETH: That the first party agrees to sell and convey unto the second party, and the second party agrees to purchase from the

first party, at and for a purchase price of ....

.... Dollars ($ ....) that certain property

described as follows, to-wit: *(If there is not room here for the full legal description, use reverse side hereof or separate sheet to be marked Exhibit "A")*

....

....

in.. County, State of.. , free and clear of all encumbrances

excepting ....Dollars ($ ....)

which encumbrances are included in the purchase price of $ ....

And in payment of the purchase price of the above described property, the second party agrees:

(a) To assume the above mentioned encumbrances of $............................... .

(b) To pay the first party in cash $ ....

(c) And to sell and convey to the first party, and the first party agrees to accept from the second party at and for an agreed price of

$ .... that certain property described as follows, to-wit:

(If there is not room here for full legal description, use reverse side hereof or separate sheet to be marked Exhibit "B")

....

....

....

in.. County, State of .... , free and clear of all encumbrances

excepting ....which the first party assumes.

Each party shall furnish forthwith to the other an abstract of title prepared by a reliable abstract company showing, or a policy of title insurance insuring, as of this date or subsequent, good and marketable title to the real property which he herein agrees to convey, free of all encumbrances excepting only those above stated; preliminary to closing, either party may furnish to the other a title insurance company's preliminary report showing its willingness to issue title insurance on his property and such report shall be conclusive evidence as to the status of such party's title; but any such report shall not excuse the party furnishing same from delivering the title insurance policy aforesaid. Each party

shall have .... days after delivery of said abstract, or title insurance policy or preliminary report, in which to examine same and a further period of 30 days after delivery of written notice of defects to correct defects in his title, should any such appear. Each party hereto agrees to accept the other's property subject to city or county zoning ordinances and to such reservations in federal patents and building and use restrictions and easements as may appear of record and none of the same shall be deemed for the purpose and within the meaning of this agreement as an encumbrance on the property. Encumbrances on either property which are to be discharged and removed by the owner thereof may be paid at such owner's option at time of closing out of moneys to be received by such owner in this exchange from the other party hereto.

Each party agrees to convey his respective property to the other by good and sufficient warranty deed. Deeds shall be delivered and transaction closed within .... days from this date.

Each party covenants and agrees to and with the other that he is the owner in fee simple of his respective property, that the same is free of all encumbrances except as above stated and that he has good right to sell and convey the same.

First party agrees that all irrigation fixtures and equipment, plumbing and heating fixtures and equipment, including stoker and oil tanks, water heaters and burners, electric light fixtures (excluding bulbs), bathroom fixtures, roller shades, curtain rods and fixtures, venetian blinds,

window and door screens, linoleum, all shrubs and trees and all fixtures, except ....

are to be left upon the premises as part of the property purchased. The following personal property is also included as a part of the property to

be offered for sale for said price: ....

Second party agrees that all irrigation fixtures and equipment, plumbing and heating fixtures and equipment, including stoker and oil tanks, water heaters and burners, electric light fixtures (excluding bulbs), bathroom fixtures, roller shades, curtain rods and fixtures, venetian blinds,

window and door screens, linoleum, all shrubs and trees and all fixtures, except ....

are to be left upon the premises as part of the property purchased. The following personal property is also included as a part of the property to

be offered for sale for said price: ....

I/we further acknowledge receipt of a duly executed copy of the above exchange contract.

....(Seal)

....(Seal)

....(Seal)

....(Seal)

NOTE—The wives of the contracting parties must also sign the above agreement.

Figure 6

5. Two purchasers of property, husband and wife, ask Broker Jones in what manner they should take title to their new home. What should Broker Jones reply?

Multiple-choice questions

1. When a seller gives equitable ownership to a buyer, the instrument used is: (a) a land contract, (b) an agreement of sale, (c) an installment sales contract, (d) all of the foregoing, (e) none of the foregoing.
2. A real estate broker used the following clause in his exclusive right-to-sell agreements: "In consideration of the execution of this contract, the undersigned broker promises to use diligence in securing a buyer." This clause is: (a) superfluous in most contracts, (b) important in the creation of a unilateral contract, (c) important in the creation of a bilateral contract, (d) to force the broker to advertise the property, (e) enforceable only against the broker's salesmen.
3. A listing agreement in which the owner promises to pay a commission under all circumstances of sale (except if he sells the property himself) is known as: (a) an exclusive right to sell, (b) an exclusive agency, (c) a net listing, (d) an open listing, (e) none of these.
4. The exclusive right-to-sell agreement contains one promise not in an exclusive agency listing. It is: (a) the owner is liable for a commission if he sells the property, (b) the broker agrees to relinquish commission if property is sold by the owner, (c) the owner can back out of contract by giving a five-day written notice; (d) none of these, (e) all of these.
5. A broker who is selling property on which he is holding an option must inform the buyer that he is; (a) an optionor, (b) a grantor, (c) a real estate licensee, (d) a grantee, (e) a vendee.
6. A contract of sale or purchase should be signed by: (a) the real estate broker, (b) the seller only, (c) the buyer and seller, (d) the buyer only, (e) none of the foregoing.
7. A purchaser withdraws his offer to purchase before it is accepted by the seller. The broker should turn the earnest money deposit made by the purchaser: (a) over to the seller, (b) back to the buyer after deducting commission, (c) over to the court, (d) back to the buyer, (e) over to his legal counsel.
8. A listing to sell property and obtain a fixed specified price for the owner is: (a) a verbal listing, (b) an exclusive listing, (c) a multiple listing, (d) a net listing, (e) an illegal instrument.
9. The relationship of a real estate broker to his principal is that of (a) fiduciary, (b) trustee, (c) salesman, (d) all of the foregoing, (e) none of the foregoing.
10. To sell a piece of property on which another broker has a listing, one should: (a) contact the owner of the property, (b) go ahead and show the property to the client, (c) call the other broker and obtain permission to show the property, (d) never work through another broker, (e) forget about the whole thing.

7

Instruments
of Real Estate Finance

Federal Consumer Credit Protection Act ("Truth in Lending")

The Truth-in-Lending regulation—a key portion of the Federal Consumer Credit Protection Act which was signed into law on May 29, 1968 —became effective July 1, 1969. The regulation applies to all real estate loans for personal, family, household, or agricultural purposes. Business loans are exempted.

The law requires the creditor (mortgage broker) to furnish the borrower with a disclosure statement. The disclosure statement must include, among other things, the finance charge and annual percentage rate (APR), which must be printed more conspicuously than the other terminology in the statement. Such disclosure shall be made before the transaction is consummated.

The *finance charge* and *annual percentage rate* are the two most important concepts in the legislation and are designed to tell the customer how much he is paying for credit and the relative cost of credit in percentage terms. In general, the finance charge is the total of all costs imposed by the creditor and paid either directly or indirectly by the borrower. *It includes such costs as interest, time price differential, discounts, service or carrying charges, loan fees, points, finder's fees or similar charges, appraisal fees, credit reports (except in real property transactions) and premiums for credit life insurance required by the creditor as a condition to granting the loan.*

Some charges paid in connection with real property transactions need not be included in the finance charge if they are bona fide, reasonable in amount, and are not contrary to the purpose of truth in lending. These include fees for title examination, title insurance, surveys, preparation of deeds, settlement statements, escrow payments to cover future taxes, insurance and utility costs, notary fees, appraisals and credit reports.

The annual percentage rate (APR) represents the relationship of the total finance charge to the total amount financed. It must be computed to the nearest one-quarter of one percent. The method of computation depends on whether the credit is open end, or of the installment type. In the case of the latter, the APR must be computed by the actuarial method. The APR must be expressed in terms of percentage.

The total dollar amount of the finance charge is not required on a first loan to finance the purchase of the borrower's dwelling.

Under the provisions of the regulation, the borrower has the *right to cancel a loan* transaction until midnight of the third business day following the date of the consummation of that transaction, or the date of delivery of the disclosure statement, whichever is later, if the loan is secured by the borrower's residence.

A first loan to finance the purchase of the borrower's residence carries no right of rescission. However, a first loan secured by the borrower's residence for any other purpose, or a second loan on the same residence, may be rescinded.

The borrower may modify or waive his right to rescind if the loan proceeds are needed to meet a bona fide personal financial emergency.

The notice of rescission must be in writing and mailed or delivered to the lender at the address shown on the notice. Telegraphic notice may also be utilized. A telephone call may not.

When a borrower exercises his right to rescind, he is not liable for any finance or other charge, and any security interest becomes void upon such rescission. Within 10 days after receipt of the notice of rescission, the lender is required to return to the customer any money or other consideration received in connection with the transaction.

The act includes civil and penal sanctions. Willful violation of the truth-in-lending law or regulations is punishable by a fine of not more than $5,000 or imprisonment for not more than one year, or both.

Enforcement of the act is assigned to nine different federal agencies as follows: the Federal Reserve Board for state banks which are members of the Federal Reserve System, the Federal Deposit Insurance Corporation for other insured state banks which are not members of the Federal Reserve System, the Comptroller of Currency for national banks, the Federal Home Loan Bank Board for federally insured savings and loan associations, the Bureau of Federal Credit Unions for credit unions, the Interstate Commerce Commission for industries it regulates, the Civil Aeronautics Board for airlines, the Agricultural Department for creditors under the Packers and Stockyards Act, and the Federal Trade Commission for all other creditors, including department stores and other retailers. See notice of right of rescission (Fig. 7).

Principal instruments of finance

Few people wish, or can afford, to pay all cash for property within their lifetime. In the real estate business, almost every transaction involves some type of financing, whether short or long term in nature. Even when the property owner could afford to pay cash, he may be able to use his funds to better advantage elsewhere.

An understanding of the principle instruments of finance, such as promissory notes (see Fig. 8) and mortgages, is essential to the real estate broker and to the property owner.

When the property buyer wishes to make only partial downpayment on a home, he must be prepared to assume an existing indebtedness. This debt will be evidenced by a promissory note in writing. As security for the promissory note, a mortgage is given, in most states. The mortgage gives the lender additional assurance that his note will be paid when due.

Negotiability

One of the attributes of negotiable instruments is their acceptability and transferability to third persons. If negotiable instruments are made payable to bearer (see Fig. 9), the instrument may be handed from one person to another. When the instrument is made payable "to the order of," it will require an endorsement by the original payee and subsequent payees, who may also become endorsers. Various types of endorsements are used. These include:

1. A *blank* endorsement. The payee signs his name on the reverse side of the instrument, and subsequent payees may do the same.
2. A *special* endorsement. The payee writes "pay to the order of John Smith" and then signs his name. Before the instrument can be negotiated further, John Smith must endorse the instrument.
3. A *restrictive* endorsement. The payee writes "pay to the order of First National Bank for deposit only" and then signs his name. This restricts the instrument to one purpose.
4. A *qualified* endorsement. The payee writes on the reverse side of the instrument "without recourse." The payee is actually saying that he

---
(Identification of Transaction)

Notice To Customer Required By Federal Law:

You have entered into a transaction on _____ which may
(Date)
result in a lien, mortgage, or other security interest on your home. You have a
legal right under federal law to cancel this transaction, if you desire to do so,
without any penalty or obligation within three business days from the above
date or any later date on which all material disclosures required under the
Truth in Lending Act have been given to you. If you so cancel the transaction,
any lien, mortgage, or other security interest on your home arising from this
transaction is automatically void. You are also entitled to receive a refund of
any downpayment or other consideration if you cancel. If you decide to cancel
this transaction, you may do so by notifying

(Name of Creditor)

at_____
(Address of Creditor's Place of Business)

by mail or telegram sent not later than midnight of _____. You
(Date)
may also use any other form of written notice identifying the transaction if it is
delivered to the above address not later than that time. This notice may be
used for that purpose by dating and signing below.

I hereby cancel this transaction.

(Date)

(Customer's signature)

EFFECT OF RESCISSION. When a customer exercises his right to rescind under
paragraph (a) of this section, he is not liable for any finance or other charge, and
any security interest becomes void upon such a rescission. Within 10 days after
receipt of a notice of rescission, the creditor shall return to the customer any
money or property given as earnest money, downpayment, or otherwise, and shall
take any action necessary or appropriate to reflect the termination of any security
interest created under the transaction. If the creditor has delivered any property
to the customer, the customer may retain possession of it. Upon the performance
of the creditor's obligations under this section, the customer shall tender the
property to the creditor, except that if return of the property in kind would be
impracticable or inequitable, the customer shall tender its reasonable value.
Tender shall be made at the location of the property or at the residence of the
customer, at the option of the customer. If the creditor does not take possession
of the property within 10 days after tender by the customer, ownership of the
property vests in the customer without obligation on his part to pay for it.

Figure 7

PROMISSORY NOTE

_____, _____
(City)   (State)

_____19____

For value received, undersigned maker(s), jointly and severally, promise to pay to the order of _____ at the above place _____ dollars ($_____) in _____ consecutive monthly payments of $_____, each beginning one month from the date hereof and thereafter on the same date of each subsequent month until paid in full. Any unpaid balance may be paid, at any time, without penalty and any unearned finance charge will be refunded based on the "Rule of 78's". In the event that maker(s) default(s) on any payment, a charge of _____ may be assessed.

1. Proceeds $_____
2. _____
   (Other charges, itemized)
3. Amount financed (1+2) $_____
4. FINANCE CHARGE   _____
5. Total of payments $_____
  ANNUAL PERCENTAGE RATE   _____ %

Signed _____

_____

_____

Figure 8

will not be responsible if the maker of the note refuses payment. Certain warranties are still implied by law, however. These warranties include assurance:

a. That the transferor has good title to the instrument
b. That the maker or endorsers of the instrument had the capacity to contract
c. That the transferor has no knowledge of any defects in the instrument that would render it valueless
d. That the instrument is genuine and is what it purports to be.

PROMISSORY NOTES

The promissory note is the principal instrument that is used to evidence the obligation or debt. The U.S. Uniform Negotiable Instruments Law, and the Uniform Commerical Code define in detail the many rules governing these instruments.

A negotiable instrument is a written promise or order to pay a certain sum in money. Examples of negotiable instruments include promissory notes, bank checks, and bank drafts. In general, three kinds of promissory notes are used:

1. *Straight note,* calling for the payment of interest periodically, the entire sum of the note being due and payable at the end of the term

S-N FORM No. 1307—Truth-in-Lending Series—DISCLOSURES—First Lien—Conditional Sale of Real Property with Dwelling Thereon.
Stevens-Ness Law Publishing Co., Portland, Oregon 97204

1307

DISCLOSURES REQUIRED BY FEDERAL LAW

Creditor _____ Customer(s) _____
                 Hereinafter called seller   *Hereinafter called buyer*

Address _____ Address _____

Summary of proposed transaction: A sale by seller to buyer for the sum of $_____, of real property and the
dwelling thereon, now free of encumbrances, known as_____

Use legal description or show Street Number, City, State and Zip

evidenced by a conditional sale contract, hereinafter called "security agreement." For a more complete legal description of
said real property and further details relative to the transaction, reference is made to the security agreement, a copy of
which, now made a part hereof, is furnished to the buyer. The security agreement will secure future indebtedness and
cover after-acquired property. The dwelling on said real property *is/is not* to be used as buyer's residence.
*Delete, by lining out, any words which are not applicable.

Amount Financed:
1. Cash price . . . . $_____
2. Down payment, cash $_____; trade-in $_____,
   total down payment . . . . $_____
3. Unpaid balance of cash price (line 1 minus 2)—**amount financed** . $_____

Interest: The purchase price bears interest on declining balances at _____ %
per annum, payable monthly. The said interest is the only **FINANCE CHARGE**
in the transaction. The total interest payable during the full term of the contract
converts into

AN ANNUAL PERCENTAGE RATE OF _____%

Payments: The total of all payments is the contract price plus the interest;
the unpaid balance of cash price (line 3 above) is payable in _____
monthly installments of $_____ each; each such payment includes
both interest and principal; the first payment will be due _____,
19_____, and further payments on the same day of each month thereafter until
the price is fully paid. (If irregular payments are required, show same with the
"Other Disclosures" below.) The total number of payments is _____.
Balloon Payments, if any, if not paid when due, will not be refinanced.
Insurance Coverage: The seller will require, for the term of the contract, insurance on the dwelling and other buildings on said property against loss by
fire with extended coverage in the amount of $_____; the premium
for the initial coverage for a term of _____ years is $_____

All premiums listed above are the cost of the insurance, if obtained through the
seller for the term stated; the buyer may choose the person through whom the

OTHER DISCLOSURES:

insurance is to be obtained, subject only to the seller's right to refuse, for reasonable cause, any insurer offered by the buyer. Credit Life and/or Disability
Insurance is not required for this credit, the purchase of the same being entirely voluntary on buyer's part. No credit insurance is involved unless the buyer
who wishes the same signs the appropriate statement below. If such insurance
is procurable, the premium therefor for the term of the credit will be: for Credit
Life Insurance $_____; for Credit Life and Disability Insurance
$_____.

☐ I desire Credit Life Insurance only ☐ I desire Credit Life & Disability Insurance

_____ _____ _____ _____
Date   Signature of Buyer   Date   Signature of Buyer
Prepayment Charges: (Show method of computation)

Delinquency Charges: (Show method of computation)

Refund Credit: If the buyer pays, before maturity, the full amount of said
obligations, interest on the unpaid balance of the cash price (line 3 above) ac-
cruing subsequent to the date of prepayment will be abated and all unexpired
insurance policies above will be released and surrendered.

Receipt is acknowledged from the seller of a copy of the foregoing disclosures and a copy of the proposed security agreement, all delivered PRIOR to the execution of any documents.

_____, 19____ _____ X_____
Date disclosures received   *Witness*   *Buyer*

_____, 19____ _____ X_____
Date disclosures received   *Witness*   *Buyer*

NOTE: This Form No. 1307 must be used in transactions involving the conditional sale of real property with
dwelling house thereon, on which the contract will be a FIRST lien. If the contract is not to be a FIRST lien,
use S-N Form No. 1308.

ORIGINAL AND DUPLICATE FOR SELLER
TRIPLICATE FOR BUYER

Figure 9

2. *Installment note*, calling for periodic payments to be made on the principal and with additional interest payable with each periodic payment ❧

3. *Amortized note*, calling for one, single-level payment which includes principal and interest and is to be made periodically over a period of time to completely pay off the note or debt obligation

To be negotiable, an instrument must be freely transferable. Such documents must conform strictly to the statutory definition as outlined in the Uniform Commercial Code. A promissory note must, therefore, have these seven essential requirements to be negotiable:

1. There must be an unconditional promise.
2. The instrument must be in writing.
3. The instrument must be made by one person to another.
4. The instrument must be signed by the maker.
5. The instrument must be payable on demand or at the predetermined future date.
6. The consideration involved must be a sum certain in money.
7. The instrument must be payable to order or to bearer.

If any of these essential elements outlined above are not present, the instrument is not considered negotiable; however, it may be valid between the two parties involved.

In a valid negotiable instrument, it may be possible for the transferee to receive more than the transferor had. When the payee of a negotiable instrument transfers it to a third party (who becomes a holder in due course), the transferee may enjoy a favored position. A holder in due course may be defined as "one who takes a negotiable instrument under certain conditions," as outlined below:

1. The instrument, when negotiated, was not overdue, and no notice of previous dishonor was given.
2. The instrument was taken in good faith and for value received.
3. The instrument was taken without notice of a defect in the title by the transferor.
4. The instrument was complete and regular on its face.

When a holder in due course brings an action to collect on a promissory note, the maker may not use certain personal defenses in order to refuse payment, such as:

1. Failure of consideration. Assume that Adam gives Brown his negotiable promissory note. Brown endorses the instrument, giving it to Cole. When Cole attempts to collect from Adam (the maker), Adam may not use failure of consideration as a personal defense.
2. Fraud. Suppose that by false statements Adam is induced to sign the instrument. This is not a good defense.

3. A claim of prior payment or rescission of the debt, evidenced by a promissory note. Suppose Adam, the maker of the instrument, pays the amount due on the note, yet fails to pick up the instrument stamped paid, and the payee transfers this to a holder in due course. Adam may not use this as a personal defense.

4. A set-off. Suppose Adam gives Brown his promissory note for $1,000. Brown owes Adam $750, evidenced by a promissory note. When Brown negotiates the $1,000 note received from Adam to a holder in due course, Adam may not use the other obligation in personal defense as a set-off.

While the personal defenses discussed above would not be good against holders in due course, they would be good against the original payees. There are real defenses that are good against all persons, including a holder in due course, such as:

1. The incapacity of the parties to contract. Suppose the maker of the instrument is a minor or an incompetent so adjudged by a court. This real defense would be good even against a holder in due course.

2. The instrument negotiated is executed in connection with gambling or other illegal conduct, or it is an usurious instrument.

3. Forgery or material alteration of the instrument, in which Adam, the alleged maker of a promissory note, never signs the instrument, or Brown, the payee of the instrument, materially changes the amount of consideration.

MORTGAGES AND TRUST DEEDS

A majority of states use the *mortgage* (see Fig. 10) as security for the promissory note. However, in a few states, the deed of trust is used. The major differences between mortgages and deeds of trust are covered below.

There are two parties to a mortgage, the *mortgagor* and the *mortgagee*. The mortgagor is the party who borrows money for purchasing the property; the mortgagee is the lender. A mortgage does not transfer title to a third party; rather, it creates a lien against the mortgaged property. Title to the property is held in the name of the mortgagor.

A deed of trust has three parties, the trustor, the trustee, and the beneficiary. The trustor is the borrower, the beneficiary is the lender, and the trustee is the party who holds *legal title* to the property (sometimes referred to as a *dry* or *bare title*). Legal title to the property is conveyed to the trustee, who reconveys the property to the trustor when he has fulfilled the obligation of the debt. In the event that the trustor fails in his obligation, the trustee sells the property at public sale to satisfy the obligation of debt to the lender or beneficiary.

Each state has adopted a statute of limitations. Such statutes provide that, after a certain time has passed, the claim on the contract will be barred. While the time limit will vary from state to state, the promissory note and the straight mortgage, which acts for the security of the obligation, are both barred under the statute of limitations four to six years from date of last payment or from due date. The promissory note that acts as the principal obligation for the deed of trust may be barred after this period, but the deed of trust is not barred, as *legal* title is held in the name of the *trustee*, who can sell anytime.

When the mortgage contains no *power of sale* clause, the only remedy available to the mortgagee is foreclosure by action. If the mortgage, however, does contain a power of sale clause, this power may be exercised. In a deed of trust the beneficiary through the trustee may foreclose by court action or by sale.

Assignment, Transfer, or Discharge of the Security. The assignment of a promissory note secured by a mortgage instrument carries the security with it. An assignment of a mortgage instrument transfers nothing without the principal obligation, the note. By the same token, if the note is transferred, the transferee is entitled to the security.

A mortgage may be recorded to give constructive notice of its existence. An assignment of a mortgage may also be recorded to give constructive notice.

When a mortgage is transferred, it may be taken either "subject to" or "assumed." If the instrument is taken "subject to," the grantee cannot be held personally liable for any deficiency on the obligation. The lender or mortgagee will look directly to the original party for the obligation. The assumption of an obligation, which may also be recorded, puts the grantee in primary position concerning his obligation. He is now responsible to the mortgagee or beneficiary. If the lender is unable to collect, however, he may go back to the original borrower. Thus, the original debtor may be held liable for deficiencies after a sale of the mortgaged property. To be completely relieved of any liability under the obligation, the original debtor must be given a release by the lender.

Mortgage instruments may contain a *partial release clause*. This clause releases certain parcels of the land when the conditions within the mortgage pertaining to partial releases have been fulfilled. Subdividers in developing residential property will use this clause to release lots. To illustrate, a partial release clause might provide that, upon payment of $10,000 by the debtor, a certain portion of the property will be released free and clear.

Offset statements are obtained when a person "assumes" a mortgage or takes property "subject to" the loan of record. An offset statement shows the current condition of the loan.

Mortgage of Real Property

This Mortgage made the..day of................................

in the year one thousand nine hundred and ....

by ....

....

....

.... *mortgagor*............

to ....

....

....

.... *mortgagee*............

Witnesseth *That the mortgagor*........*do*...............*hereby mortgage to the mortgagee*...............
....*that certain real property*
situate in the..*County of*....................
State of.., *particularly described as follows, to wit:*

Together *with all and singular the tenements, hereditaments, and appurtenances thereunto*

belonging, and the rents, issues, and the profits thereof...

....

This Mortgage *is made to secure the payment of*..............................*promissory note*..........,
of even date herewith, in the words and figures following, to wit:

Also, *to secure the payment to the mortgage*........*of all money expended by*...............*under*
the provisions of this mortgage hereinafter contained, together with interest thereon as herein-
after provided; ALSO, if suit be commenced to foreclose this mortgage, to secure the payment
of a reasonable counsel fee to be fixed by the court, the expense of the examination of the title
to said property, and the costs and expenses of such suit; and ALSO to secure the performance
of all the covenants and agreements of this mortgage.

    The mortgagor........*hereby agree*........*to keep insured against loss by fire*...............
....*the buildings now on or which shall hereafter be*
erected on said property, with loss payable to the mortgagee........, *as*...............*interest may*
appear; and also to pay when due, all taxes, assessments, and other encumbrances whatsoever,
which now are, or may be, or may hereafter appear to be liens on said property, or any part
thereof. If the mortgagor........*shall fail so to do, the mortgagee*........*may, without notice to the*
mortgagor........, *effect such insurance and pay such taxes, assessments, and encumbrances, and*
in such event, the mortgagee........*may expend such sums therefor as*...............*shall deem*
necessary and shall be the sole judge of the legality thereof.

Figure 10

The mortgagor........further agree........to pay to the mortgagee........the principal sum of said promissory note........, and the interest thereon, according to the terms thereof, and also, on demand, the amounts of all sums of money which said mortgage........shall have paid by reason of the provisions, or any of them, hereinbefore contained, together with interest on each of said amounts from the time of the payment thereof by said mortgagee........until paid, at the rate of ....per cent per annum.

In case default be made in the payment of the principal sum of said promissory note........ or the interest that may grow due thereon, or any part of said principal or interest according to the terms of said note........, or in the payment of any other moneys herein agreed or provided to be paid by the mortgagor........, or the interest thereon, or in the performance of any of the covenants or agreements herein contained, then the mortgagee........ may consider the entire indebtedness secured by this mortgage as immediately due, and the mortgagee........ may thereupon, or at any time during such default, institute legal proceedings for the foreclosure of this mortgage and the sale of said property, and out of the net proceeds of such sale shall receive all indebtedness hereby secured, with counsel fee and costs.

In Witness Whereof the said mortgagor........ha........executed these presents the day and year first above written.

Signed and Delivered in the Presence of

....

....

State of California,

County of.. } ss.

On this................................day of................................

in the year of our Lord one thousand nine hundred and................................, before me,

....

a Notary Public, State of California, duly commissioned and sworn, personally appeared

....

....

....

known to me to be the person........described in and whose name................subscribed to the within

instrument, and acknowledged to me that................executed the same.

In Witness Whereof I have hereunto set my hand and affixed my official seal in the................................County of................

the day and year in this certificate first above written.

....
Notary Public, State of California.

My commission expires................................

Figure 10 (continued)

97

When a mortgage has been paid in full, a *satisfaction of mortgage* is recorded in most states.

When the promissory note and the deed of trust are paid, a deed of reconveyance is executed by the trustee for the beneficiary. A deed of reconveyance reconveys the legal title from the trustee to the trustor.

Generally, liens on the same property take priority according to the time of their creation. A mortgage instrument may be valid between the parties though it is not recorded. The notice of a lien may be actual or constructive, the latter accomplished by filing in the county recorder's office in the county in which the property is located. All persons are presumed to know that which is a matter of public record. To safeguard his interests, the lender should take the precaution of seeing that the mortgage instrument is recorded.

Most mortgages will carry an *acceleration clause*. This states that the entire sum of the obligation becomes due and payable upon a certain event, usually the default of the debtor, or upon the sale of subject property or conveyance without consent or approval of the lender.

Default may occur through such events as nonpayment of taxes or failure of the debtor to maintain adequate insurance. The definition of a default will be outlined in the instrument itself. The debtor may usually remedy a default by paying the amount of default, plus costs and attorney's fees. Many mortgage notes contain an alienation clause with a provision that the note shall become due and payable in full if the mortgagor sells the property, since he is then able to pay the mortgage.

Release of the mortgage instrument. When the debtor maintains payments during the life of the loan, the lender must release the lien of record upon demand. When the instrument is a mortgage, a satisfaction of mortgage is recorded. If the instrument is a deed of trust, the trustee or beneficiary will issue a deed of reconveyance to the trustor. Should the lender fail to release the lien within a specified period of time, some state statutes provide penalties in addition to the actual damages suffered by the debtor.

REMEDIES OF LENDER IN EVENT OF DEFAULT

If the debtor should default on the obligation, certain remedies are available to the lien holders. Under the *mortgage,* the mortgagee may decide to go along with the mortgagor and continue the loan, or he may agree to extend the loan with certain modifications. If the mortgagee decides that the loan is excessive and wishes to collect his money, he may pursue one of the following courses of action: (1) foreclosure by action; (2) exercise assignment of rents clause; or (3) exercise power of sale clause.

The purpose of a *foreclosure by action* is to sell the title and interest in the subject property on which the mortgage was first executed. The debtor and all others who have any interest in the property subordinate to the mortgagee are made parties to the action as codefendants. Prior lien holders to the subject mortgage being foreclosed need not be joined, as their interests will not be affected by the action. A "notice of pendency" (lis pendens), a notice of action, should also be filed in the county clerk's office under the jurisdiction of which the property is located. The purpose of such a notice is to warn all persons that an action has commenced on the subject property.

The complaint filed describes the promissory note and mortgage, states that a default has occurred, and claims that a certain amount of money and interest is due the mortgagee. It further asks for a judgment in favor of the plaintiff mortgagee and asks that the property be sold free from the interest of all defendants, that costs, expenses, and claims be deducted from the proceeds of the sale, and that, if said sale does not realize enough to do same, a *deficiency judgment* be given against the maker of the promissory note.

The summons and complaint must be served on all defendants. A certain amount of time is given defendants to answer the allegations of the complaint. Should any of the defendants answer the complaint, the case must be tried. If the defendant debtors make no answer within the time period specified by statute, the mortgagee proceeds to judgment and the defendants lose by default. The amount due the mortgagee is determined, and a judgment is entered in his favor directing a sale by the sheriff or a commissioner appointed by the court in accordance with the state statutes. Defendants are given notice of the sale and such notice must also be advertised in accordance with the statutes. Any person is permitted to bid at the sale, and the property usually must be sold to the highest cash bidder. When several parcels are covered by the same mortgage, each lot is generally offered separately for sale.

The mortgagee (or his agent) may bid at the sale to protect the amount that is due him. In this way, if the property does not bring enough to satisfy his claim, he gets the property. If the property brings over and above the amount needed to satisfy the mortgagee's claim, perhaps even all costs and expenses, so much the better for the mortgagee. The bid is paid to the officer in charge of the sale, who pays the expenses of sale and the expenses of the court action. The mortgagee's claim is then paid, and any surplus is deposited with the court.

The officer of the sale then makes his report to the court, which will show, among other things: (1) the amount of sale; (2) the amount of any deficiency—the mortgagee may enter a judgment against the maker of the mortgage in that amount providing it is not a purchase money mortgage;

(3) court costs and expenses of the sale; and (4) any surplus remaining after everything has been paid.

Surplus money proceedings may be commenced by persons having valid claims against the property to protect their rights, in order of priority. When all such priorities and claims have been determined, the money will be divided as proportionally among the claimants.

The successful bidder, upon paying his bid, will receive a deed of possession to the property. If there are persons in possession of the property who refuse to vacate, the court will aid the purchaser in removing such persons. It is important, therefore, that all persons with any claim subordinate to the mortgagee be joined in the action.

Some state statutes provide for an *equity of redemption* for a certain period of time after the foreclosure by action sale. This redemption period will vary among states, but the usual period seems to be one year. In this case, the successful bidder at the sale is given a certificate of title, which acts as a conveyance of title to the property. It is actually a conditional title. The mortgagor may redeem the property at any time during the redemption period by paying, to the successful purchaser or the court officer who conducted the sale, the full purchase price plus any statutory charges and other advances made by the successful purchaser for such items as taxes, insurance, and assessments. The right to redeem is not limited to the mortgagor alone; it may be exercised by any successor in interest. When a creditor of the judgment debtor redeems the property, he becomes an assignee of the certificate of sale, and if the property is not redeemed by the mortgagor, he will become entitled to a deed to the property when the full period has expired.

A foreclosure sale transfers to the successful bidder only the title which was encumbered by the mortgage or deed of trust. Although the deed on such sale may appear to convey full title, it will contain no warranty or representation concerning the title, and this title will remain subject to any liens or encumbrances prior or superior to the foreclosed instrument.

Another remedy known as the *mortgagee in possession* may be utilized with the owner's consent, under an assignment of rents clause. This clause gives the mortgagee the right to collect rents, pay expenses, and apply the balance towards the reduction of the debt. Once the default is remedied, the owner is returned to possession. The mortgagee, of course, must make a full and accurate account to the owner.

The mortgage with *power of sale* clause is provided for in some states. Under this method of foreclosure, the owner is given notice—if he can be found—and the property is advertised for sale. Unless the mortgagee is in possession at the time of sale, it may be difficult for the purchaser to obtain possession if the debtor refuses to vacate. An action in ejectment is expensive and the proceedings may be lengthy. In addition, no deficiency judgment may be obtained against the mortgagor.

The laws of each state vary, and the student of real estate should check the state statutes of his state to determine foreclosure proceedings.

Trustee's Sale. When the trustor defaults under a deed of trust, the beneficiary notifies the trustee of such default. The trustee notifies the trustor of the default by recording in the county recorder's office a notice of default, and sending a copy of the same to the trustor. This notice will identify the deed of trust, and will include such items as the legal description of the property, the name of the trustor, and a description of the default.

When other lien holders, such as holders of second deeds of trust, have requested that a copy of a notice of default be mailed to them, this must be done within a certain time, usually ten days after the recording of the notice of default. Such requests for notices of default may be included in the deed of trust itself, or may be obtained by recording with the county recorder a request for notice of default. A time period, usually three months, must elapse between the recording of the notice of default and the first published notice of the sale of the property in a newspaper of general circulation. (At any time during this period, the trustor may reinstate his loan, a statutory right which may not be waived. If he remedies his default during this time, his loan is reinstated.) Statutes provide that a certain number of days must pass between the first notice of the sale and the date the sale is to take place. During this period the trustor may redeem his property. If he does so, he must pay the entire principal of the note, including all costs incurred and the trustee's fees. Such fees will normally be regulated by state statute. The above penalty also applies if the trustor reinstates his loan during the three-month period between the recording of the notice of default and the advertising period.

The trustee's sale is final, and not subject to any right of redemption by the owner foreclosed against, or by any inferior lien claimants affected by the sale; further, the purchaser is entitled to a trustee's deed. In conducting a trustee's sale, trustees will be sure to have complied with all statutory provisions. A defect in the proceedings may require that the process be started again.

JUNIOR MORTGAGE INSTRUMENTS

In many real estate transactions, funds are required over and above those obtainable under a first mortgage. In some cases a first, second, and even third mortgage may be placed on certain property. A second or a third mortgage on a property is a *junior lien*, and such liens take priority according to their creation. Except for the junior position of the lien, these mortgages appear, on the surface of the instrument, to be the same as a first mortgage, but they usually carry a higher rate of interest. To illustrate, where a first mortgage may carry an interest rate of 8 percent, a second mortgage on the same property might carry an interest rate as high as 9 or 10 percent. The amount of equity the owner has in the property may also make a difference to the interest rate. A junior lien holder is well advised to keep informed on his security, and to take advantage of any laws within his state that may afford him protection.

TYPES OF MORTGAGES

Purchase money mortgage.   A purchase money mortgage is one given as a part of the purchase price in the sale of real property. Assume that Adam buys Brown's home for $30,000 cash. He obtains a personal loan from a lending institution for the amount of $20,000 and gives Brown a purchase money mortgage for the amount of $5,000, paying the balance in cash. The lending institution actually loaned Adam money, and should Adam default on his obligation to pay, a deficiency judgment could be obtained through court action. In the mortgage delivered to Brown, no actual cash changed hands. Brown merely gave Adam an extension of credit. Brown's mortgage is, further, a purchase money mortgage, and no deficiency judgment could be obtained. Such a mortgage does, however, become a lien at the time title passes. When the mortgage is given as a part of the purchase price—by the seller, lender, or another individual—it is a purchase money mortgage, and is prior to any liens against the purchaser in existence at time of sale.

Package mortgage.   A package mortgage not only covers the real property but covers other fixtures and equipment as well. Under this principle, the fixtures and equipment become realty and are included in the mortgage loan, providing that: (1) they are appropriate for use in the home; (2) the parties intend that they become realty; (3) the fixtures and equipment are paid for under the loan; and (4) they are actually affixed in some manner to the realty.

Open-end mortgage.   Under the principle of the open-end mortgage, it is possible for the mortgagor to secure additional advances to add an extra room, build a garage, or make a major improvement on the existing structure. If the mortgagor were to refinance his property to accomplish these improvements, it might prove too costly. Under this type of mortgage, the mortgagor may secure additional advances, up to but not exceeding the original amount of the loan.

Blanket mortgage. A blanket mortgage covers several parcels of property. The usual manner for release of the individual parcels is through parcel release clauses in the mortgage. These clauses were discussed earlier in this chapter.

The FHA-insured mortgage and the "G. I." guaranteed mortgage will be discussed in Chapter 8.

AGREEMENTS OF SALE

Agreements of sale have been discussed in Chapter 6. The title to the property remains in the name of the vendor, and the vendee obtains title when he has fulfilled the conditions of the contract. When a seller is willing to take a small downpayment on property, these instruments may be used. They are also useful for tax purposes to spread out the taxpayer's capital gain on the sale of property. These instruments are also known as installment sales contracts, land contracts, and agreements for purchase and sale.

SECURITY AGREEMENT

In a mortgage or deed of trust, real property is pledged as security for a loan. A *security agreement* is used when personal property is pledged for a debt or obligation owed. This instrument then gives the vendor or seller a security interest in the goods or personal property. The security agreement in conformance with the U.S. Uniform Commercial Code must be in writing and signed by the buyer. The agreement must reasonably identify the personal property pledged, which may be by manufacturer's model number or by serial number. Although a *financing statement* is not recorded it is valid between the parties, but will not be valid against subsequent purchases for value and in good faith.

The forerunner of the security agreement, provided for in the Uniform Commercial Code, was the chattel mortgage. While the code does not rule out such instruments, the chattel mortgage must contain all provisions therein.

FINANCING STATEMENT

The instrument filed to perfect the security agreement is the *financing statement*. Whether it is recorded with the county recorder or with the secretary of state of the state where the personal property is located will depend upon the statutes of the state.

The financing statement must be signed by the secured party and the debtor. It must contain the following: (Uniform Commercial Code 9-402[1])

1. Address of secured party and debtor
2. Statement indicating types, or describing items of collateral

If the debt extends over a five year period, the filing is effective for five years only, unless a *continuation statement* is filed identifying the original statement by file number and stating that it is still effective. The continuation statement will continue until the debt is perfected, or for an additional five year period. The secured creditor may continue to file such statements. If the obligation is due within less than five years, the filing will be effective for the entire period and for 60 days thereafter.

When the debt has been paid in full, a termination statement is filed by the creditor releasing the claim. The debtor should make a written demand on the secured creditor for such a release.

Review questions

1. What is the purpose of the Federal Consumer Credit Protection Act known as "Truth in Lending"?
2. Name and discuss the various types of endorsements of negotiable instruments; include the purpose of each type.
3. Give the common rules governing negotiability, and discuss the types of promissory notes in common use.
4. Explain the conditions under which a person may become a holder in due course of a negotiable instrument.
5. Discuss the differences between mortgages and deeds of trust, as they are commonly used.
6. Explain the use of a security agreement and the financing statement.

Multiple-choice questions

1. A person who is an innocent purchaser of a negotiable instrument for value without knowledge of any defects is called: (a) a holder in due course, (b) an assignor, (c) a principal, (d) all of these, (e) none of these.
2. A promissory note calling for one, single-level payment which includes principal and interest and is to be made periodically over a period of time to completely pay off the note or debt obligation is called: (a) a straight note, (b) an amortized note, (c) a straight note with interest, (d) a straight-amortized note, (e) an interest note.
3. A deficiency judgment is allowed: (a) on a purchase money mortgage to seller when buyer lacks cash to buy the property, (b) on a mortgage to a private money lender for the purpose of purchase of a car, (c) on any mortgage, (d) on a deed of trust only, (e) on all mortgage instruments.

4. If a person endorses a note in such a way as to indicate he is not responsible for payment in the future to the person or subsequent persons receiving the note, this endorsement is called: (a) an endorsement in blank, (b) an endorsement without recourse, (c) an endorsement at will, (d) none of these, (e) all of these.

5. The finance charge and annual percentage rate need not include which of the following, if the charge is bona fide, reasonable in amount, and is not contrary to the purpose of truth in lending? (a) discounts, (b) title examination fees, (c) service or carrying charges, (d) loan fees, (e) appraisal fees.

6. A mortgage is usually released of record by recording: (a) a quitclaim deed, (b) a satisfaction of mortgage, (c) a deed of reconveyance, (d) a mechanic's lien release, (e) a financing statement.

7. A security agreement is executed to secure: (a) a lease, (b) real property, (c) mineral, oil, and gas rights; (d) an eviction, (e) a loan on personal property.

8. The blanket mortgage covers: (a) a single parcel of land only, (b) personal property, (c) more than one parcel of land, (d) farm property, (e) none of the foregoing.

9. To be jointly and severally liable on a promissory note means that: (a) only the person that signed first is liable, (b) each party is equally liable, (c) each party is liable for his share, (d) all parties must be sued to enforce collection, (e) none of the foregoing.

10. A financing statement may be released from the public records by: (a) payment in full, (b) a satisfaction of mortgage, (c) filing a release statement, (d) the death of the debtor, (e) the death of the seller.

8

Financing the Real Estate Transaction

Types of financing

In the previous chapter the principal instruments of finance were considered. In negotiating a real estate transaction, the broker must know the best sources of loans for real property.

The field of finance is one of constant change. The real estate licensee who would be successful in his business must keep abreast of current practices of local lending institutions.

The mortgage money market may be classified as *primary* and *secondary*. In the primary money market lenders loan money directly to the borrowers. They must bear the inherent risk involved in both long- and short-term financing until the obligation is discharged. In a secondary mortgage money market existing mortgages or deeds of trust are sold or used as collateral against new loans.

Institutional lenders or investors make up the largest groups loaning money on real property. Among the institutional lenders are commercial banks, savings and loan associations, insurance companies, and mutual savings banks (see Table 1).

COMMERCIAL BANKS

Commercial banks may operate under either federal or state charter. Federal laws or statutes govern the national banks, and state laws control the activities of state-chartered banks. Limitations placed on loans will differ between national and state-chartered banks. Lending policies

Table 1
Conventional Mortgage Loan Limitations

Type	State S&L LTV	State S&L Term	Federal S&L LTV	Federal S&L Term	State Bank LTV	State Bank Term	National Bank LTV	National Bank Term	Insurance Company LTV	Insurance Company Term
Single F	[1]90	30	[1]90	30	—	—	—	—	—	—
Single F	80/70	30	80	30	80	25	80	25	75	25
2–4	80/70	25	80	30	80	25	80	25	75	25
5–15	70	25	75	25	80	25	80	25	75	25
16 or more	75	25	75	25	80	25	80	25	75	25
Planned Development	[2]80/70	25	80	30	80	25	80	25	75	25
Com'l-Ind'l	70	20	70	25	80	25	80	25	75	25
Nursing Homes	70	20	75	25	80	25	80	25	75	25
Construction	As above		As above		[4]Single F— 18 mos. Other—85% 36 mos.		[4]As 3 yrs above		Limited Activity	
Unimproved Land	70	20	70	[3]1	80	25	80	25	—	—
Leasehold	LTV same— 10 yrs beyond loan term		LTV same— 10 yrs beyond loan term		LTV same— 10 yrs beyond loan term		LTV same— 10 yrs beyond loan term		LTV same. Term 2/3 lease term.	

[1]Maximum loan $31,500, no secondary financing, owner-occupied
[2]Condominium, cluster, coop. 70/75 percent multiple limitation until owner-occupied, (50 percent)
[3]Can be renewed one year if offsites commenced, maximum three years
[4]Takeout required
[5]Pattern noted is general, state of incorporation governs
The above percentages and terms may change from time to time

Key: LTV—loan to value; 80/70: 80 percent first $40,000, 70 percent above

among the banking institutions themselves will differ widely, and the lending policies of the individual banks will depend upon the area in which they operate. To illustrate, the ratio of mortgage loans to time deposits (or the bank's combined capital surplus, whichever is greater,) is limited by law to a certain maximum percent. The individual banking institution, however, may limit this ratio below the maximum, but in no case may it exceed the maximum. Commercial banks, by law, must maintain a liquid position at all times; therefore, they tend to favor short-term loans.

Straight loans are generally restricted to 60 percent of the appraised value of improved real estate, and carry a maximum term of five years. When the loan will be paid within this time period, it may extend over a ten-year period. State-chartered banking institutions, on fully amortized loans, may loan 75 percent of the appraised value of the improved property and extend the period of amortization up to 20 years. A recent change in the law permits national banks or those with federal charters to loan up to 80 percent of the appraised value of the property, and to extend the loan up to 20 years. These percentages and time periods allowable by law do not necessarily reflect the lending policies of the individual banking institutions. To illustrate, a national bank within a given community may decide to lend only 60 percent of the appraised value of the property, and limit the amortization period to 15 years.

In most cases loan applications and appraisals of property are submitted to a loan committee of the banking institution, which will approve or disapprove the loan. Properties may be graded according to type, location, and so on. Prime or excellent property may be accepted at a full 75 or 80 percent of the appraised value with amortization extending over a period of 20 years. A 66.66 percent loan, however, may be granted on acceptable or class B property with an amortization period limited to 15 years. The policies of the individual banking institutions will govern here. Generally speaking, commercial banking institutions will loan up to 66.66 percent of the appraised value on agricultural properties operating on a sound basis, and a maximum of 50 percent on special purpose properties or industrial and commercial properties.

Commercial banks will also make FHA-insured loans and Veterans Administration–guaranteed loans. These loans will be discussed later in the chapter.

The current rates of interest charged by commercial banking institutions will vary from 7 to 10 percent, depending upon the security. Banks rank third in importance in the residential mortgage money market, following savings and loan institutions and insurance companies.

In *qualifying the buyer* for the loan, commercial banks look to the character, capacity, and capital of the individual, sometimes referred to as the three C's of credit. If the individual has good character and earning capacity and a sound motivation for home ownership, he can normally qualify, assuming the property meets the other standards required by the loan committee.

SAVINGS AND LOAN ASSOCIATIONS

Savings and loan associations make more home loans than any other lending institution. Like commercial banks, savings and loans are both federally-chartered and state-chartered. The federally-chartered institutions are governed by the Federal Home Loan Bank, and the state-chartered institutions operate under the supervision of the savings and loan commissioner. State-chartered savings and loan associations may also qualify as members of the Federal Home Loan Bank system. As members of this system, the institution may borrow from its district home loan bank to finance additional loans or to pay withdrawal demands.

Most savings and loan associations today are also members of the Federal Savings and Loan Insurance Corporation, and individual accounts in these associations are federally insured up to $20,000 for each account. With prudent lending policies and federally insured savings accounts, the savings and loan associations have moved to the front in the home loan market.

State-chartered savings and loan associations are usually *stock companies* owned by the stockholders of the corporation. Those savings and loan associations which hold federal charters, however, are owned by their depositors. One of the chief purposes of the savings and loan associations has been to loan money on single-family dwellings, although many of their loans extend to commercial and, in a few cases, industrial properties. Today, savings in the institutions are at an unprecedented high and the interest rates paid to their depositors are very competitive. Many are paying as high as 5 and 7.25 percent interest on time deposits, depending upon the length of time deposits are left. Savings and loan associations normally maintain a margin of approximately 2 percent between interest paid to depositors and that charged to borrowers. In a competitive money market, a full 2 percent margin may not be realistic. To illustrate, in some cases savings and loan institutions in 1964 were paying 4.85 percent interest to their investors and charging 6 percent interest on a home mortgage loan. In such cases, a real estate point or, perhaps, two points, depending upon the loan, may be charged. (*Note*: "point" is synonymous with "percent.") If one point is charged on a $10,-000 loan, this is a bonus to the lender for making the loan of $100 which is paid at the time the loan is taken out. Real estate points will be discussed later in the chapter.

When a savings and loan association is operating under the Federal Home Loan Bank regulations, a conventional loan may be made up to 90 percent of the appraised value of the home. Such a loan may not exceed $31,500 and must be amortized over a period of 30 years or less. State-chartered institutions may make similar loans when the sales price or the appraised value of the property does not exceed 90 percent of such amount or $31,500, whichever is greater. A second mortgage or a deed of trust is not allowed under this type of financing.

Straight loans may be made for 50 percent of the appraised value of property and for a maximum loan period of five years. This amount may be increased to 60 percent, providing the loan is for three years or less.

Savings and loan associations may further restrict their loans to a fixed distance from the home office (a 50- or 100-mile radius). Conventional loans for property improvements may be made to a maximum of $1,500 over a five-year period, and FHA modernization loans may be made for a $3,500 maximum period of five years.

The *interest rates* charged for conventional loans by savings and loan institutions will vary from time to time. Service charges or loan fees to 2.5 percent of the full amount of the loan may be made. In most cases, a prepayment penalty is charged if the loan is paid off during the first five years. Savings and loan associations will usually limit themselves to 75 percent of the appraised value or sales price of the property, whichever is greater, and extend the loan over a period of 15 to 30 years.

Savings and loan associations may now make loans, advance credit, and purchase obligations representing loans and advances of credit for financing the acquisition of mobile dwellings. This type of activity is subject to the rules and regulations of the savings and loan commissioner.

INSURANCE COMPANIES

Insurance companies, as lenders, are interested in large long-term loans, including industrial properties, shopping centers, and so on. Large amounts of money are also invested in the single-family dwelling, particularly when they are FHA-insured or VA-guaranteed. In many cases, the FHA and VA loans are purchased in large blocks from the Federal National Mortgage Association.

Since many of the large insurance companies have their main offices on the East Coast, they operate through loan correspondents who are paid a fee for placing a loan. These loan correspondents may be mortgage banking companies or individuals. In many cases, the loan correspondent also services the loan on a fee basis that is negotiated between the mortgage banking institution and the insurance company. To illustrate, the servicing fee might be 66 percent of the loan. On a volume basis, when the mortgage company is servicing many of these loans, this can be a profitable item. Insurance companies are governed by the laws of the state in which they are incorporated and also by the laws of the state in which they operate. These companies are restricted to loans of 75 percent of the market value of the property of a single-family residence and 66.66 percent for all other types of property. In most cases the terms of insurance loans will not exceed 25 years, but no state restriction is imposed. The term of the loan is further governed by the age or remaining economic life of the property.

As with most other lending institutions, the life of these loans must be amortized over a period maximized at ten years less than the remaining economic life of the building. As is true of the commercial bank regulations, the three C's of credit (character, capacity, capital) are important. In most cases the payment for the loan, which will include taxes, insurance, principal, and interest, may not exceed 20 percent of the borrower's monthly take-home pay. Some insurance companies will not make a loan exceeding two and one-half times the individual's annual income.

MUTUAL SAVINGS BANKS

Mutual savings banks, as the name implies, are owned by depositors of such banks and, as owners, they share in the earnings of the bank. These institutions are located principally in the New England states and although funds do flow as far west as California, they represent only a small amount. They are more active in the secondary than in the primary mortgage money market.

MORTGAGE BANKING COMPANIES

Mortgage banking companies operate under the laws of the state in which they are located. They act primarily as loan correspondents for various lending institutions including insurance companies, savings and loan associations, commercial banks, mutual savings banks, and sometimes, individual lending institutions. In many cases they have funds of their own.

These mortgage companies perform the task of taking loan applications and shopping them among the various lending institutions. They receive a loan fee for placing the loan.

The greatest asset of the mortgage banking company is its loan source book. Ideally, the mortgage company prefers to be appointed the exclusive loan correspondent for several insurance companies, commercial banks, savings and loan associations, pension funds, and private investors. Many of the administrative expenses incurred by the lending companies can be saved by operating through the mortgage banking companies, permitting them to select the loans of their choice.

OTHER SOURCES OF REAL ESTATE FINANCING

Individuals. Real estate brokers and salesmen may find individuals within their community who are willing to loan money on good first and second deeds of trust, particularly when the interest rates paid on these loans will be from 6 to 12 percent and the property is adequate security for such a loan. Individuals are limited to a maximum interest rate in most states; anything in excess is usury.

Individuals are particularly helpful in the second mortgage money market and in short-term loans extending up to three or, on a straight loan basis, five years.

Syndicates. A syndicate is a small group of individuals who band together to finance, develop, or purchase a piece of property. A syndicate may take the form of a *joint venture*, a *limited partnership*, a *partnership*, or a *corporation*. A joint venture is organized for a single purpose. It may include two or more individuals, although the smaller the number in a joint venture, the more flexible it is to operate. The members of a joint venture have unlimited liability, which is one of the disadvantages of such an organization. Unless otherwise stated, all share equally in the expenses and profits of the venture.

A syndicate may also take the form of a general partnership. Under a partnership, all members have unlimited liability and also share in the profits and expenses of the project.

Under a limited partnership, individuals act as general partners with unlimited liability. There may be any number of limited partners, however, and such partners are liable only for the amount of their investment in the project. A corporation may be formed to finance, purchase, or develop a piece of property. The advantage of a corporation is the limited liability of the investors. Under a subchapter ("S") corporation of ten or fewer members, the corporation may elect to be taxed as a partnership at the end of the taxable year. This may be an advantage to individuals planning to purchase or develop a piece of property.

FEDERAL HOUSING ADMINISTRATION INSURED LOANS

Prior to 1934, ours was a nation of renters. Many uncertainties existed when lending institutions made a property loan. A loan was made for a maximum of only 50 to 60 percent of the appraised property value, on a straight loan basis. Property owners would pay the interest periodically during the life of the loan, usually a four- or ten-year period after which the entire loan would become due. Consequently, many were unable to pay their loans in full at this time, and they faced one of two choices—having their loans refinanced by the same institutions or obtaining a new loan (sometimes an impossible achievement).

The Federal Housing Administration was created under the National Housing Act of 1934. Among other things, it provided insured loans which could be amortized over a period of years. The Federal Housing

Administration does not lend money. It merely insures loans made by supervised lending institutions which include banks, life insurance companies, federal savings and loan associations, some state associations, and any other institutions where deposits are insured by the Federal Deposit Insurance Corporation. Other lenders included in this group are approved mortgage companies, pension funds, and individuals.

All approved insured mortgages must be serviced in accordance with practices of prudent lending institutions. If the borrower defaults on his obligation, the lender may apply to the FHA, which will take over the property and pay the lender in cash or government debentures for any portion of the loan remaining. The individual lender may also decide to hold the property and dispose of it through a trustee's sale or foreclosure by court action. The latter may be a time-saving device to the individual lender.

FHA-insured loans have many advantages over other types of conventional financing. These include:

1. Low interest rates, plus 0.5 percent mortgage premium, based on the average outstanding balance of the loan in any one year
2. Elimination of short-term financing, second trust deeds, and mortgages
3. A larger ratio of the loan to the appraised value
4. Protection of the lender providing him with a ready secondary market through the sale to the Federal National Mortgage Association
5. Improved housing standards through minimum specifications and building standards set up by the Federal Housing Administration
6. Provision for one monthly payment which includes principal, interest, insurance, taxes, and so on

The Federal Housing Administration has developed a system to reduce the risks in loaning money on real property by careful evaluation of the individual borrower and by establishment of standards for the appraisal of the property involved.

An individual's *rating* includes an investigation of his credit characteristics, property buying motives, ratio of effective income to total obligations owed, adequacy of other available assets, and the stability of his effective income. Generally speaking, an individual can afford to pay two and one-half times his annual income for a home. His monthly payments on the home should be limited to twenty percent of his effective take-home pay, excluding certain deductions. Property appraisal is based upon livability, the estimated economic life of the property, and appropriate adjustments for economic and social deterioration.

Two types of commitments may be made by the FHA. *Firm commitment* is requested when the mortgagor desires a definite commitment on a specific piece of property with a definite borrower. When the borrower or mortgagor is not known, a conditional loan commitment is requested. A conditional commitment is usually good for six months, and is contingent upon a mortgagor qualifying for such a loan.

A pamphlet entitled "Digest of Insurable Loans" may be obtained from the local FHA District Office or from the Federal Housing Administration, Washington, D.C. 10025. This pamphlet outlines the many minimums and maximums allowable under FHA-insured loans and the many titles under which such loans are made.

Basically, the National Housing Act permits the Federal Housing Administration to insure loans for the purpose of (1) improvements, repair, or alterations to the property; and (2) insuring lending institutions making loans on one- to four-family dwellings and large rental developments.

Property Improvement Loans. Title One of the National Housing Act permits FHA-insured loans made by prudent lending institutions for improvements, alterations and repairs to property. FHA limits their liability to 90 percent of the loss on such individual loans and to 10 percent of the total of such loans made by the individual institution.

Individuals must own the property involved or have a lease expiring not less than six months after the expiration of the loan. Such loans must not exceed $5,000, and, on single-family homes, must be amortized in seven years or less. A permissible loan on a multi-family dwelling is $2,-500 per unit, or $15,000, whichever is less, and must be amortized in seven years and 32 days or less. An insurance charge is paid by the lender on each loan. This program has been self-supporting and has been sufficient in amount to establish a surplus.

Home Mortgage Insurance. Under Title Two in the National Housing Act, loans may be insured on individual mortgage loans. There are several sections under this act; however, this textbook is concerned with section 203b, which deals with loans for construction or purchase of one- to four-family dwellings. The other sections in Title Two are more properly considered in a course in real estate finance.

FHA Maximum Mortgage Amounts. Under the emergency housing law revised by the Federal Housing Administration, maximum insurable loans to purchase a single-family home may be made up to $33,000; for two- and three-family dwellings, $37,750; and for four-family dwellings, $41,250. Such loans may not exceed: (all figures subject to change)

1. 97 percent of the first $15,000 of value, plus 90 percent of the next $10,000, plus 80 percent of the value in excess of $25,000 to a mortgage of $33,000. In order to obtain the maximum loan, then, a single-family dwelling must be appraised at $37,000. Mortgage amounts are adjusted to the next lower multiple of $50. Monthly payments include principal, current interest rate, and one-twelfth of the first annual premium at 0.5 percent per annum. These percentages apply

to proposed or existing construction that has existed or been proposed for at least one year.

2. 90 percent of the first $25,000 of value, plus 80 percent of the value in excess of $25,000 to a maximum mortgage of $33,000 where the existing dwellings have been completed less than a year, or in the case of new construction, not approved prior to its beginning.

3. For a nonoccupant owner, 85 percent of the amount that an owner-occupant may obtain under an FHA loan.

4. For an FHA-VA combination loan, 100 percent of the first $15,000, 90 percent of the next $10,000, and 85 percent of anything beyond this, to a maximum of $33,000. The mortgagor must have a minimum of $200 in prepaid items.

In addition to the above programs, the federal government, through the Federal Housing Administration, is interested in the mobile home industry. Perhaps this industry will aid in solving the housing crisis in this country. Under new FHA regulations, buyers will be able to obtain personal loans of up to $10,000 for mobile home units. The loans may be for terms up to 12 years and 32 days, and will bear an effective annual interest rate ranging from 7.9 to 10.67 percent, depending on the amount and term.

Mortgagor Loan Cost. Loan cost to the borrower will include current interest plus 0.5 percent mortgage insurance premium based on the average outstanding balance of the principal for any 12-month period. The borrower will also be required to place in a loan trust fund a proportionate amount for taxes, special assessments, and hazard insurance. These items will be included in his monthly payments. Other expenses include an FHA application fee, initial service charge, recording fees, credit reports, and a survey of title and title insurance.

VETERANS ADMINISTRATION LOANS

The Servicemen's Readjustment Act, sometimes referred to as the *G.I. Bill*, was passed in 1944 to provide benefits which include loans, hospitalization, education, re-employment, and unemployment allowances.

Title Three of this act authorizes the Veterans Administration to guarantee or insure loans made by private or public lenders to veterans. The act further provides for direct loans to be made to veterans when loans are difficult or impossible to obtain.

FHA loans and VA loans are similar in many respects. Both may be used for the purchase or construction of homes, farms, and business properties. They are designed to enable the borrower to get a maximum loan and to encourage lenders to make loans because of the protection provided. Both VA and FHA loans provide for equal payments, low rates of interest, and a high ratio of loan to value, and both provide for minimum building requirements and prescribed appraisal techniques to determine the reasonable value of the property.

The 1958 Emergency Housing Act extended the VA bill to include Korean veterans. It has since been extended to include Vietnam veterans. Additional benefits of VA loans include:

1. A low rate of interest.
2. No initial service charge; under FHA loans, however, a service charge of one percent of the loan on existing structures, and 2.5 percent on new construction is made.
3. Maximum loans. No limit is placed on the amount of loan that may be made on VA loans. FHA loans do place maximum limits.
4. No down payment, or a minimum down payment as required by the lender.
5. All VA loans must be amortized, but may be amortized under any accepted plan used extensively by established lending institutions. No prepayment penalty is provided; under FHA loans, such penalties may be charged.
6. The veteran, in order to avoid default, may refinance his loan. This may be done by the mortgagee if at least 80 percent of the loan is within the maximum period for loans in its class. FHA limits such refinancing to 75 percent of the economic life of the structure.
7. In the appraisal for VA loans, the reasonable value or cost in light of current conditions is considered; thus, maximum loans are provided.
8. Loans may be made for purposes other than the purchase, construction, and improvement of homes. Loans may be guaranteed for the purchase of farms or farm equipment. Business loans will be considered if the borrower can qualify through his experience, and is able to show favorable conditions under which he proposes to operate.

Usually, the Veterans Administration *guarantees* loans rather than insuring them. When such loans are insured, they must be made by supervised lending institutions which maintain insurance accounts with the Veterans Administration. The Veterans Administration will pay the lending institution up to the amount of its insurance account, in the event of default.

Where the loan is guaranteed, the specified maximum that will be paid to the lender by the government is reduced proportionately as the loan is paid. The amount of guarantee will depend upon the type of loan made. On a single-family residence, 60 percent of the loan is guaranteed to a maximum of $12,500. For farms or business loans, 50 percent of the loan is guaranteed to a maximum of $4,000; and on nonreal property loans, 50 percent is guaranteed to a maximum of $2,000.

In some cases, if the veteran can show that adequate financing is not available, a *direct loan* may be made to a maximum of $13,500. The loan will be conditional upon the ability of the veteran to pay, based upon his present and future income and expenses. Further, the loan must be for the construction or purchase of a home or farm house. The property also must be situated in an area where no private capital is available at the interest rate fixed for VA loans.

No maximum limit is set to the amount the veteran may borrow, but such loans must be amortized over the 30-year period in the case of homes. Farm loans may not exceed 40 years.

Every veteran who receives a discharge other than dishonorable from the service is a candidate for a potential VA loan. If he is planning to purchase a home and use his Veterans Administration–guaranteed loan, he should first find the property. When the veteran makes a deposit to bind the transaction, the deposit receipt or other contract used should provide for the return of the deposit in case the veteran fails to procure the loan. After such an agreement is signed, the veteran should present the contract to the lending institution from which he expects to secure the loan. The property is then inspected by a qualified appraiser from the Veterans Administration, who will determine the reasonable value. The certificate of reasonable value issued by the Veterans Administration is then sent to the prospective lender who will decide whether to approve or disapprove the loan.

Real Estate Points. A real estate point may be defined as a bonus to the lender for making a loan on real property; one real estate point is equal to 1 percent. To illustrate, a lending institution may be making good conventional loans and securing 9.25 percent per annum interest on these loans. Why then, would a lender be willing to make a loan at 8.5 percent? The lending institution may be willing to do so, providing two to four points can be charged. Points increase the total yield to the lender.

If a lender were to make a $10,000 loan for 20 years at 9.5 percent, the payments amortized over this period would be $93.33. This same loan under FHA or VA, bearing interest at 8.5 percent, would return payments of only $86.80. To make up this difference in yield, the lending institution may charge two points, or 2 percent of the loan. This means that the lender will receive a bonus of $200 when the loan is made.

In the case of FHA loans, although the borrower may not be charged more than one point, there is no limit to the number of points which may be made by the seller. This is true of all classes of loans. Under an FHA loan, the lender would receive $100 from the buyer and $200 from the seller, a total of $300. The $100 paid by the buyer would be deducted from the loan and the proceeds would be $9,900. The $200 bonus paid by the seller would be deducted from the amount he received from escrow.

The Internal Revenue Service has ruled that "points" paid by a seller of real property may not be deducted as interest costs, but they may be added to selling expenses. Thus, the amount in dollars represented by payment of "points" may be used to reduce the seller's capital gains.

The buyer may, however, deduct points provided they are compensation for the use or forebearance of money per se and not a payment for specific services which the lender performs in connection with the borrower's account.

FEDERAL NATIONAL MORTGAGE ASSOCIATION

The Federal National Mortgage Association was organized under Title III of the National Housing Act in 1938 to provide a secondary market for mortgage loans that were federally-insured or guaranteed. The industry often refers to this organization as "Fanny May."

One of the purposes of this agency is to assure lenders a ready secondary market for FHA and VA loans. The original capital for the purchase of these loans was obtained from the Treasury of the United States, and the first purchases were made at 100 cents on the dollar.

Loans are currently purchased by FNMA on a "bid" and auction basis. The amount of FNMA funds available for bid are announced every two weeks—time period subject to change—and sealed bids presented by lenders are opened on Monday morning and awarded to the successful bidders. Quotations are in terms of percentage, such as 95.8, which would mean $958 for each $1,000 in loans being bid. The total any one mortgagee can bid at each auction is $1,500,000, which can be split among the classifications below. The classifications are based upon promised delivery by the lender of the loans.

Time period for delivery	Charge made by lender at time bid is submitted[1]
90 days	½%
6 months	¾%
1 year	1%
15 months	1¼%
18 months	1½%

[1]Based on total dollar volume of loans being bid.

In addition to the above, there is a fee of $100 per million that is payable at the time the bid is submitted, and this fee is also nonrefundable. Under the present rules, sellers of mortgages are required to buy capital stock in the amount of 2 percent of their sales to the organization, and must further agree to service the loans for a fee. There is no guarantee, however, that the lender can continue to service. FNMA can withdraw servicing at any time, assign the servicing to another mortgagee, or sell the loans to another mortgagee. Formerly, a mortgagee was permitted to repurchase the loans he had sold to FNMA at the same price within nine months, in case the market price went up. There is no such guarantee today.

In 1968 a separate new corporation was formed known as the Government National Mortgage Association (dubbed Ginnie May). GNMA is a wholly-owned corporate instrumentality of the United States within the Department of Housing and Urban Development. It is authorized to conduct its business in any state of the United States, the District of Columbia, the Commonwealth of Puerto Rico, and possessions of the United States. The principal office of GNMA is in Washington, D.C.

GNMA is authorized by section 306(g) of the National Housing Act to guarantee the timely payment (in accordance with the terms set forth in the security instrument) of principal and interest on securities which are based on or backed by a pool composed of mortgages insured by the Federal Housing Administration or the Farmers Home Administration, or guaranteed by the Veterans Administration. GNMA's guaranty of mortgage-backed securities is backed by the full faith and credit of the United States.

A detailed analysis of either the Federal National Mortgage Association or the Government National Mortgage Association is not possible in this text. The laws, rules, and regulations are subject to change and are more properly covered in a real estate finance textbook.

Creative financing

Lender participation in today's mortgage financing is a new concept and is bringing about a basic change in the character of the industry. Creative financing is the term now generally used to describe this development.

Equity transactions now command such attention that it is predicted a two-rate structure is not only prevalent but will remain with us permanently; that is, a rate at a specified percentage on a straight interest mortgage, and a lower rate that is applied with an equity or income participation provision. The inflationary spiral of the past several years, and the firm belief that it will continue for several years, is generally credited with triggering this phenomenon, since investors are seeking means to avoid being caught with fixed interest rates and a fixed yield that is actually a declining yield in the face of inflation.

The new approaches require infinitely more sophistication and are being applied to every type of property. There are many formulas but they divide basically into: (1) a participation in equity ownership, and (2) a participation in income or cash flow.

Equity participations usually follow one of the following:

1. *Joint venture.* The joint venture is often referred to as the front-money deal. The lender supplies the money and the developer supplies the land and the know-how. Usually profits are divided equally.

2. *Sale and leaseback.* This is probably the oldest of such devices but new refinements have been added such as prepaid interest or "soft" money.

3. *Sale and leaseback of land and leasehold mortgage.* A current favorite, where only the land under a structure is sold and then leased back to the developer with a mortgage placed on the resulting leasehold.

4. *The sale-buyback* (sometimes termed an installment sales contract). This is a refinement of the sale-leaseback with a difference: the contract vendee has an interest in the title so he can take depreciation.

Income participations have several variations of the following:

1. *Contingent interest* or the variable interest rate. This rate is stated in two parts: a fixed rate and an additional rate based on the performance of the property—an add-on of the percentage of the gross income or a percentage of the net income.

2. *Purchase of mortgaged land.* The lender buys land subject to an existing mortgage, leases it back for 40 or more years. Ground rents are approximately 10 percent or more per year with additional rent provided if the project's own rents increase.

3. *Wrap-around mortgage,* sometimes referred to as a blanket mortgage or an extended first mortgage. A borrower may need additional capital which the original lender does not wish to advance. A new lender may advance this additional capital, writing a longer term mortgage for the entire amount of debt outstanding.

Some of these applications have been used for many years, while others are comparatively recent in their origin. There are, of course, numerous variations of each, tailored to fit each particular application. The combination of a "tight" money market and inflation with the mounting competition from other types of investments with high yields has spurred the use of these devices in the real estate lending field. The firm belief of institutional investors of a continuing inflationary period for several years has given such financing an assured continuing future.

Review questions

1. List the most common sources for real estate loans and discuss the current lending practices of the local lenders in your community.
2. What sources of real estate financing are available to real estate brokers other than institutional lenders?
3. Discuss the part the Federal Housing Administration plays in the real estate market. What is the purpose of the Federal National Mortgage Association?
4. What are the advantages of FHA-insured loans over other types of conventional financing of real estate loans?
5. Contrast the Veterans Administration–guaranteed loans with FHA-insured loans. Under what conditions is a veteran eligible for such loans?

Multiple-choice questions

1. A client requests you to advise him concerning how much he can afford to invest in a home. To arrive at this figure, you should multiply his gross annual income by: (a) 1, (b) 2, (c) 2½, (d) 5, (e) 6.
2. Who would most probably pay the initial one point allowed on an FHA-insured loan? (a) seller, (b) buyer, (c) lender, (d) FNMA, (e) mortgage broker.
3. When the Veterans Administration "guarantees" a loan, it does so to protect the: (a) veteran, (b) seller, (c) lending institution, (d) assets of the Federal National Mortgage Association, (e) none of the foregoing.
4. Which of the following is *not* an advantage to FHA financing: (a) reasonably low interest rates, (b) monthly payments within buyer's ability to pay, (c) mortgage insurance at low cost to protect the buyer, (d) improved housing standards, (e) none of the foregoing.
5. When a borrower defaults on an FHA-insured loan, any losses sustained by foreclosure are made up through: (a) the Federal Treasury, (b) the Mutual Mortgage Insurance Plan, (c) an attachment lien against the borrower, (d) an assessment against the lending institution, (e) none of the foregoing.
6. The purpose of "Fanny May" is to: (a) lend money to builders, (b) make loans that regular lenders may not make, (c) stabilize the money market, (d) make loans on subdivisions.
7. A bank will ordinarily make a conventional loan at a higher interest rate than an FHA-insured loan on the same property. What would be the determining factor in deciding to give an FHA-insured loan instead of the conventional? (a) higher return, (b) degree of risk, (c) needs of borrower for interest, (d) number of properties sold by seller, (e) none of the foregoing.
8. The maximum amount that may be loaned to a qualified veteran on a VA-guaranteed loan is limited to: (a) the assessed value of the property, (b) 60

percent of the appraisal, (c) $12,500, (d) $33,000, (e) the amount shown on the VA Certificate of Reasonable Value (CRV).

9. A man listed a property for $16,000 and was willing to take back a mortgage and note for $2,000 as part of the purchase price. The broker secured a buyer who wanted to secure an FHA-insured loan for $12,000, pay $2,000 cash and execute a second mortgage and note in favor of the seller. The broker should: (a) write up the offer subject to the FHA-insured loan and second mortgage, (b) write up the offer "subject to better financing," (c) write up the offer subject to $12,000 FHA-insured loan and a personal loan for $4,000, (d) refuse to accept this offer, (e) do any of the foregoing.

10. Which of the following would give a lender the best protection? (a) an increase or decrease in the value of money, (b) credit of the buyer, (c) value of the property, (d) all of the foregoing, (e) none of the foregoing.

9

Leases

In discussing ownership of real property in Chapter 3, two major classifications of estates were covered: (1) freehold estates, and (2) less-than-freehold estates. The latter category will be explored in this chapter.

Less-than-freehold estates are referred to as *leases* or *leaseholds*. The person who holds the leasehold interest and has the right to exclusive possession of the land is called the tenant or lessee. The landlord or lessor is the one who grants exclusive use of the property to the lessee. The distinguishing feature between lessees and hotel guests, licensees, or employees, is that the latter have no exclusive right of possession; therefore, they are not governed by the laws relating to landlord and tenant.

Leases, more properly referred to as leasehold estates, are called *chattels real*. The term chattels refers to personal property and real refers to real property. A lease is a personal interest in real property and, therefore, is governed by the laws applicable to personal property.

Types of leasehold estates

Four types of leases exist and are recognized in most states. These may be classified according to length of duration:

1. Estate for years
2. Estate from period to period
3. Estate at will
4. Estate at sufferance

ESTATE FOR YEARS

An estate for years is an interest possessed by a tenant having exclusive possession of real property for a fixed period of time.

This may be for a fixed number of years or for a period less than a year. To illustrate, a lease for five years from date of acceptance, or a lease for six months from date of acceptance, is considered an estate for years.

ESTATE FROM PERIOD TO PERIOD

An estate from period to period, sometimes referred to as a *periodic tenancy*, is one that runs from one period to another. This may be from year to year, quarter to quarter, or month to month. The period should be designated in the rental or lease agreement. Statutes in some states require a 30-day notice on the part of the landlord or tenant before terminating such a leasehold estate.

ESTATE AT WILL

An estate at will is one that may be terminated by either the landlord or the tenant at will. No specified period of time is designated in the lease agreement. Notice of termination is usually necessary in most states but the statutes will vary in the several states.

ESTATE AT SUFFERANCE

When the tenant has come into rightful possession of property under a lease agreement and wrongfully remains in possession of the property after the legal term of the lease, it is referred to as an estate at sufferance. The landlord may treat the individual as a trespasser or a tenant. A *tenancy at sufferance* exists, however, until the landlord makes his election. In the states of California and New York, a tenant at sufferance must be given 30 days notice to vacate.

Essential elements of leases

The fourth section of the statute of frauds applies to leases, as to other types of real property contracts. An owner of real property may lease it for as long as he wishes (within statutory maximum limitations), but most states provide that a lease for one year or less need not be in writing; however, if the lease agreement is to extend over a year, it must be in writing. In these states, a term of exactly one year but which is to commence at some future date must also be in writing.

An agent usually has oral authority to lease property for less than one year. However, when the lease extends over one year, such authority may be granted only in writing.

All lease agreements should contain the following items:

1. Date of execution
2. Names of the parties
3. Sufficient description of the premises
4. An agreement for the rent to be paid
5. Time and manner of such payment
6. Signature of the parties

There must be a proper execution of the lease by the lessor or landlord, the lease must be delivered to the lessee, and such delivery must be actual. In some states, however, when the lease is properly executed by the lessor, the acceptance of the premises by the lessee and his actual taking of possession may constitute a delivery. The latter is evidenced by the lessee paying rent and entering into possession of the real property. After acceptance of the lease, both parties become bound under the lease agreement. The lessee need not sign the lease for it to be valid; the signature of the lessor is sufficient in most states.

RECORDING

In most states, contracts of real property may be recorded, and such contracts would include the lease agreement of real property. Recording statutes vary in the many states, however. In California all lease agreement of real property may be recorded. In New York a lease for more than three years may be recorded. In any case, the signature of the lessor must be acknowledged. Where the property is located in more than one county, the agreement should be recorded in both counties. The recording will give constructive notice to all persons that such lease agreement exists; however, in some cases, actual possession of the premises is sufficient. It is advisable to record all long-term commercial and industrial leases.

Covenants, conditions, and provisions of the lease agreement

All pertinent terms should be covered even in the simplest lease agreement. These terms cover such items as the duration of the lease, rent, possession, maintenance and improvements, liability of the parties for injuries, special covenants, conditions, restrictions, and the termination of the lease agreement.

A *covenant* within a lease agreement (or any contract) may be defined as a promise to do or not to do something. Thus, when the tenant or landlord promises to make repairs, it is called a covenant to repair. Failure to perform said covenant makes the tenant or landlord, as the case may be, liable for breach of contract, which may be in the form of monetary damages. The agreement may provide for a forfeiture of the leasehold or a termination thereof which is a condition rather than a covenant. When the condition is not clearly stated, the courts will usually interpret the wording as a covenant rather than a condition.

RENT

Most lease or rental agreements will provide that the tenant shall pay rent in the *manner specified* in the agreement. Assume that this is a *condition* of the agreement giving the landlord the right to declare a forfeiture in the event the tenant does not pay as provided. As a general rule, when the tenant habitually pays his rent late and the landlord does nothing to enforce his rights, then later declares a forfeiture, he may be estopped to deny that he did not in fact give the tenant permission to be late. This is called "late because of habit."

The *time* of the rent payment is normally fixed in the term of the lease agreement. When no mention is made in the lease concerning the advance payment of rent, rent is normally due at the end of the period; however, statutes or customs in a particular state may provide otherwise.

Most residential leases are based on a flat sum of money each month. Others may be based on a sliding scale with stated increases over the term of the lease. Still others may be based on a cost of living index.

POSSESSION

Unless the agreement specifies otherwise, the tenant is entitled to possession at the beginning of the lease, and has the right to retain possession until the expiration of the lease. When a building is under construction, there is an implied covenant that the building will be ready for occupancy on the date the lease agreement is to commence.

The tenants' right to possess is exclusive even to the landlord, unless the landlord reserves the right to make reasonable inspection of the property. There is an implied covenant on the part of the landlord that the tenant will have quiet enjoyment of the leasehold. The covenant, however, is against the landlord's own acts and not those acts of strangers. An eviction of the tenant is a breach of this covenant. What is an eviction? An eviction occurs when the landlord ousts the tenant or allows him to be ousted by someone with a superior title. The eviction need not be actual; it may be a constructive eviction. A *constructive eviction* occurs when the quiet enjoyment of the premises is disturbed by either the lessor or by other tenants. Such an eviction may give the tenant the right to abandon the premises and to pay no further rent. When the tenant remains in possession of the property, he is obligated to continue paying the rent. When the property is taken under the right of eminent domain, the tenant is released from his obligation to pay rent, providing the whole leasehold is taken. Generally, if only a portion of the property is so taken, the lessee is obligated to pay his rent in full and the lessee, not the lessor, is entitled to money damages from the condemnation action. Condemnation should be covered, particularly in long-term lease agreements.

ASSIGNMENT OF LEASEHOLD

An assignment of the leasehold interest transfers all rights and interests that the assignor had, but the assignor remains secondarily liable on the lease agreement unless he is specifically released by the landlord. If the lease agreement so assigned contained an option to purchase the property, the option would also transfer. The assignee, then, has all rights that the assignor had in the contract, while the assignor has the same remedies against the assignee that the landlord had against him. The assignee pays the rent directly to the assignor, unless it is otherwise specified in his contract.

When the lessee *sublets* the premises or leasehold estate, he remains primarily liable to the landlord for payment of the rent and for upholding all covenants, conditions, and provisions of the lease agreement. The assignee (sub lessee) in this case becomes the tenant, and he is liable to the assignor (original lessee) for fulfillment of the lease agreement. In long-term commercial and industrial tenancies, "sandwich" leases are sometimes arranged. To illustrate: A landlord leases a commercial building for 21 years to Adam for $.40 per square foot. Some time later, Adam subleases the property to Brown for 45 cents per square foot. Brown in turn subleases the property to Cole for $.55 per square foot. Cole is responsible to Brown for the payment of rent, Brown is responsible to Adam for the payment of rent, and Adam would remain liable to the landlord for the fulfillment of the contract.

Lease agreements may provide a covenant against the assignment or subletting of the leasehold interest. As a general rule, when the contract does not forbid an assignment or sublease, an assignment may be made on the part of both the landlord and tenant of their contract interests.

REPAIRS

A lease agreement should provide a covenant for repairing the property. When no agreement has been made, and in absence of any statutory requirements, the tenant must make repairs necessary to prevent waste or decay of the property. Failure to make such repairs may make the tenant liable for permissive waste. In some states there may be a statutory duty placed on the landlord to keep the premises in a fit condition for human occupation. What is "fit for human occupation" may depend upon the condition of the property at the time the tenant accepted the property. When there is a statutory duty on the part of the landlord, an exception is usually made for depreciation or waste caused by the tenant's negligence. Generally, when the landlord fails to perform his duty, the tenant may spend up to one month's rent for the repairs, or he may abandon the premises and be discharged of his obligation to pay rent and to perform under the other conditions of the lease. Notice must be given to the lessor by tenant before he moves out or exercises his right. As long as the tenant remains on the property, he is obligated to pay rent.

The tenant should receive written permission from the landlord before he installs fixtures which may be considered real property if he wishes to remove them upon the expiration of the lease. When such fixtures are removed, the lessee must restore the property to its original condition.

USE OF THE PREMISES

As stated in an earlier paragraph, the tenant's right of possession is exclusive and, therefore, he may use his possession in any legal manner he sees fit. The tenant must, however, not allow permissive waste.

The parties to the lease may agree on a limited use of the property. The lease may state "for residential purposes only." This phrase would also include multi-family dwellings.

LIABILITY FOR INJURIES

The lessor may place a covenant in the lease whereby he attempts to exempt himself from any liabilities for injuries to the lessee or any other party while they are on the property. These clauses are referred to as *exculpatory* clauses. When, however, the lessor has been negligent and such contributory negligence can be proved, he may, in some cases, be held liable, even though this provision is contained in the lease. In any case, the landlord may have a right of action against the tenant.

PARTIES BINDING CLAUSE

Contrary to popular belief, a lease does not terminate upon the death of the lessor or lessee. When the landlord enters into a long-term lease agreement and the tenant expends a sum of capital in improving the property for his business, this would constitute an *unjust enrichment*. Most lease agreements will carry a clause that may read: "the terms and conditions of this lease agreement shall bind the heirs, successors, and assigns of the respective parties."

COVENANT TO PAY UTILITIES

In residential lease agreements, the landlord may agree to pay for water charges, but in commercial and industrial leases this is usually the responsibility of the tenant. Other utilities, such as electric lights and fuel, will be paid by the tenant.

A sewage tax has recently been instituted by some cities. This is a special tax and is calculated on the amount of water entering the property. Thus, as the water bill goes up, so does the sewage tax. Since the sewage tax is billed with the water bill, the landlord may want to protect himself by making a provision in the lease agreement.

OPTION TO RENEW LEASE

The lease agreement may contain a provision or option to renew the agreement. The agreement may provide for a stated time period prior to the termination of the lease. The renewal may be automatic or for a definite period of time. If it is automatic, it gives either the lessor or lessee the right to notify the other that he does not choose to renew the agreement. Generally, the right to renew is given only to the lessee, but either party has the right to refuse to renew. Under the definite renewal period, the lessee may notify the lessor within the stated period of time exercising his right to renew. Such a renewal would generally not carry with it the right to renew a second time.

OPTION TO PURCHASE PROPERTY

Lease agreements may provide the tenant with the right to purchase the property in which he has a leasehold. This is particularly common when a tenant has leased for commercial or industrial purposes an area of ground and erects a building thereon. The option to purchase may give a stated price or it may provide for negotiation of the purchase price between the lessor and lessee. The negotiation would normally provide for an appraiser to be appointed by the lessor and another to be appointed by the lessee. The two appraisers would then select another to act as umpire. Each appraiser would then appraise the subject property and most agreements would then provide that the decision of any two would be binding upon the parties.

SALE AND LEASEBACK AGREEMENT

Under a sale and leaseback, the owner of the property sells it to another and then leases it back for a term of years. The term of the lease is normally determined by the economic life of the structure. The pros and cons of this agreement are too numerous to discuss in this text.

SALES CLAUSE

When the landlord has entered into a lease agreement, he may find that said lease will restrict the salability of the property. The landlord may, therefore, wish a cancellation clause in the event of a sale. Thus, if the property sells, the lease would be cancelled. The lessee may want to protect himself against this clause by adding a "first right of refusal." This would give the tenant the right to have the property offered to him first in case of a sale.

SECURITY AND CLEANING CHARGES

The tenant may be required to post with the landlord a sum of money, a security, or a bond as a guarantee of his performance or protection against breakage or waste of the property leased. The amount of such deposit may vary. It may be equal to one month's rent or even a percentage of value of the property. The security is held in trust by the landlord for the tenant and is a fund against which the landlord may draw or retain as damages in the event the tenant breaches his agreement. Otherwise, it must be returned to the tenant upon expiration of the lease.

Cleaning charges are sometimes collected in advance by the landlord to insure that the property will be returned in a clean condition. Some agreements will provide that if the tenant returns the leased property in good condition, all or part of such charges will be returned to the tenant.

Termination of lease agreement

A leasehold estate may be terminated in any one of the following manners:

1. Upon expiration of the lease
2. By the lessee acquisition of the fee title or a title superior to that of the lessor
3. By mutual agreement of the lessor and lessee
4. By destruction of the premises
5. By cancellation at the option of the aggrieved or injured party in case of a breach of any covenant or condition stated in the lease agreement

Lease expiration. The expiration of the lease provides notice to the lessor and lessee that it has expired, and no further notice is usually required. When the lessee continues in possession, fulfilling all conditions of the expired lease, and the landlord continues to accept rent and no provision is made otherwise, the lease is presumed to be renewed for a like period of time and under the same conditions over the period of time in which rent is collected. When rent is collected on a month-to-month basis or quarterly basis, and so on, such renewal of the lease shall not be considered to extend beyond this period.

Acquisition of fee title. There can be no lease agreement when the lessee acquires fee simple title to the property or any title superior to that of the lessor himself. A party may not pay rent to himself.

Mutual agreement. The lessor and lessee may agree mutually to rescind the lease agreement. To illustrate: When the lessee is transferred to another part of the state or country, making it impossible for him to complete his lease agreement, the landlord or lessor may release the lessee from his contract. Otherwise the tenant may be held to his agreement. When the tenant is transferred often, he may desire a clause in his lease to this effect.

Destruction of premises. When destruction of the premises has occurred through fire or other cause and the lessee has paid rent in advance, he may usually not recover such rent. The lease agreement may provide for an apportionment of the rent. To illustrate: When a fire occurs or another damage makes the premises uninhabitable and the lessee remains in possession, he may be liable for the rent. Also providing such damages are minor and the landlord makes immediate repairs the lessee must complete his leasehold estate. A lessee cannot have a leasehold estate longer than the estate of the lessor. To illustrate: When the holder of a life estate has leased his estate in the property, the lease agreement bcomes invalid upon the death of such a life tenant.

Cancellation. When the tenant or landlord breaches a covenant or condition of the lease, the aggrieved party may cancel the lease agreement. Written notice usually is asked of the aggrieved party on such cancellation.

Remedies of the landlord in case of default

LANDLORD'S LIEN

In the absence of an agreement between the parties and in absence of a statute, the landlord does not have a lien upon the personal property of the tenant. The parties may, however, create such a lien.

Some states have created a *baggage lien* law. This law gives the lessor of furnished apartments, bungalows, boarding houses, and hotels the right to place a lien upon the baggage and other personal property of the tenant who has not paid his bill. The lessor may sell such personal property after the time provided by statute (usually 60 days) if the bill remains unpaid. A notice of the sale must be published stating the time and the place of the sale, the name of the debtor, the amount due, and giving a description of the property. The notice must be placed in a newspaper of general circulation in the county and must be published once every week for four consecutive weeks prior to the date of the sale. A copy must also be mailed to the tenant or guest at his last known address at least 15 days prior to the sale. If the address is unknown, the copy is addressed to the location of the apartment house in question. Before exercising this right, the lessor is advised to consult his attorney.

SUIT FOR PAYMENT OF RENT

The landlord may sue the tenant on his contract to pay rent as specified in the lease agreement. If payment of rent is not specified, the lessor may enforce a quasicontractual obligation to pay. When the lessee defaults in the payment of rent, the landlord may sue for each installment as it becomes due. This is true whether the tenant remains in possession or not. Since this is not very practical, it is not often used. Usually, when the tenant abandons the premises, the landlord takes immediate possession and rerents to another tenant. Upon the expiration of the lease, the landlord may sue the defaulting tenant for the difference between the sum for which he was able to rent the property and the rent stipulated in the original lease agreement.

LANDLORD MAY RECOVER POSSESSION

Most lease agreements provide that if the tenant breaches the covenants or conditions of his agreement, such as payment of rent, the landlord may reenter, take possession, and declare the lease terminated. Such reentry may not, however, be automatic. In the event the tenant refuses to leave, it may be necessary for the landlord to file a complaint in the form of an *unlawful detainer action*. The statutes of the state must be complied with fully; these statutes vary in requirements.

Common lease agreements

NET LEASE

There is sometimes confusion in the real estate industry concerning net leases. A *true net lease* (net, net, net) provides a net figure to the landlord. All expenses, including taxes and insurance, are paid by the tenant. The term *net, net, lease* is sometimes used. In this case, the tenant usually pays for everything except insurance and taxes. Another term sometimes used is a *broker's net*. Usually only a portion of the major expenses are stated. Under the real estate law of most states such representations are illegal.

PERCENTAGE LEASE

The percentage lease is one in which the rental consideration is based upon the gross sales of a business. It may also provide for a guaranteed amount against a percentage of gross sales. Below are examples of percentages paid by some retail stores.

Auto accessories	8–10	Groceries, chain	3–5
Barbershops	10–15	Hardware	6–8
Cleaners and dryers	10–12	Theaters	8–10
Drugs, regular	6–10	Variety stores	6–8

The above percentage figures vary throughout the country.

GROSS LEASE

In this type of lease, the premises are leased at a flat rate. The landlord usually pays all expenses and the rent is the total consideration involved.

OIL AND GAS LEASES

Real estate brokers in many states become involved with oil and gas leases. An oil and gas company may wish to lease a piece of land, believing that oil and gas may be found on the property. A flat sum of money is usually paid by the oil company for a stated period of years, giving the company the right to drill for oil and gas during the period. If oil and gas are found, a royalty is usually paid (approximately one-eighth of a barrel of oil, and one-eighth of the gas sold) to the lessor. The lease will normally provide that, in the event operations are not started within one year, another flat sum of money will be paid for the continued oil and gas rights.

Review questions

1. Distinguish between freehold and less-than-freehold estates.
2. Discuss the four common types of leases that exist in most states.
3. Give reasons for recording of a lease, and its legal significance.
4. Explain leasehold assignment and subletting of the premises of a leasehold, with reference to responsibility of parties.
5. State the ways in which a lease agreement may be terminated, and the remedies of the landlord in case of default in rent.

Multiple-choice questions

1. A tenant who continues in possession of a property after the expiration of a lease is said to have: (a) an estate of inheritance, (b) an estate for years, (c) an estate at sufferance, (d) a life estate, (e) a fee simple estate.
2. Which of the following is true regarding the termination of a lease? (a) a lease terminates upon the death of a lessor, (b) a lease terminates upon the death of a lessee, (c) a lease does not terminate upon the death of a lessor or lessee, (d) all of the foregoing, (e) none of the foregoing.
3. Which of the following applies to whether or not a lease must be in writing? (a) it must always be in writing, (b) it is better verbal than written, (c) it is required to be in writing if for a period of one year or more, (d) it is re-

quired to be in writing if for a period of more than one year, (e) it should never be in writing.

4. A lease: (a) creates an interest of both real estate and personal property, (b) conveys an interest in real estate, (c) is a *chattel real*, (d) all of the forego-going, (e) none of the forgoing.

5. Before filing an unlawful detainer action, a landlord usually must: (a) obtain judgment for possession, (b) secure a sheriff's eviction, (c) serve the tenant with a three-day notice to pay rent or quit the premises, (d) none of the foregoing, (e) all of the foregoing.

6. In a lease, assigning means: (a) subletting, (b) paying rent in advance, (c) changing managers, (d) transferring all rights to another person, (e) doing all of the foregoing.

7. What is the interest between the holder of a fee title and the final sublessee called? (a) in-between lease, (b) sandwich lease, (c) lease in sufferance, (d) redemption lease, (e) any of the foregoing.

8. A landlord leases a store to a men's clothing shop on a "percentage lease." On which of the following is the percentage usually based? (a) market value, (b) assessed value, (c) appraised value, (d) tenant's gross sales, (e) tenant's net income.

9. A lease by a minor lessor is: (a) voidable by lessee, (b) voidable by lessor, (c) not renewable, (d) void, (e) valid.

10. When real property under a lease agreement is sold, the lease: (a) must be renewed, (b) expires, (c) is broken, (d) remains binding upon the new owner, (e) is voidable by lessee.

10

Deeds and Instruments
of Conveyance

The development of land transfer

Years ago, under English Common Law, the transfer of property was accomplished by "livery of seisin." The seller of the land would meet the purchaser on the property and pass a clod of dirt, a small branch from a tree, a stone, or some other symbol and say, "This land belongs to you," and the transfer was accomplished. If any questions were raised in future years concerning this transfer, a witness was usually around to say, "Yes, I saw the transfer take place." Ownerships of property were common knowledge and transfers were few, usually from father to son.

Later, in 1677, when the Statute of Frauds became part of the law in England, the symbolic transfer or delivery described above was replaced by the delivery of a written instrument. This was developed into our present-day *deed*, which is generally now uniform throughout the states.

The general nature of deeds

A deed is a written document transferring property from the owner, called the *grantor*, to another person, called the *grantee*. Such document must be properly executed by the grantor, delivered to and accepted by the grantee. A deed is a contract and, therefore, must contain the essential elements of a contract discussed in Chapter 5.

Essential elements of deeds

A valid deed should contain certain elements, including:
1. Proper writing
2. Description of the parties

3. Parties capable of conveying and receiving real property
4. Consideration
5. Adequate legal description
6. Grantor's clause
7. *Habendum* clause
8. Proper execution by grantors
9. Proper delivery

A state's statute of frauds requires that all transfers of real property be made in writing. Legal instruments such as the deed may only be drawn by a person licensed to practice law. *Form deeds*, deeds in printed form, usually may be filled in by a properly licensed real estate broker, provided such forms are essential to the real estate transaction being handled, or escrowed by the licensee. In California, for example, a licensed real estate broker may escrow those transactions in which he participated as the broker. (Escrows will be discussed in Chapter 12.) Real estate brokers and others using form deeds are cautioned concerning the giving of legal advice on how title to property should be taken. The licensee may generally point out the various ways to take title, but the decision should be left to the grantee and his attorney.

While the form of deed is somewhat standardized in the many states, no particular form for the written instrument is generally required if it contains the essential elements of the statutes of that state. The following would be proper in most states for the transfer of property:

I, Harvey Jones, grant to John Q. Smith all that real property situated in Santa Clara County, State of California, described as follows: Lot 1, Tract 122, recorded in book 11 at Page 83 of maps of Santa Clara County, filed February 13, 19___. Witnessed by hand, this first day of March, 19___.

Signed_____

The types of deeds in general use will be discussed later in the chapter.

The parties to a deed must be properly described. To illustrate: Jane Doe, a single woman, acquires title to property under her name. She later marries and wishes to transfer the property to another individual. Jane Doe would be described in the following manner: "Jane Doe Jones, formerly Jane Doe, under which name said title was acquired." The above situation is also true when partnerships, corporations, or businessmen change their names.

The parties to a deed must be *competent* to convey and receive real property. Most persons are capable of receiving property; exceptions are felons and other persons deprived of their civil rights. Even they may receive property when the state statutes so provide. The difficulty lies, however, in the transfer of property when such a person acts as the grantor. Minors and persons of unsound mind must have their contracts approved by a court-appointed guardian. Married minors, in some states, between the ages of 18 and 21 are considered adults in the eyes of the law and may enter into valid contracts or deeds. The real estate broker should investigate the status of parties if a question concerning their competency should arise.

All valid contracts should state the consideration. A few state statutes require that the consideration be set forth in the deed. In others, the actual amount of consideration is not stated, and the words, "for a valuable consideration," are used in a deed. The actual consideration is, however, stated in the sales agreement or contract of sale. The deed may state the actual consideration, and may contain a statement such as the following: "in consideration of the sum of fifteen thousand five hundred and no/100 Dollars, in lawful money of the United States, paid by the grantee. . . ."

In the initial sales agreement or contract of sale, or contract to sell, the street address of residential property will normally suffice. When title to a parcel of land is deeded (conveyed or transferred), the exact legal description by one of the methods described in Chapter 2 becomes very important. Although the deed must contain the exact legal description, a minor portion left out may not defeat the instrument. In a block, tract description, for example, where the page number on which the map is recorded is omitted, the deed would not be defeated because a competent survey engineer or other person could readily locate the parcel with exactness. The real test, then, is whether or not the property can be located with certainty.

Appurtenant means belonging to, and includes anything that is by right used with the land for its benefit. This may be a right of way or another type of easement. A clause is usually added following the legal description which may read: "together with all appurtenances thereto and all the estates and rights of the party of the first part in and to said premises."

A valid deed must contain a *grantor's clause* or operative words of conveyance. The law does not specify an exact wording, but any phraseology should be definite in meaning. To illustrate, "I grant to John Q. Jones," or "I, a married man, do hereby give and grant to John Q. Jones," will suffice. Such words as "grant and release, grant and convey, or grant, bargain and sell" are also operative words of conveyance.

An additional recital may follow after the operative words of conveyance denoting the quantity of estate granted. For example: "the party of the first part, does hereby grant and release unto the party of the second part, his heirs and assigns for ever." The latter portion—"heirs and assigns"—in a majority of the states, creates a fee simple estate. When these words are left out in those states that require same, a life estate would be created in the grantee, rather than a fee simple interest.

The deed should be dated, but this is not essential to its validity, as the date of delivery will be presumed to be the date of the deed.

The *habendum* clause will set forth reservations or declarations of trust. It may be done in the following manner: "to have and to hold the premises granted herein unto the party of the second part. . . . (Herein said reservations and declarations of trust are set forth)."

The deed must be signed by the parties making the grant or conveyance of the real property, and, finally, there must be a proper delivery of the instruments. It is not necessary that the grantee sign the deed. For the instrument to be valid the grantors or the persons making the conveyance must sign, as this is a charge against their title. Form deeds are void when the instrument is signed in blank by the grantor with the provision that it is to be filled in later by the broker.

In some states, including Alaska, Connecticut, Florida, Georgia, Maryland, Ohio, and Texas, the execution of the deed must be witnessed by one and, in some cases, two persons.

When the grantor is unable to write, he may affix his *mark* to the deed. Such a mark must be properly witnessed. The same would also be true of a *signature* in a *foreign language*. Note the examples that follow:

J. Adam, being unable to write, made his mark in my presence, and I signed his name at his request and in his presence.

J. X Adam

Witnesses   1. _____
            2. _____

Witness to the signature of X.Y. whose name is written in Greek.

Witnesses   1. _____
            2. _____

J. Adam by R. Brown, his attorney-in-fact

Signature _____

While the statutes of the individual state in which the student is residing should be checked to make certain that compliance is made therein, the spouse may normally sign as one witness and the notary or other person taking the acknowledgment may be the additional witness.

For a valid conveyance, some states require that a deed must be sealed. Some other states have deleted the seal by statute. A seal is a particular sign or impression made on the deed to attest to the execution in a formal manner. The seal may simply be the letters "L.S." (*locus sigilli*), meaning the place of the seal.

There must be a *proper delivery* of the deed for it to be valid. The mere turning over of the possession of the instrument does not transfer title. The grantor must intend title to pass immediately. When Adam gives a deed to his son with instructions to record the deed upon Adam's death, the intention to pass title immediately is not present and there is no proper delivery. In addition, in cases when a husband and wife give each other deeds on their separate properties with instructions to the other to record upon the death of either, no proper delivery has occurred. Such a delivery must be absolute with the intention to transfer title immediately. There is a presumption at law of valid delivery in some states, where the deed is recorded in the office of the county recorder and the deed is found in possession of the grantee. These presumptions, however, may be open to repudiation in a court of law.

Acknowledgment and recording of deeds

ACKNOWLEDGMENT

An acknowledgment is made by a duly authorized officer or person and is a formal declaration that the instrument so executed is his act or deed. An instrument must be acknowledged to be recorded by the recorder of the county in which the property is situated. Recordation gives constructive notice of the content and will allow such instrument to be used as evidence without additional proof. Unless provided otherwise by statute, an instrument may be valid between two parties having actual notice of it without an acknowledgment.

The time of acknowledgment is immaterial, if the rights of innocent third parties do not intervene. To illustrate, Adam transfers his real property to Brown by grant deed. Brown, trusting Adam, does not record. The deed is valid in most states between Adam and Brown. Assume, however, that Adam now transfers his property also to Cole by deed. Cole has no knowledge of the first deed and records his deed. Cole's deed will prevail over Brown's. If, however, Cole had knowledge of the prior deed when he recorded his deed, Brown's deed would prevail. Recording is a privilege and is not required by law.

Where may *acknowledgments* be taken and by whom? Acknowledgments may be taken by a justice or clerk of the supreme court or district court of appeal, the judge of a superior court, the clerk of a court of record, a county recorder, a county clerk, a court commissioner, a notary public, or a judge of a municipal or justice court. In the military, certain officers are authorized to take acknowledgments of persons serving in the armed forces.

When an acknowledgment is taken outside the state in which the property is located and is not in accordance with the forms and provisions of that state, a certificate is usually required to be attached thereto by a clerk of a court of record in the county or district where the acknowledgment was taken in accordance with the law of that state. It will further affirm that the officer who took the acknowledgment was authorized to do so, and that his signature is true and genuine.

When an acknowledgment contains all of the essentials required by law but does not include the date, this will not invalidate the instrument. Under these circumstances the date of execution of the instrument will be considered the acknowledgment date.

A *notary public* is usually appointed by the secretary of state or the governor. The notary must have a seal, and on it must be engraved the words "notary public," the name of the county, and the coat of arms of the state. An acknowledgment will usually be considered void if a person who is an interested party to the transaction—a grantee, mortgagor, trustee, and so on—executes an acknowledgment. Employees or officers of corporations may take acknowledgments when the corporation is involved in a transaction if they do not have a personal interest in it. Officers may not acknowledge the document as an officer of the corporation. They must do so as a notary public. Once the instrument has been delivered, the acknowledgment may not, under most statutes, be amended. To be recorded, the instrument must have a new acknowledgment. When a proper acknowledgment has been made but is defectively certified, it may be amended by a superior court action.

RECORDING OF INSTRUMENTS

The recording of a deed protects the grantee's right. All deeds must be acknowledged to accord the privilege of recording. Today, most transactions are completed in escrow and routine escrow procedures generally take care of recording. The possession of real property gives actual notice of the rights of those in possession. Such notice is the same as if the party in possession had recorded his deed; however, he would be well advised not to depend upon his possessory rights alone but to record his instrument. The purchaser of property should not rely upon recordation rights alone, but should make a physical inspection of the property. If persons are found to be in possession, he should determine what rights such persons have therein. The purchaser may find that a legal interest exists in the property. Those in possession may be there under a contract of sale; these are prior contract rights with title still remaining in the name of the seller.

DOCUMENTARY STAMP TAX

Until January 1968, federal transfer documentary stamps, in the amount of $.55 per $500 or fraction thereof, were required to be affixed to the deed. The amount of stamps required was based upon the difference between an existing mortgage and the purchase price of the property. When a new purchase money mortgage was involved and created, the dollar amount of the new encumbrance was not deducted.

Some states, and counties within states where permitted by statute, have enacted legislation similar to the federal tax.

VOID DEEDS

We pointed out in an earlier part of this chapter that a deed will be void if the grantee's name is inserted in a blank deed without proper authorization. A deed to a fictitious person is also void. However, a deed to a person with a fictitious name that he has assumed for purpose of taking title to property is valid. A distinction must be made between a fictitious person and a fictitious name.

QUITCLAIM DEED

The grantor in a quitclaim deed releases any right or claim that he may have in property. The deed may convey a fee simple title or any title that the grantor may have in the property. The quitclaim deed makes no warranties and guarantees nothing; neither does it convey after-acquired property. In most states, such deeds are used to clarify the title. Quitclaim deeds also have other uses; they may be employed to convey title interest (such as sole and separate interest to a spouse), or to clear types of recorded instruments (such as leases or agreements for sales).

A practical illustration of a quitclaim deed follows: Adam has purchased a tax deed from a county. He may wish to obtain a quitclaim deed from the former owner as additional protection of his title interest.

In some states, Adam could go through a *Torrens proceeding* and register the title, but a quitclaim deed would be much less expensive and time consuming.

WARRANTY DEEDS

The warranty deed is the deed generally used throughout the country, with a few exceptions. In California, for example, while the warranty deed is rarely used, it is legal but the grant deed (discussed later) is used in its place. The owner of the property being conveyed in a warranty deed warrants that he has a good and merchantable title to the property. The warranty deed usually specifies the interest of the grantor being conveyed, and will include covenants to protect the grantee in the event the title should not be as represented and the grantee suffers damages. In a majority of states, the warranty deed is considered the best deed that can be given.

There are five common covenants found in a warranty deed. These include: (1) legal possession seisin, (2) quiet enjoyment, (3) further assurance, (4) encumbrance, and (5) warranty of title.

The grantor warrants, in his *covenant of seisin*, that he has full possession of the premises in fee simple and any other quantity (quantum) of estate he is conveying. The covenant would be broken, then, if title were in the name of a person other than the grantor.

The grantor warrants that the grantee will have *quiet enjoyment* of the premises being conveyed. If said grantee is evicted by the grantor, anyone claiming under him, or a third party, the grantee would have a right of action against the grantor. If the grantee later sold the property to another and his grantee were evicted, the same right of action would apply.

In the *covenant of further assurance*, the grantor may be obligated to perform certain acts to perfect the title of the grantee. These might include perfecting a defective legal description or obtaining quitclaim deeds from others who may have had an interest in the property. This covenant is usually enforced by an equity action for specific performance, rather than by a suit for damages.

The *covenant against encumbrances* says, in effect, that the property being conveyed is free from all liens and encumbrances of the grantor or any person claiming under him, except those set forth and known to said grantor. These would include taxes, assessments, and other such liens.

The *covenant and warrant of title* states that the property has not previously been conveyed by the grantor and that he will forever warrant title to the property conveyed. The covenant warrants both title and possession and, should the grantee suffer a loss in either case, the grantor will be liable for damages.

The special warranty deed used in a few states is one in which the grantor gives a warranty of title against defects arising only during his tenure of title, and not against defects arising before that time. It is similar to the bargain and sale deed, discussed later.

In a few states, a grant deed is used in lieu of the warranty deed. The warranty deed is not illegal in those states, but because of the implied warranties, it is not used as a matter of practice. The two implied warranties not written in the deed but recognized are:

1. That the property has not previously been conveyed to another by the grantor.
2. That the property being conveyed is free from all liens and encumbrances of the grantor or any person claiming under him except those set forth in the transaction. Such warranties include encumbrances made during the ownership of the grantor, and no other.

No representation or guarantee of good title is made in this deed, but there is an absolute conveyance of the grantor's title. The bargain and sale deed may be made with or without covenant. In either case, however, the grantor asserts that he has possession of a claim to or the interest in the property. The latter is that which distinguishes the bargain and sale deed from the quitclaim deed discussed earlier.

The bargain and sale deed *with covenants* adds a representation that the title is good and that the grantor has done nothing to encumber it.

When the grantor, in some states, decides to make a gift of property to the grantee, he may do so either by gift deed or quitclaim. The usual method is by gift deed. The consideration involved in the gift deed is one of love and affection which is termed a good consideration. When the gift deed is used to defraud creditors, it may be set aside and voided by the creditors. Because of its many tax implications, a gift deed should be used cautiously and only with proper legal counsel.

SHERIFF'S DEED

The sheriff's deed is one given by court order in connection with the sale of property to satisfy a judgment that has been rendered by the court. Such a deed carries no warranties and conveys only that title acquired by the state or the sheriff under a foreclosure.

REFEREE'S DEED IN FORECLOSURE

A referee is a court-appointed official whose duty it is to sell property and execute a deed to the successful purchaser in accordance with the laws of the state where the property is located. When a mortgage is foreclosed by action, for example, it would be the duty of the referee to sell the property and execute the referee's deed in foreclosure.

REFEREE'S DEED IN PARTITION

This is much like the deed described above. Assume that Adam and Brown are tenants-in-common of a parcel of land. Adam's attorney files a partition action on behalf of Adam to have the partnership dissolved. A referee is appointed and the property is sold. The proceeds of the sale are divided between the co-owners, Adam and Brown. The referee then executes a referee's deed in partition to the purchaser at the auction.

GUARDIAN'S DEED

A guardian, an official usually appointed by the court, conveys the interest in real property of a minor child. The guardian's deed includes the following: (1) court order appointing the guardian, (2) application of the guardian to the court for permission to convey said property, and (3) court order authorizing the sale.

COMMITTEE'S DEED

The committee's deed is similar to the guardian's deed discussed above. This deed is used for such incapacitated persons as the insane and mentally retarded. A committee is appointed by the court, with instructions to administer the affairs of the incompetent person. The committee, in the conveyance of real property will recite the court order of appointment, the application for permission to sell, and the court order authorizing the sale.

CORRECTION DEED

When an error has been made in a prior deed, a correction deed is used. It may also be called a deed of confirmation. For example, if a deed has been recorded with a defective legal description, a correction deed may be used, provided the grantor of the prior instrument is willing to do so. The same thing may also be accomplished by a quitclaim deed reciting the purpose of the instrument. When the seller refuses to correct the error in the deed, a court order may be obtained to correct the error in the deed. This is referred to as reformation of an instrument.

DEED OF SURRENDER

A quitclaim deed may be used in lieu of the deed of surrender in which a life tenant, for example, quitclaims his interest to the remainderman. In summary, a deed of surrender mergers an estate of life or years with either a remainder or reversionary interest.

CESSION DEED

This form of deed is used to convey street rights of an abutting owner to a city or municipality. The purpose of the conveyance will be set forth in the instrument. Developers and subdividers usually do this by dedication with formal acceptance from the municipality.

DEED OF RELEASE

The deed of release is generally used with mortgages and deeds of trust. When the mortgagor pays his debt, he is entitled to a release and the return of his mortgage and the promissory note, stamped "paid." A partial deed of release would be used in the case of a subdivision. In some states, a satisfaction of mortgage is recorded to show the release. The deed of release may also be used to release the premises from a dower interest, a reverter for a breach of condition subsequent, or a remainder interest.

DEED BY ASSIGNEE FOR BENEFIT OF CREDITORS

When an insolvent person does not wish to file a petition of bankruptcy, he may hold a meeting of his creditors. The creditors and the debtor may decide to draw up a trust agreement wherein a trustee, often called an assignee, is appointed for the benefit of the creditors. The trustee will gather the assets of the debtor, convert them to cash and distribute the proceeds to the creditors based on the terms of the agreement. When real property is involved, the debtor conveys same to the trustee by deed of assignment. The assignee is free thereafter to convey it to third persons by deed of assignee for the benefit of the creditors.

TRUST DEED

The trust deed is actually a mortgage instrument used in a few states. It should be remembered that there are three parties to a trust deed, the trustor, trustee, and beneficiary. The trustor is he who signs the promissory note and trust deed conveying legal title to the trustee, with the trustor retaining an equitable title. The trustor retains possession of the property. The trustee holds a "dry or bare title," sometimes referred to as a "naked title." He has only such interest in the property as will allow him to sell under a trustee's sale, in case of a default by the trustor. He holds the property in trust for the beneficiary or lender.

TRUSTEE'S DEED

When the borrower or trustor defaults in his obligations under a deed of trust, the trustee may foreclose through a trustee's sale. Under power of sale clause in deed of trust, a trustee's deed will be executed to the successful cash bidder of the property by the trustee. A trustee's deed sells the trustor's right and interest in the property, and it is final.

DEED OF RECONVEYANCE

A deed of reconveyance may take two forms, a full deed of reconveyance or a partial deed of reconveyance. A deed of reconveyance conveys legal title to the property from the trustee to the trustor when the trust has terminated. Termination occurs when the obligation or balance of the note has been paid in full. A partial deed of reconveyance is issued in subdividing property. This instrument permits the trustee to release parcels of a blanket encumbrance after certain monies have been paid according to the terms of the contract. The satisfaction mortgage referred to in Chapter 7 can be used in a similar manner.

Review questions

1. What are the essential elements of a deed? What statute requires the use of a deed?
2. What protection is given to a purchaser by the recording of a warranty deed?
3. In the conveyance of property, what will constitute proper delivery of a deed?
4. Do a fictitious person and a fictitious name mean the same thing in taking title to property? Explain.
5. Give five types of deeds and a description of each with its proper uses.

Multiple-choice questions

1. A deed can be: (a) assigned, (b) transferred, (c) foreclosed, (d) signed by a mark, (e) none of the foregoing.
2. A quitclaim deed conveys only the interest of the: (a) vendee, (b) grantee, (c) grantor, (d) lessor, (e) claimant.
3. Of the following, which must a deed contain to be valid? (a) signature of grantor, (b) legal description, (c) granting clause, (d) all of the foregoing, (e) none of the foregoing.
4. A deed made and delivered but not recorded is: (a) invalid between the parties and valid to third parties with constructive notice, (b) valid between the parties and valid to subsequent recorded interests, (c) valid between the parties and invalid to subsequent recorded interests without notice, (d) invalid between the parties, (e) void.
5. Recording a deed: (a) guarantees possession, (b) insures ownership, (c) presumes delivery, (d) does none of these, (e) does all of these.
6. The person who conveys under a deed is called the: (a) grantor, (b) grantee, (c) lessee, (d) lessor, (e) vendee.
7. There are seven basic elements essential to a valid deed. Which of the following is not essential to a valid deed? (a) The grantor must be competent to convey. (b) The deed must be acknowledged. (c) The property conveyed must be adequately described. (d) There must be a granting clause. (e) None of the foregoing are essential elements.
8. The most common deed used to convey real property in a majority of the states is the: (a) a quitclaim deed, (b) grant deed, (c) sheriff's deed, (d) trust deed, (e) agreement of sale.

9. The grantor's guarantee that he is the owner of property and has the power to convey title is called the covenant of: (a) quiet enjoyment, (b) warranty, (c) further assurance, (d) seisin, (e) release.
10. Deeds are usually recorded: (a) in the county courthouse, (b) in the city hall, (c) in the governor's office, (d) in any of the foregoing, (e) in none of the foregoing.

11

Real Estate Mathematics

The purpose of this chapter is to review for the real estate student the elementary principles of arithmetic (addition, subtraction, multiplication and division) and to show their application to practical situations in the field of real estate.

Fractions

METHOD 1

Fractions may be proper or improper. A proper fraction is part of a whole number; for example, $\frac{3}{4}$. An improper fraction is a whole number plus a fraction; for example, $\frac{27}{4}$. This improper fraction may be changed into a whole or mixed number by dividing the denominator (4) into the numerator (27). The answer, of course, would be $6\frac{3}{4}$, as in the first example below. By the same token, the whole number plus the fraction may be changed back to an improper fraction by multiplying the denominator by the whole number and adding the numerator, as in the third example:

$$\frac{27}{4} = 6\frac{3}{4} \qquad (27 \div 4 = 6\frac{3}{4})$$
$$\frac{15}{2} = 7\frac{1}{2} \qquad (15 \div 2 = 7\frac{1}{2})$$
$$\frac{21}{11} = 1\frac{10}{11} \qquad (21 \div 11 = 1\frac{10}{11})$$
$$6\frac{3}{4} = \frac{27}{4} \qquad ((4 \times 6 + 3) \div 4 = 27 \div 4 \text{ or } \frac{27}{4})$$
$$6\frac{7}{8} = \frac{55}{8} \qquad ((8 \times 6 + 7) \div 8 = 55 \div 8 \text{ or } \frac{55}{8})$$
$$5\frac{2}{3} = \frac{17}{3} \qquad ((3 \times 5 + 2) \div 3 = 17 \div 3 \text{ or } \frac{17}{3})$$

In adding or subtracting fractions, it is desirable to find the lowest common denominator. Three principal methods may be used: (1) inspection, (2) multiplying all denominators together, and (3) the prime numbers method. Usually the student can determine the common denominator by inspection, simply looking at the denominators. If this method fails or is too time consuming, methods 2 or 3 may be used.

METHOD 2

Add:

$4 \times 6 \times 8 = 192$ (common denominator)

$\frac{3}{4} = \frac{144}{192}$ (192 ÷ 4) $\times$ 3 = 48 $\times$ 3 = 144

$\frac{5}{6} = \frac{160}{192}$ (192 ÷ 6) $\times$ 5 = 32 $\times$ 5 = 160

$\frac{7}{8} = \frac{168}{192}$ (192 ÷ 8) $\times$ 7 = 24 $\times$ 7 = $\dfrac{168}{472}$

$\frac{472}{192} = 2\frac{88}{192} = 2\frac{11}{24}$

Note that fractions should be reduced as far as possible. In the above example:

$$\frac{88 \div 8}{192 \div 8} = \frac{11}{24}$$

To subtract fractions, find the lowest common denominator, then subtract the numerators. Subtract $\frac{3}{10}$ from $\frac{7}{8}$ as follows:

$$\frac{7}{8} = \frac{35}{40}$$

$$\frac{3}{10} = \frac{12}{40}$$

$$\frac{35 - 12}{40} = \frac{23}{40}$$

The lowest common denominator for fractions may be found by the prime number method. A prime number is divisible only by itself or by 1. Examples include: 1, 2, 3, 5, 7, 11, 13, 17, and so on.

METHOD 3

Take any prime number that is divisible into *two or more* of the denominators and continue to divide until it is no longer possible.

Add:

$\frac{1}{4}$	÷2	4	6	18	20
$\frac{5}{6}$	÷3	2	3	9	10
$\frac{1}{18}$	÷2	2	1	3	10
$\frac{7}{20}$		1	1	3	5

Now multiply the divisors and remainders together; the result is the lowest common denominator:

$$2 \times 3 \times 2 \times 1 \times 1 \times 3 \times 5 = 180 \quad \text{(lowest common denominator)}$$

$$\frac{1}{4} = \frac{45}{180}$$

$$\frac{5}{6} = \frac{150}{180}$$

$$\frac{1}{18} = \frac{10}{180}$$

$$\frac{7}{20} = \frac{63}{180} \qquad \frac{45 + 150 + 10 + 63}{180} = \frac{268}{180} = 1\frac{22}{45}$$

Multiplying or dividing the numerator and denominator by the same number does not change the value of the fraction:

$$\frac{3 \times 5}{4 \times 5} = \frac{15 \times 2}{20 \times 2} = \frac{30}{40} \quad \text{or} \quad \frac{3 \times 10}{4 \times 10} = \frac{30}{40}$$

$$\frac{7 \times 5}{8 \times 5} = \frac{35 \times 2}{40 \times 2} = \frac{70}{80} \quad \text{or} \quad \frac{7 \times 10}{8 \times 10} = \frac{70}{80}$$

$$\frac{30 \div 2}{40 \div 2} = \frac{15 \div 5}{20 \div 5} = \frac{3}{4} \quad \text{or} \quad \frac{30 \div 10}{40 \div 10} = \frac{3}{4}$$

$$\frac{70 \div 2}{80 \div 2} = \frac{35 \div 5}{40 \div 5} = \frac{7}{8} \quad \text{or} \quad \frac{70 \div 10}{80 \div 10} = \frac{7}{8}$$

When multiplying fractions, simply multiply numerator by numerator and denominator by denominator:

$$\frac{3}{4} \times \frac{5}{6} \times \frac{7}{8} \times \frac{1}{4} = \frac{105}{768} = \frac{35}{256}$$

Numerators may also be cancelled into denominators before performing the above process:

$$\frac{\overset{1}{\cancel{3}}}{4} \times \frac{5}{\underset{2}{\cancel{6}}} \times \frac{7}{8} \times \frac{1}{4} = \frac{35}{256}$$

To divide fractions, the divisor must be inverted and the fractions multiplied:

$$\tfrac{7}{8} \div \tfrac{3}{4} = ? \qquad \tfrac{7}{8} \times \tfrac{4}{3} = \tfrac{28}{24} = 1\tfrac{4}{24} \quad \text{or} \quad 1\tfrac{1}{6}$$

$$\tfrac{1}{2} \div \tfrac{1}{6} = ? \qquad \tfrac{1}{2} \times \tfrac{6}{1} = \tfrac{6}{2} = 3$$

SAMPLE PROBLEM

Broker Thompson sold $\tfrac{1}{4}$ of Mr. Green's ranch for \$25,000, leaving Mr. Green with 90 acres of land. How many acres were there in the ranch before the sale?

Answer: One-fourth of the ranch was sold, leaving Mr. Green with $\tfrac{3}{4}$ or 90 acres of land (90 acres = $\tfrac{3}{4}$).

$$90 \div \frac{3}{4} = \frac{\overset{30}{\cancel{90}}}{1} \times \frac{4}{\cancel{3}} = 120 \text{ acres}$$

DECIMALS AND PERCENTS

Decimals and percents are equivalent to common fractions that have 100 for a common denominator. Note the illustrations below:

$$\tfrac{1}{2} = \tfrac{50}{100} = .50 = 50\%$$
$$\tfrac{1}{4} = \tfrac{25}{100} = .25 = 25\%$$
$$\tfrac{1}{5} = \tfrac{20}{100} = .20 = 20\%$$
$$\tfrac{1}{10} = \tfrac{10}{100} = .10 = 10\%$$
$$\tfrac{1}{20} = \tfrac{20}{100} = .05 = 5\%$$

It is important to remember that if a percent sign (%) follows a number, it indicates that the number has been multiplied by 100. To change a fraction to a decimal or percent, divide the denominator into the numerator:

$$\tfrac{1}{4} = .25 \quad \text{or} \quad 25\%$$

```
      .25
  4 ) 1.00
       8
      ──
      20
      20
```

$$\tfrac{1}{5} = .20 \quad \text{or} \quad 20\%$$

```
      .20
  5 ) 1.00
      1 0
```

The decimal point separates the whole number from the fraction: 36.2. Thus 36 is a whole number and 2 indicates two-tenths of a number.

A fraction may be expressed as a decimal by dividing the denominator into the numerator and placing a decimal point in the proper location. The result may be expressed as a percentage by moving the decimal point two places to the right and adding the percent sign (%).

$$\frac{1}{6} = .16666 = 16\frac{2}{3}\% \qquad \frac{7}{8} = .875 \quad = 87\frac{1}{2}\%$$
$$\frac{1}{8} = .125 \quad = 12\frac{1}{2}\% \qquad \frac{1}{16} = .0625 \quad = 6\frac{1}{4}\%$$
$$\frac{1}{4} = .25 \quad = 25\% \qquad \frac{1}{3} = .33333 = 33\frac{1}{3}\%$$
$$\frac{3}{8} = .375 \quad = 37\frac{1}{2}\% \qquad \frac{2}{3} = .66666 = 66\frac{2}{3}\%$$
$$\frac{5}{8} = .625 \quad = 62\frac{1}{2}\% \qquad \frac{3}{5} = .60 \quad = 60\%$$
$$\frac{3}{4} = .75 \quad = 75\% \qquad \frac{4}{5} = .80 \quad = 80\%$$

Note the importance of the decimal point location:

$$2.00 \quad = 200\%$$
$$0.20 \quad = 20\%$$
$$0.020 = 2\%$$
$$0.002 = .2\%$$

When adding or subtracting decimals, it is important to align all decimal points:

Add:

1.246	1.246
24.1	24.100
2.13	2.130
.7	.700
28.176	28.176

Subtract:

2,741.72	2,741.7200
28.9437	28.9437
2,712.7763	2,712.7763

In multiplication of decimals, the number of decimals in the answer must equal the sum of decimals in the multiplicand, plus the multiplier:

746.28	2 decimal places
.167	3 decimal places
522396	5 decimal places in answer
447768	
74628	
12462876 = 124.62876	

In the division of decimals, move the decimal point in the dividend as many places to the right as there are decimal points in the divisor:

$$2\,498.2289$$
$$7.\underline{284}\,\overline{|18197.1\underline{00}.}$$

$$.7804$$
$$124.\underline{6}\,\overline{|97.\underline{2}.403}$$

When dividing a larger number into a smaller number, it is necessary to add zeros to the dividend:

$$.83\tfrac{2}{6} = .833\overline{3}$$

$$\tfrac{5}{6} \qquad 6\,\overline{|5.00}$$
$$\underline{4\,8}$$
$$20$$
$$\underline{18}$$
$$2$$

Percentage problems

Any simple percentage problem contains three basic elements; picture it as a triangle:

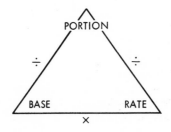

RULES

Base   × Rate = Portion
Portion ÷ Base = Rate or percent
Portion ÷ Rate = Base

$$2{,}500 \times .20 \ (20\%) = \quad 500$$
$$500 \div .20 \ (20\%) = \ 2{,}500$$
$$500 \div 2{,}500 \qquad = .20 \text{ or } 20\%$$

In certain percentage problems, it will be necessary to perform some mathematical process to determine the base, rate, or portion:

1. 375 is 25% less than 500 (base)

$$\begin{array}{ll} 500 & \text{Base} \\ -375 & \\ \hline 125 & \text{Portion} \end{array} \qquad 125 \div 500 = 25\%$$

2. 625 is what percent greater than 400?

$$\begin{array}{ll} 625 & \\ -400 & \text{Base} \\ \hline 225 & \text{Portion} \end{array} \qquad 225 \div 400 = .5625 \quad \text{or} \quad 56.25\%$$

3. A lot cost $6000. It sold for $8500. What is the percentage of the profit on the cost and on the selling price?

Based on cost

$$\begin{array}{ll} \$\ 8500 & \text{Selling price} \\ -6000 & \text{Cost (Base)} \\ \hline \$\ 2500 & \text{Profit (Portion)} \end{array}$$
$$\$\ 2500 \div \$6000 = .4166 \quad \text{or} \quad 41.66\% \quad \text{or} \quad 41\tfrac{2}{3}\%$$

Based on selling price

$$\begin{array}{ll} \$\ 8500 & \text{Selling price (Base)} \\ -6000 & \text{Cost} \\ \hline \$\ 2500 & \text{Profit (Portion)} \end{array}$$
$$\$\ 2500 \div \$8500 = .294117 \quad \text{or} \quad 29.41\%$$

4. A house and lot cost $25,000. The property later was sold making a profit for the owner of 20% *based on the selling price*. Find the selling price.

$$\begin{array}{ll} 100\% & \text{Selling price} \\ -20\% & \text{Profit} \\ \hline 80\% & \text{Cost or } \$25{,}000 \end{array}$$
$$\$25{,}000 \div .80 = \$31{,}250$$

$$\text{Check:} \quad 20\% \text{ of } \$31{,}250 = \begin{array}[t]{ll} \$\ 6{,}250 & \text{Profit} \\ + \$25{,}000 & \text{Cost} \\ \hline \$31{,}250 & \end{array}$$

5. A home sells for $45,000, making the owner a profit of 30% *based on the cost price* of the house. Find the cost.

$45,000   Selling price
  30%   Profit based on cost

  100%   Cost (unknown)
+ 30%   Profit based on cost

  130%   Selling price or $45,000
$45,000 ÷ 1.30 = $34,615.3846 = $34,615.39

6. Mr. Jones gives a real estate salesman a net listing. To cover costs and expenses of the sale (except for the real estate commission) the property must sell for $86,500. The real estate salesman wishes a six percent commission *based on the selling price*. Find the selling price.

  100%   Selling price (unknown)
   6%   Commission

   94%   Net selling price or $86,500
$86,500 ÷ .94 = $92,021.2765 = $92,021.28

Closing statements (prorations)

Sales price, $45,000. Closing date, September 30, 1972. Annual taxes of $900, 1972–73, have been paid in full. Seller has a three-year fire insurance policy, effective July 5, 1970, on which the premium is $162.50. Buyer will take over the policy. Seller owes a balance of $32,123.43 on an existing first mortgage which buyer will assume. Monthly payments, including principal and interest, are $322, payable on the first of each month. There will be $158 in the loan trust fund as of September 30, 1972. Buyers deposited with X.Y.Z. Realty $4000 which the firm will deposit in escrow. Buyer will pay balance in cash. Sellers will pay six percent real estate commission and title insurance, which will be $238. All instruments to be recorded will be $2 each, and the cost of drawing of all instruments will be $5 each.

SOLUTION

(1) Taxes 1972 − 73, $900: = $75 per month
      Buyer 9 months ($675)   Seller 3 months ($225)
(2) Insurance (3 years, policy due July 5, 1973)

Year	Month	Day	
1972	18	35	
1973	7	5	Due date
1972	9	30	Prorata date
	9	5	Buyer's share

$162.50 \div 36 = \$4.5139 \quad \text{per month}$
$\$4.5139 \div 30 = \$.15046 \quad \text{per day}$
$9 \times \$4.5139 = \$40.6251 \quad \text{(9 months)}$
$5 \times \$.15046 = \$ \quad .75230 \quad \text{(5 days)}$
$\overline{\qquad\qquad\qquad \$41.37740} \quad \text{(9 months} + \text{5 days)}$

Seller's Closing Statement

Seller: *Escrow No.:*

	Dr.	Cr.
Sale Price		$45,000.00
Prorate Taxes		$ 675.00
Prorate Insurance		$ 41.38
Existing Loan Assumed by Buyers	$32,123.43	
Loan Trust Fund		$ 158.00
Real Estate Commission (X.Y.Z.)	$ 2,700.00	
Title Insurance Policy	$ 238.00	
Drawing Deed	$ 5.00	
Transfer Tax Stamps	$ 14.30	
Balance to Seller	$10,793.65	
	$45,874.38	$45,874.38

Buyer's Closing Statement

Buyer: *Escrow No.:*

	Dr.	Cr.
Sale Price	$45,000.00	
Prorate Taxes	$ 675.00	
Prorate Insurance	$ 41.38	
Existing Loan Assumed		$32,123.43
Loan Trust Fund	$ 158.00	
Deposit: Los Altos Properties Inc.		$ 4,000.00
Recording: Deed	$ 2.00	
Deed of Trust	$ 2.00	
Cash Needed from Buyer		$ 9,754.95
	$45,878.38	$45,878.38

Additional problems involving prorations may be found in Chapter 12 in escrow procedures.

Amortization of loans

Amortization is the liquidation of a mortgage debt on an installment basis. Generally recognized methods of amortization are (1) principal plus interest, and (2) principal including interest.

PRINCIPAL PLUS INTEREST

Under this plan of amortization, each payment toward the principal is constant, with the interest in addition calculated on the unpaid balance to the loan.

EXAMPLE

Mr. Smith borrows $1,000 from Jones and agrees to repay the money in 12 monthly installments with interest in addition thereto at 6 percent per annum.

SOLUTION

Each payment toward the principal will be $100, and interest will be based on the unpaid balance at 0.5 percent per month.

Month End	Beginning Balance	Principal Payment	Interest Payment	Total Payments	Unpaid Balance
1	$1000.00	$100.00	$5.00	$105.00	$900.00
2	900.00	100.00	4.50	104.50	800.00
3	800.00	100.00	4.00	104.00	700.00
4	700.00	100.00	3.50	103.50	600.00

PRINCIPAL INCLUDING INTEREST

The distinguishing feature of the principal including interest payment is that each installment is the same as the preceding installment. Interest is always calculated on the unpaid balance. The payments, like the premiums on an insurance policy, are level payments, or of a constant amount.

To amortize a loan, the interest for one month is calculated by multiplying the unpaid balance at the time of the payment by the interest rate, and dividing by 12, regardless of the balance.

The following table shows the first ten installments on a loan of $10,000 payable $100 per month with 6 percent interest:

Unpaid Balance	Interest Amount	Principal Amount	Total Amount	Installment Number
$10,000.00	$50.00	$50.00	$100.00	1
9,950.00	49.75	50.25	100.00	2
9,899.75	49.50	50.50	100.00	3
9,849.25	49.25	50.75	100.00	4
9,798.50	48.99	51.01	100.00	5
9,747.49	48.74	51.26	100.00	6
9,696.23	48.48	51.52	100.00	7
9,644.71	48.22	51.78	100.00	8
9,592.93	47.96	52.04	100.00	9
9,540.89	47.70	52.30	100.00	10

Calculating interest

Remember that interest should always be calculated on the unpaid balance of the loan.

Formula: Interest = Principal × rate × time $I = Prt$

Interest is always calculated in terms of 360 days per year, unless exact interest is specified. If time is stated in terms of months rather than days, the same formula applies.

EXAMPLE

What is the interest on $900 for 60 days at 5%?

$$I = 900 \times .05 \times \tfrac{1}{6} = 7.50$$

Whenever any three parts of the formula are given, the other may be found easily:

$$I = Prt \qquad r = \frac{I}{Pt} \qquad P = \frac{I}{rt} \qquad t = \frac{I}{Pr}$$

EXAMPLE

How many days will it take $900 to earn $7.50 at 5 percent simple interest?

$$t = \frac{I}{Pr} = \frac{7.50}{900 \times .05} = \tfrac{1}{6} \text{ of a year} \quad \text{or} \quad 60 \text{ days}$$

Amortization tables are available to real estate brokers and salesmen from many sources such as banks, title insurance companies, and savings and loan institutions.

Short-cut in calculating interest

60-day 6% Method ($5000):

$5000.   To find the interest for 6 days at 6%, move the decimal point three places to the left.

$5000.   To find the interest for 60 days at 6%, move the decimal point two places to the left.

$5000.   To find the interest for 600 days at 6%, move the decimal point one place to the left.

When the interest has been found at 6 percent for the desired period of time, the interest at any other rate may also be found by making minor adjustments.

EXAMPLE

Find the interest on $5,000 for 8% for 73 days.

$50.00	60	days at	6%
8.33	10	days at	6% ($\frac{1}{6}$ of 60)
2.50	3	days at	6% ($\frac{1}{20}$ of 60)
$60.83	73	days at	6%

8% is $\frac{1}{3}$ more than 6%:

$$\begin{array}{ll} \$ \ 60.83 & 6\% \\ +20.27 & 2\% \\ \hline \$ \ 81.10 & 8\% \quad \text{or} \quad \$81.10 \end{array}$$

Check: $\$5000 \times \frac{8}{100} \times \frac{73}{360} = \$81.10$

Other percentage problems

CAPITALIZATION

Mr. Smith wishes to purchase a duplex and to obtain a 7.5 percent return on his total investment. How much can he pay for the duplex and maintain a 7.5 percent return on his total investment if the property produces $150 per unit and has the following monthly expenses?

$ 48.00   Taxes
   3.50   Insurance
  24.00   Maintenance
  48.00   Management
$123.50 × 12 months = $1482

$ 300   Gross income per month
  ×12   Months
$ 3600   Gross income
 −1482   Expenses
$ 2118   Net income ÷ .075 = $28,240   property value

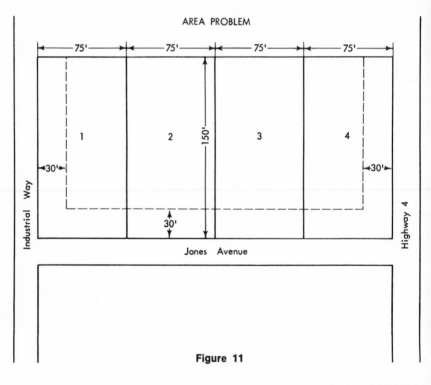

AREA PROBLEM

Figure 11

AREA PROBLEM

In Fig. 11, X.Y.Z. industrial firm wishes to build a 15,000 sq. ft. plant fronting on Industrial Way and Jones Avenue. Taking into consideration the 30′ setback lines, how many lots must the firm buy?

Lot 1: $(75-30) \times (150-30)$ or $45 \times 120 =$ 5,400 sq. ft.
Lot 2: $75 \times (150-30)$ or 75×120 $=$ 9,000
                                                              14,400 sq. ft.

The firm needs 15,000 square feet; therefore, Lots 1, 2, and 3 will be needed.

Additional mathematical problems are in Chapter 14, which concerns appraisal. The same basic principles of mathematics will apply in that chapter.

Review problems

1. Add $\frac{1}{8}$, $\frac{5}{6}$, and $\frac{3}{4}$
2. Subtract $\frac{7}{8}$ from $1\frac{3}{4}$
3. Multiply $1\frac{3}{4}$ by $\frac{7}{9}$
4. Divide $\frac{3}{4}$ by $\frac{1}{3}$
5. Change to decimals and percents:
   a. $\frac{3}{4}$ c. $\frac{7}{8}$
   b. $\frac{1}{6}$ d. $1\frac{1}{4}$
6. Change to fractions:
   20%   40%
   $16\frac{2}{3}\%$ $12\frac{1}{8}\%$
   80% $\frac{2}{3}\%$
7. What is (a) 20% of 1200, (b) .784 of 525, (c) 160% of 200?
8. A salesman sold a property for $36,000; his broker's commission was 6%, out of which the salesman was to receive 60%. How much was the salesman's commission?
9. Adam receives $150 per month on an investment; his return is equal to 7.5%. How much money did he invest?
10. An apartment house cost $120,000 and returns a net income of $7440. What percent is made on the investment?
11. A loan of $4650 is paid at the rate of $15.50 per month. How many years will it take to pay off the loan, excluding interest?
12. A lot with a frontage of 80.12 feet and a depth of 172.23 feet was sold for $1.50 per square foot. What was the selling price?
13. An investor receives $18.50 per month interest. The interest rate is 6%. How much is the loan?
14. An investor makes a loan of $3600 and receives $18.00 per month interest. What percent is he making on his money? (straight loan).
15. What is the monthly interest on a mortgage of $6500 at 7.2% annual interest?
16. Adam wishes to receive $9250 net for his property after paying a 6% sales commission. What should the sale price of the property be?
17. Salesman X agrees to list a home owned by A. A does not know the current balance of his 7% Int. loan, but out of the last monthly installment, $52.50 went to pay the 7% interest and the balance of the payment was applied toward the principal. What is the current balance of the loan?

18. Four lots were sold for a total of $20,000. The first was sold for $1,000 more than the second. The fourth was sold for $500 more than the third and the third was sold for $100 more than the first. What was the sale price of each lot?

19. The insurance on a house is $90 or $.80 per $100. The tax rate on the same property is $4\frac{1}{2}\%$ and the taxes are $520. What is the difference between the insurance value and the assessed value?

20. A broker made a 15-year lease at $250 per month at the rate of commission of 5% for the first five years, 3% on the next five years, and $1\frac{1}{2}\%$ on the balance. What is his commission?

21. The gross annual rent on a 36-unit apartment house is $54,000. What is the average rent per month per unit?

22. Brown buys a lot for $8400 and builds a house costing $2\frac{1}{2}$ times the price of the lot. If he wishes a 7% return on his total investment, what must he rent the house for each month?

23. Fifteen lots remain in a subdivision which represents $16\frac{2}{3}\%$ of the total lots in the tract. How many lots were there in the subdivision?

24. A 780-acre ranch sold for $125 per acre. A salesman received 60% of a 5% commission from his broker. What did the broker receive as his share of the commission?

25. The value of three lots is $18,000. Lot one is worth $3000 more than the second, and the third is worth $1200 more than the first. What is the value of each lot?

12

Title Search, Examination, and Escrows

Before we start our study of title search, examination, registration, and closing, let us examine the major steps in a real estate transaction.

The first step in the transaction is made when the seller lists his property with a realtor. If the realtor has obtained complete information from the seller, and if the property is priced to compete with the sale of similar properties in the market, the property should sell when exposed to the market for a reasonable length of time.

The realtor now advertises the property to attract purchasers who may be ready, willing, and able to buy it. When the buyer is found and a contract to purchase has been signed by both the seller and purchaser, the realtor is ready to start the title search and proceed to the closing of the real estate transaction. The purchaser should avail himself of the best title examination possible. Deeds and mortgages should not be accepted by the purchaser unless a proper search of the title has been made. When a proper search has been completed and the purchaser and his attorney are satisfied with the title examination, the closing of the transaction may take place. A deed will be delivered by the grantor to the grantee, who will record it to give constructive notice to "the whole world" of his interest in the property.

Title search

When a title search is made on a parcel of real property, a condensed history of that property is developed into what is known as an "abstract of title." The abstract is a summary of the operative parts of instruments of conveyance which affect the land, title, or interest therein. It will include the current vesting (ownership) of title, statements of any liens, charges, encumbrances, and other liabilities to which the property may be subject. In summary, all material facts affecting the title or chain of title, to which the purchasers should have notice, will be set forth in the abstract of title.

In some states *title insurance* is used exclusively and the purchaser may not see the abstract of title although the title company may have one kept for its own use. In these states, a preliminary title report is given to the purchaser. This report is preliminary to the issuance of the title insurance policy. It will show the current vesting of title, taxes and special assessments, deeds of trust, mortgages, easements in gross, and any exceptions which the title insurance company may wish to exclude from its policy.

PURPOSES OF TITLE EXAMINATION

A title search or examination is made in order to discover whether there are defects in the grantor's chain of title or whether clouds exist on the title that might prevent the grantor from granting a merchantable title to the purchaser. The title search may be ordered and paid for by either the seller or purchaser, depending upon their contract of sale and custom in the particular state or area. The contract of sale will usually provide that the purchaser, at his option, may rescind the contract if the seller is unable to convey merchantable title.

A title search may be ordered by a mortgagee at the mortgagor's expense if a new loan is being placed on the property. The lender, in placing a new loan on property, will want to make sure that there will be no superior liens to jeopardize his security. Banks, for example, only make first mortgages. The lender will want to assure himself that the taxes, assessments, and water charges are current, because these are paramount liens on real property. The lender may further require that the new owner establish a loan trust fund account (impound account) to protect his loan. If the title search shows delinquencies, these can be disposed of in closing the transaction.

A title search may be made by a mortgagee prior to the foreclosure of a mortgage. The same would apply to a mechanic's lien foreclosure. When inferior liens are discovered by the forecloser, he will be required to join these inferior lien holders in the action; otherwise, the foreclosure action against the mortgagor will be defective. Thus, all persons having a title interest in the foreclosed property will be disclosed.

THE CHAIN OF TITLE

When a deed is given by the grantor to the grantee and said deed is recorded by the county recorder in the county and state where the property is located, the deed is cross-filed under the names of both the grantor and grantee. This system is known as the *grantor–grantee system of indexing*. In this way, the vested ownerships on a single parcel of land can be checked back to the earliest records kept in that county. Each deed recorded will show the legal description of the property, the acknowledgment, the internal revenue stamps (see Chapter 10), the date and time of recording, the easements, the restrictions, or other special covenants or conditions.

To simplify the system, some large title and abstract companies have developed a system of indexing by parcel of land. The student of real estate may recognize the difficulties that might arise from very common names like Smith and Jones. In a very large county there may well be 100 James Smiths. When there is a question of liens that have been filed, title companies frequently use identification sheets filled in by the individual.

LIS PENDENS INDEX

A *lis pendens* is a notice of pendency of action and is filed with the county clerk or recorder when legal action commences on a particular parcel of property. The index is set up alphabetically according to plaintiffs and defendants. When the plaintiff's attorney files a lawsuit, a file number will be assigned to the case. All future documents including a record of the disposition made will be filed in the folder bearing this case number.

In addition to the names of the plaintiff and defendant, the index will include the date of filing, a column for file numbers, and the file number of the action. Before title can pass to the grantee, the legal action must be settled, or dismissal filed, and the docket marked "cancelled."

MORTGAGES

The mortgage index should be checked to determine whether or not persons in the chain of title had a mortgage on the property, and whether or not this lien remains in force. The title examiner starts with the most recent mortgage and works in reverse. A search may disclose that a mortgage remains in force which was paid off by a mortgagor without a proper release having been recorded. Assignments may have been made by both the mortgagee and the mortgagor over a period of time. The validity of these assignments must be checked. A mortgage may still remain of record when the time period specified by the statute of limitations has run its course. Such an instrument cannot be ignored by an abstract company guaranteeing the title, or by the title insurance company.

JUDGMENTS

When an abstract of judgment is recorded, it is a lien on all the real property of the debtor within the jurisdiction of the court. The length of time the judgment lien remains will vary according to the statutes of each state. In some states it is a lien against the property for a period of ten years. In a few states, the lien can be renewed for an additional ten years. Thus, the title examiner must search the title back for at least ten years, because those persons who had title during this period of time may have had a judgment lien against the property that continued until the date of the current search. The judgments are entered alphabetically on the judgment rolls in the county clerk's office. These rolls indicate the judgment creditor, the judgment debtor, time, date, and entry of judgment, and the file number. It will indicate further whether or not the judgment was satisfied.

TAXES—CITY AND COUNTY

In most parts of the country it is difficult to examine the county records and determine whether or not the city taxes have been paid. When the city has arranged with the county to collect taxes in their behalf, it may not be as difficult. The purchaser of property will sometimes require that the seller sign a statement that certifies that the city taxes have been paid in full.

Real property taxes are due and payable at a time specified in the state statute. Taxes and assessments are superior to all other liens; therefore, a search of the tax records is necessary to determine whether the taxes are current or whether, in fact, they have not been paid. The tax records will disclose a sale to the state and any existing penalties. These liens must be cleared before title passes; otherwise, they will carry over to the new owner. The tax rolls are usually found in either the tax assessor's office or in the county treasurer's office of the county in which the property is located. Indexing will normally be done according to the property description.

PROBATE COURT RECORDS

It may be necessary to examine the records of the surrogate or probate court when the searcher finds a break in the chain of title or when an executor's or administrator's deed is found in the chain of title. Assume that in searching the title a deed is found with Susan Adams as the grantor but that no deed is found conveying the title to Susan Adams. The probate records must be searched for the death of a certain deceased Adams from whom Susan may have inherited the property. If no records are found whereby she did inherit title, an invalid deed may exist and steps must be taken to perfect the title.

In those states that have an inheritance tax it must be determined whether or not the tax has been paid. If there is no record of tax payment, an inquiry of the tax department should be made to determine whether any tax is yet due, or to receive a tax waiver from the department.

DOWER RIGHTS

In those states where dower rights still exist it will be necessary to determine said rights. Dower rights are those that a wife has in her husband's estate after his death. Some states have abolished dower rights, but it is still necessary to check because the particular rights may have been created prior to the time such rights were abolished statewide.

CHATTEL MORTGAGES AND SECURITY AGREEMENTS

Chattel searches are usually not a part of the title examination of real property. When the purchaser is in doubt about such liens, however, a chattel search may be in order. Usually a search over approximately the previous six months will disclose such liens.

Security agreements and the financing statement were discussed in Chapter 7. The security agreement is used when personal property is pledged for a debt or an obligation due. The financing statement is filed to perfect the security agreement. When the seller has purchased personal property, has attached it to the real property, and a financing statement has been filed, the vendor of said goods has a lien therein that will run with the title. To illustrate, the seller may have had installed and built into the real estate stereo units, television sets, or intercom systems, and the vendor may have his security interest perfected.

PETITIONS IN BANKRUPTCY

Bankruptcy proceedings must be disposed of before a merchantable title to property can pass. Generally, the same procedures apply here as apply in judgments.

Preparation of abstract of title

The searcher or title examination officer will keep notes on all transactions that may affect the title to the subject property. When he has completed his examination, his notes will be organized into a brief history of the property.

This history will be concluded with a certification of the search with any exceptions set forth. This certification will contain an opinion of title whereby the searcher states that he has searched the title for deeds, mortgages, judgments, and so forth, and that no defects have been found except . . . (here follows a list). The opinion of title may also come from the purchaser's attorney, who may examine the abstract of title for his client.

How far back should an abstract company or title insurance company go in searching a title? This may depend upon the statute of limitations within the state; however, 40 years seems to be sufficient, according to many title examiners.

Title insurance

The opinion of title, in many cases, does not guarantee that the purchaser has or will acquire a clear title to property, although some abstract companies do issue a guarantee of title.

The title insurance policy was developed to eliminate as many hazards as possible, and to insure the purchaser's title on a "one-time" premium basis. Generally, two major types of policies are in existence: (1) the standard policy of title insurance, and (2) the American Land Title Association policy of title insurance.

The standard policy of title insurance protects the new owner of property against risks of record, against such off-record hazards as forgery, impersonation, or incapacity of the parties to transfer, against loss from a lien of federal or state taxes (which is effective without notice upon death), and against attorney's fees and other expenses connected with defending the title, whether or not the plaintiff prevails.

Certain risks are inherent in acquiring title to property against which the standard policy of title insurance does not protect the insured. These include: any existing defects in the title up to the date of the policy and known to the buyer, but not previously disclosed to the title insurance company; easements and liens not shown by the public records; any right or claim which is not of public record of any party in physical possession of the property; any rights or claims not of public record that could be ascertained by physical inspection of the land, by inquiry of persons on the land, or by a correct survey. The standard policy does not protect against mining claims, reservations, patents, water rights, or zoning ordinances. Riders, however, may be attached to this policy to cover these items.

Lenders will usually require the American Land Title Association title insurance policy. Such a policy expands the risks insured under the standard policy of title insurance to include *unrecorded liens of record,* easements, rights of those in physical possession of the property, including tenants or vendees, rights and claims of a correct survey or physical possession, mining claims, reservations, patents, and water rights. The ALTA policy still gives no protection against defects concerning the title known to the insured at the date the policy was issued but not communicated to the insurer. Further, it will not provide against governmental regulations concerning occupancy and use of the property.

Closing procedures through escrow

A grant may be deposited by the grantor with a third person, to be delivered on the performance of some condition, and to take effect on delivery by the depository. While in the possession of the third person and subject to the condition, the grant is called an *escrow.*

The escrow agent, then, is a stake holder. He is the agent of both parties until the escrow is closed, and he then becomes a trustee for documents and money until distributed in accordance with the instructions of the escrow.

Escrows are not limited to the conveyance of real property, but may be used for other instruments such as chattel mortgages. The escrow agent acts as a custodian of funds and documents and makes concurrent delivery when the escrow is completed. The escrow also provides a clearing house for the payment of liens and refinancing and for computing proration of such items as taxes, insurance, and so forth.

ESSENTIAL REQUISITES OF A VALID ESCROW

Essential requirements for a valid escrow include a binding contract between the buyer and the seller and the conditional delivery of the transfer instrument to a third party. The binding agreement may be a *deposit receipt*, agreement of sale, exchange agreement, option, or the mutual escrow instructions of the buyer and seller. Escrow instructions supplement the original contract, which may be any one of the accepted binding agreements, and, in case of litigation, they are interpreted together wherever possible. If there exists a conflict between the original contract and the escrow instructions, the latter constitute a subsequent contract and, therefore, will prevail over the original agreement. It is important that the original agreement be concise and contain all of the conditions binding on each of the parties.

Second, there must be a conditional delivery of the transfer instrument to a third party. The conditional delivery of such instrument must be accompanied by instructions to the escrow agent that he deliver the instrument, usually the grant deed, upon the fulfillment of the condition. The escrow agent must be neutral to the transaction. Before the delivery of the transfer instrument and the fulfillment of the condition on the part of the grantee, the transaction is termed an "escrow."

COMPLETE OR PERFECT ESCROW

A complete or perfect escrow is one that contains all necessary instructions, instruments, and monies, and reflects an understanding of the transaction by all parties.

Generally, in order to have a proper escrow, a valid and binding contract must be entered into between the buyer and the seller. Such contracts should contain an irrevocable deposit of documents or monies with the escrow holder. When no such contract exists, the grantor generally may recover his deed from the escrow agent at any time before the condition is performed. The escrow agent exceeds his authority if he attempts to deliver the instrument (the grant deed) *before* the performance of the conditions specified.

ESCROW INSTRUCTIONS

An escrow must be confidential. Only the parties to the transaction are entitled to information concerning the escrow. For example, if the seller is paying off a loan and the buyer is obtaining a new loan, the buyer is not entitled to know the terms and conditions of the seller's loan, nor is any acquaintance of either party entitled to obtain information from the escrow agent without written permission of the party involved.

The agent is a distinterested stranger to the transaction. He must be impartial to the transaction, and he may not give legal advice. Advice on all legal matters should be referred to the attorney of the respective parties. Such advice would include information on how title to the property should be taken.

An escrow agent may not exceed the authority granted him in the escrow instructions. He should see that unnecessary elaboration is avoided; the instructions should be positive rather than negative, and they should be brief, to afford the parties to the transaction little or no difficulty in interpreting them at a later date. Questions asked by the escrow agent should be pertinent to the instructions, and these instructions should be prepared while the concerned parties are present. Questions might include:

Who is the seller?
Is he married or single?
Who is the buyer?
How does he wish to take title?
What is the purchase price?
How will it be paid?
What monies have been taken outside of escrow?
Will these be transferred to the escrow agent?
Have the parties agreed on how much money is to be deposited?
At the inception of escrow, will the buyer "assume" the loan, or take the loan "subject to"?
Will normal prorations and adjustments be made (taxes, fire insurance, rent)?
Upon what basis will they be prorated?
Are leases involved in the transaction?
If so, is the buyer familiar with the terms of the lease agreement(s)?
Will an assignment be made of such agreement(s)? Will water stock be transferred with the property?
Is personal property involved in the transaction?
If so, is personal property transferred by a bill of sale rather than a conveyance?
In the case of personal property, will a chattel search be made?
If so, will the escrow agent make such search and if so, how many years back?

The escrow agent will request an *offset statement* (statement of condition) from the lender, to check the terms of the loan as shown in the escrow instructions. If such statement differs from the escrow instructions given, the approval of the buyer must be obtained. If a loan installment falls due during the escrow period, such payment should be made to the escrow agent so that the offset statement may be kept up to date. If the buyer is obtaining a new loan as a part of his purchase agreement, he should state that the closing of the escrow is contingent upon his obtaining a loan, and should indicate the desired amount. The following statement may suffice as a part of his escrow instructions:

> The closing of this escrow is contingent upon obtaining a loan in amount of $20,000.00 on the following terms and conditions: a minimum loan in the amount of $20,000.00, payable at $137.58 per month, including principal and interest, at not more than 7.5 percent per annum, said loan to be for not less than 20 years. The execution of loan papers by myself in connection with this escrow is my waiver of said contingency, provided the loan is consummated.

The subject of a *termite clearance* or report should not be mentioned by an escrow officer. As a matter of practice the buyer will usually request a termite report. An agreement between the parties is usually reached prior to escrow. It should be pointed out, in connection with this report, that it would be impossible for an escrow officer, real estate broker, or other individual to give a termite clearance. The only way that a "clearance" could be obtained would be to tear down the entire structure piece by piece to make certain that no termites were in the building. The termite reports say, in effect, that there is no *visible evidence* of termites. In the Appendix is an example of an agreement between buyer and seller that could be attached to the original contract prior to entering escrow.

When all monies and documents have been deposited, the escrow agent becomes the *trustee* for all parties to the transaction. After all conditions of the escrow have been performed, the escrow holder is agent for the buyer concerning the deed or other items to which the buyer is entitled. He is agent for the seller concerning money and any other items to which the seller is entitled. The delivery of the deed or other instruments must comply strictly with the escrow instructions.

The escrow agent may not legally concern himself with any controversies between the parties to the escrow. When the parties to the escrow cannot agree and a distribution of monies or documents cannot be made by the escrow holder, an action of interpleader to compel them to litigate between themselves may be obtained by such escrow agent.

The buyer's interest in the escrow is an "equitable" ownership. This is evidenced by the deposit receipt, agreement of sale, exchange agreement, option, or the escrow instructions. Such rights may be transferable by deed, assignment, contract, or mortgage instrument, and may pass to the buyer's heirs or devisees upon his death. In the event that the seller dies or becomes an incompetent or a bankrupt, however, the buyer may be put to additional expense to obtain title. The seller, as the legal owner, may transfer all of his interest in the contract by deed. Such grantee must take title, but only subject to the original contract.

PRORATION OF CHARGES

Escrow customs may differ between various states but, in general practice, the distribution of charges will be as follows. The *seller* is usually responsible for:

1. The drawing of instruments in favor of the purchaser, including the deed that passes title from seller to buyer, and any quitclaim deeds (or others) necessary to clear the title
2. The transfer of tax stamps on the deed, when necessary
3. Notary fees on instruments in favor of the purchaser
4. The real estate broker's commission; legally, the broker has earned his commission when he has furnished a buyer ready, willing, and able to purchase property. As a matter of practice, however, real estate commissions are paid out of escrow through the seller's instructions.

The *purchaser* is usually responsible for:

1. The drawing of instruments in favor of the seller and, if financing is involved in the transaction, the drawing of instruments in favor of the lender. Such instruments include a purchase money trust deed to the seller, or a trust deed to the beneficiary.
2. Recording fees in favor of himself, including the recording of the deed giving constructive notice of the new ownership
3. Recording fees for mortgages in favor of the lender
4. The title insurance policy fee, but this may vary according to state or county
5. Notary fees on instruments in favor of the seller or lender (such acknowledgments will permit the instruments to be recorded)

CHECK LIST

Thus, after a written listing on a piece of property is secured and a client ready, willing, and able to purchase the property is located, there remain certain facts to ascertain and certain preparations to be made before the executing of the contract of sale:

1. The date of the contract
2. The name and address of the seller

3. Whether the seller is a citizen of full age and competence

4. The name of the seller's wife

5. The name and address of the purchaser

6. A full description of the property

7. The purchase price, including the amount to be paid upon signing the contract and the amount to be paid upon delivery of the deed

8. The kind of deed that is to be delivered; that is, separate, community, joint tenancy, or tenancy in common

9. What agreement has been made with reference to any specific personal property on the property to be conveyed, such as gas ranges, heaters, machinery, fixtures, window shades, carpets, rugs, hangings, or TV antenna

10. If purchaser is to assume the mortgage, or take the property subject to it

11. If mortgages contain acceleration or restrictive provisions (alienation clause)

12. If there are to be any exceptions or reservations in the deed

13. If there are any special specifications or conditions to be inserted in the contract

14. The stipulations and agreements with reference to tenancies and rights of persons in possession

15. The stipulations and agreements with reference to any facts the survey would show, such as party wall, easements, and so forth

16. The items to be adjusted on the closing of the title

17. The name of the broker who brought about the sale, his address and the amount of commission to be paid

18. The agreements concerning liens, easements, assessments, taxes, covenants, or restrictions affecting the title, and who is to draw the purchase money mortgage or trust deed and pay the expense thereof

19. The place and date on which the title is to be closed

20. If time is to be the essence of the contract

21. Any alterations to be made on the premises between the date of the contract and the date of the closing

22. The name and address of escrow holder

23. Who is to pay title and recording charges

24. Whether structural pest control report is to be furnished, and who shall pay the cost, or any recommended corrections or replacements

25. The date of possession and adjustments of taxes, interest, and so on

Upon the closing of title, the seller should be prepared to furnish the following:

1. The seller's copy of the contract

2. The latest tax, water and receipted assessment bills

3. The latest possible water meter readings

4. His receipt for the last payment of interest on mortgages or trust deeds, if any

5. The fire, liability, and other insurance policies

6. A certificate or offset statement from the holder of any mortgage or trust deed on the property, showing the amount due and the date to which interest is paid

7. Any subordination agreements which may be called for in the contract

8. A certificate showing satisfaction of mechanic's liens, chattel mortgages, judgments, or mortgages which are to be paid at or prior to the closing of the title

9. A list of the names of the tenants, amounts that are paid and unpaid, the dates when rents are due, and an assignment of unpaid rent

10. An assignment of all leases affecting the property

11. The letters to tenants to pay all subsequent rent to the purchaser and reaffirm conditions of tenancy

12. The authority to execute the deed for his agent, if any

13. A bill of sale of the personal property covered by the contract

14. The seller's last deed

15. Any unrecorded instruments affecting the title, including extension agreements

16. The deed, and other instruments which the seller is to deliver or prepare

The purchaser should have the following:

1. The purchaser's copy of the contract

2. The certificate of title or policy of title insurance, showing title vested in the grantor

3. An examination of the deed to see if it conforms to the contract

4. A comparison of the description to see if it coincides with the description of the deed and a true description of the property to be conveyed

5. An examination of the deed to see if it is properly executed

6. Sufficient cash to make payments required in accordance with the provisions of the contract

7. The disposition of all liens that must be removed

8. The names and details of tenants and rent

9. An assignment of unpaid rent and assignment of leases

10. A certificate with reference to mortgages, showing the principal due, and the date of the last payment

11. Letters to tenants from seller reaffirming conditions of tenancy

12. An examination of the authority if the seller acts through an agent

13. The bill of sale of personal property covered by the contract

14. The seller's deed

15. An examination of the survey

16. An examination to see if the policy or certificate of title shows any

covenants, restrictions, or other matters affecting the title or the use of the property

17. All bills for any unpaid tax, water, or assessments, and have interest computed up to the date of the closing
18. The adjustments completed if called for in the contract
19. An examination of purchase money mortgages
20. Any unrecorded instruments affecting the title, including extension agreements

Termination of escrow

An escrow may be terminated in one of the following ways:

1. Full performance by both parties
2. Mutual consent to cancellation
3. Revocation by one of the parties
4. Death or incapacity of one of the parties

When both parties to the escrow have fully performed and a proper distribution of the monies and instruments has been made, the escrow is closed.

Both parties may agree to the cancellation of the escrow. In this event, certain costs and expenses have been incurred. The payment of these expenses may be made by agreement of the parties.

One of the parties to the escrow may revoke the escrow agreement. The escrow agent will then enter an action of *interpleader,* asking the court to compel the parties to litigate between themselves. When a valid and binding contract is in effect prior to escrow, an attempted revocation by one of the parties is ineffective. If no valid or binding contract existed prior to escrow, then the offer is revocable until its acceptance by the other party. When there is a breach of the contract by one of the parties not performing as agreed upon, the other party may withdraw, and he is discharged from his obligation.

If one of the parties to an escrow dies or is adjudged incompetent and a legal escrow has been established, it may not be revoked by either party during the time fixed for the performance of the escrow. When the person entitled to the benefits of the instrument performs within the time limit prescribed, he is entitled to receive the delivery of the deed.

When no binding contract exists prior to escrow and the grantor deposits a deed with the escrow holder with instructions to deliver it to the grantee upon payment of a specified price, no contract exists until the grantee deposits his money and issues his escrow instructions; thereafter, an offer exists to be terminated only upon the death of the grantor.

After the grantor and grantee have signed escrow instructions that result in a binding contract but the grantor has not delivered a deed to the escrow holder, then, should the grantor die, the grantee may not acquire title through the escrow. When the grantee is not in default on his obligations, he may acquire title by action of specific performance against the representatives of the grantor. If he is successful, they will be required to deliver title to the property.

Prorations

Prorations were discussed in the chapter on real estate mathematics. The student should review them.

Review questions

1. Discuss the purposes of making a title search of real property.
2. Why might it be necessary for the title examiner to check the probate court records?
3. Visit a title insurance company or an abstract company in your community. Describe your experiences in a report to your instructor.
4. Explain what is meant by "chain of title."
5. Discuss the essential requisites of a valid escrow.

13

Property Insurance

Insurance is a broad and specialized field; however, its basic concepts must be considered in real estate principles and practice. The real estate practitioner may find it profitable to engage in the property insurance business as a side-line or to associate with an insurance broker. Whether or not the practitioner engages in the insurance business, he must be aware of the necessity for insurance, and the types of insurance that would be most suitable for his client. All property owners face the possibility of loss due to fire or other hazards. In this chapter we will discuss the types of risk that can be shifted to other parties in the form of insurance.

Insurance contract

Insurance is a contract (policy) whereby one party, called the insurer, agrees to indemnify another, called the insured, upon the occurrence of a stipulated event. The consideration paid for the contract is called a *premium*.

It is almost impossible for an individual to project what his losses through fire may be in a given period of time, but the fire insurance company, through its vast data accumulation, can predict the probability of such losses with a high degree of accuracy. The premiums paid by a large number of property owners will indemnify those few that suffer the losses.

The insurance company, similarly, will try to spread its risk. In very large policies, the issuing company will allow the participation of other insurance companies. Further, it will not place all of its insurance contracts in a single city or area, where one major fire could wipe out its entire assets.

Insurable interest

The insured in the insurance contract must have an insurable interest in the subject property; otherwise, it would be considered a gambling contract.

Any individual who has a right in the subject property that would cause him to suffer a monetary loss in the event of its destruction or damage has an insurable interest. Thus, an insurable interest in property exists not only for the property owner himself, but also for creditors of the owner, such as lienholders and possessory interest holders.

While the insurable interest must exist at the time the loss occurs, it is generally not necessary that it existed at the time the contract to insure was entered into. Assume, for example, that Adam is negotiating to purchase real property from Brown and that during the negotiations he insures the improvements on it with Acme Insurance Company. Adam completes his contract to purchase from Brown and six months later the improvements are destroyed by fire. The insurance company refuses to indemnify Adam for his loss, on the grounds that Adam had no insurable interest at the time the contract was made. Adam, in most states, would prevail because his insurable interest existed at the time of loss.

Types of insurance contracts

Today it is possible to obtain from some source an insurance contract to cover almost every conceivable risk or loss. The comments in this chapter, however, will deal with the most common insurance contracts covering risk of loss to real property. These will include fire, extended coverage endorsement, and liability insurance.

Fire insurance

All states, with the exceptions of one or two, have adopted the New York Standard Fire Insurance Form (1943). A copy of it can be secured from your local insurance agent.

ASSUMPTION OF RISK

For a loss to occur, there must be a hostile fire, that is, one which has escaped from its proper place accidentally. The fire must further be the immediate or proximate cause of the loss that has occurred. If there is a reasonable connection between the loss sustained and the fire, the insurer is generally liable.

Those losses that are reasonably foreseeable as incidental to the fire are also covered provided clauses within the insurance contract do not state otherwise. Thus, damage caused by smoke, water where used to extinguish the fire, theft of personal property during the fire, and explosions caused by the fire are generally covered.

The standard policy lists several perils not included in the contract. These include:

(a) Enemy attack by armed forces, including action taken by military, naval or air forces in resisting an actual or an immediately impending enemy attack
(b) Invasion
(c) Insurrection
(d) Rebellion
(e) Revolution
(f) Civil war
(g) Usurped power
(h) Order of any civil authority, except acts of destruction at the time of and for the purpose of preventing the spread of fire, provided that such fire did not originate from any of the perils excluded by this policy
(i) Neglect on the part of the insured to use all reasonable means to save and preserve the property at and after a loss, or when the property is endangered by fire in neighboring premises
(j) Loss by theft

PROOF OF LOSS AND INSURER'S LIABILITY

The fire insurance policy will provide that proof of loss be given within a certain period of time and in a specified manner by the insured. Failure of the insured to provide such proof will generally release the insurer from liability.

The insured may never collect more than the actual extent of his loss. The amount of loss is the actual cash value at the time the property was destroyed. Most insurance policies will provide that the insurer has the right either to replace or to restore the property destroyed, or to pay the actual cash value thereof. When property is under-insured, the company is not liable for more than the face value of the policy.

A total loss may occur and yet the property may not be completely destroyed. When the unconsumed portion of the property is of no value for the purposes for which it was built, a total loss has occurred.

A standard policy provides for arbitration in the event that the insured and insurer cannot agree upon the actual amount of loss. Upon written demand of either party, each will select a competent and disinterested appraiser to act as umpire. If they fail to agree upon an umpire, then the selection will be made by the court in accordance with the contract. The amount paid to the insured is the actual cash value, and the decision of any two appraisers will be binding upon the parties. Each party pays for his own appraiser, and the two parties pay the umpire equally.

Most insurance companies pay a loss immediately after the amount of loss has been agreed upon. A loss must be paid within 60 days after the agreement has been reached by the parties or by the appraisers.

ASSIGNMENT

Insurance is a personal contract between the insured and the insurer. A personal contract cannot be assigned without the consent of the insurer unless a particular state statute so provides. This is an important point for the purchaser of property to remember.

CANCELLATION

Insurance contracts will frequently contain a cancellation clause. In absence of such a clause, however, cancellation requires the agreement or consent of both the insurer and insured.

Generally, if the insurer is permitted in the policy to cancel the contract, the unused premiums are refunded in full. If the policy contract is cancelled by the insured, "short rates" are applicable for the period of time the policy was in force. The short rate is slightly higher than the prorata rate and gives the insurance company a little more for the extra work involved. It is computed from a short rate table. Cancellation requires that actual notice be given to the insurance company and such notice may usually be oral or written.

COINSURANCE

The average or coinsurance clause in a contract provides that the insurance company shall not be liable for a loss greater than the proportion of insurance carried to the amount of insurance required. Because the rates are cheaper, it encourages the property owner to insure to the full value of his property.

Most fires do not produce a total loss; therefore, the property owner might reason in this manner: My property is worth $75,000, and if the building is completely destroyed, the foundation worth $5,000 will remain, so the insurable value is only $70,000. However, the building is entirely framed of steel and concrete, and the wooden portion of the building is worth $25,000; therefore, I will only insure for this amount, $25,000.

The most popular coinsurance clause is the "80 percent clause," but there are other percentage clauses. Assume that the full value of a building is $100,000. Under the 80 percent clause, the owner agrees to keep 80 percent of its value insured, $80,000. The formula works in this manner:

$$\frac{\text{Amount of Insurance}}{\substack{\text{Amount of Insurance that} \\ \text{should be carried}}} \times \text{Actual Loss} = \text{Insurance Company Liability}$$

$$\frac{\$80,000}{\$80,000} \times \$5,000 = \$5,000 \quad \text{Liability of Insurance Company}$$

In the above example, assume a loss of $5,000 with the owner carrying the full amount of insurance required. Note that the insurance company would pay the full amount of the loss because the proper amount of insurance was carried.

Now let us assume a loss of $5,000 in the same example except that the owner only carried $60,000 in insurance. The insured is penalized because he failed to carry the proper amount of insurance.

$$\frac{\$60,000}{\$80,000} \times \$5,000 = \$3,750 \quad \text{Liability of Insurance Company}$$

Assume the same loss in the above examples, but that the owner has the building insured for $110,000. It would appear from this example that the insured might profit from his loss but, as stated earlier in the chapter, this is not permitted. The insured will collect only the amount of his loss, $5,000.

$$\frac{\$110,000}{\$\ 80,000} \times \$5,000 = \$6,875$$

The property owner should periodically review his insurance program to make certain that he is carrying the proper amount of insurance on his property.

MORTGAGEE'S CLAUSE

The mortgage will carry a clause that states that the mortgagor will further provide that the mortgagee will be a beneficiary to the insurance contract. Therefore, when a total loss occurs to the property, the mortgagee will be paid first, with any remaining money going to the mortgagor.

SUBROGATION

After the insured has collected from the insurance company, the company may require that the insured assign his rights of recovery against any other party to the extent of the payment made by the insurance company. This right is used only when a third party negligently causes the loss.

PRO RATA INSURANCE LIABILITY

This clause states, in effect, that the insurance company shall not be liable for a loss greater than the proportion of insurance it has to other existing insurance policies. For example: Assume Adam had the following insurance policies on his office building:

Company A	$30,000
B	20,000
C	10,000
	$60,000 = Total insurance carried by Adam

Each company would be liable for a loss in the following manner: Company A, one-half; Company B, one-third; and Company C, one-sixth.

REDUCTION BY LOSS

When a loss to property occurs, the policy is reduced by the amount of the loss. If the face of the policy is $50,000 and a loss of $10,000 occurs, the policy will remain with a value of $40,000. For an additional premium, the full amount of insurance may be reinstated.

CONCEALMENT AND FRAUD

The standard policy of fire insurance provides that the insurance contract shall be void if, before or after the loss, the insured has concealed or misrepresented material facts concerning the insurance contract.

Extended coverage endorsement

The standard policy of fire insurance provides that any peril to be insured against, or any subject of insurance to be covered in the policy, shall be by endorsement in writing. This clause grants permission to extend the insurance policy to include wind storm, hail, explosion, aircraft, civil commotion, vehicles, and smoke. Extended coverage gives full protection to the mortgagee and the property owner. Many lenders require this endorsement but neither time nor space is permitted in this text for further discussion of it.

Liability insurance

Liability insurance is actually "third party" insurance in that it protects the insured when injuries result to another person while he is on the insured's property. It does not cover loss or damage to the property of the owner, but when the owner may be negligent in protecting the public and the law may impose liability on the owner, liability insurance gives the owner peace of mind. For example, let us assume that a guest, while staying at another's home, falls and breaks a leg on a defective step and sues the owner for damages. Chances are that the guest will be able to obtain a judgment against the owner, but if the latter has proper liability insurance, he will be protected against this suit.

A distinction should be made between three types of visitors, because the obligation owed to each is different under law.

Trespassers. A trespasser is one who comes upon the property of another without the legal right to do so. His only legal protection is against violence or willful injuries inflected upon him by the owner or persons under the owner's jurisdiction. The exceptions to the rule are infants of tender age who fall under the doctrine of *attractive nuisance.* Under this doctrine, the owner must use ordinary care, prudence, and foresight to prevent an injury to such children, if this can be accomplished without placing an undue burden upon the owner. The *nuisance* consists of any dangerous thing, attractive to such children, placed in an area frequented by them.

Licensed persons. Licensed persons include those who enter upon property for a special purpose only, with *permission* of the owner, such as a hunter granted the right to hunt on one's land; there is one right of use only. This category also includes policemen, firemen, utility service men, such as the reader of a meter, purchasers of theater tickets, and so forth. Ordinary care must be exercised to protect these individuals, and to keep the premises in a reasonably safe condition.

Guests. The *business visitor* or *invitee* are guests of the owner, and usually enter the premises at the *invitation* of the property owner or his agent. The highest degree of care must be exercised for the protection of these persons.

It would be impossible to discuss all the existing forms of liability insurance in a single chapter, so only the more important ones will be mentioned here.

OWNERS', LANDLORDS' AND TENANTS' LIABILITY POLICY

This type of policy will cover, to the limitations outlined, liabilities that occur from the ownership of apartment houses, motels, hotels, office buildings, resorts, and so on. It will cover the use and maintenance of the premises as outlined in the insurance contract.

The policy covers bodily injury for which the insured may become legally obligated to pay, including sickness, disease, and death resulting therefrom, and it covers injury or destruction of property, including the loss of use caused by an accident in any one of the hazards outlined in the contract.

Exclusions in the policy may be covered by the payment of an additional premium. The policy will not cover cases that fall within, or are covered by, workmen's compensation.

ELEVATOR LIABILITY INSURANCE

Elevators are an exclusion under the owners', landlords', and tenants' liability policy, unless an additional premium is paid. This type of insurance covers the risk of liability that results from the use, maintenance, and ownership of elevators, hoists, or shafts. Serious accidents may result from the use of elevators and like equipment; therefore, the owner may find it desirable to carry a greater amount of insurance for this type of liability.

WATER DAMAGE AND SPRINKLER LEAKAGE
INSURANCE POLICIES

The water damage liability policy is used to protect property damaged by water from refrigerator units, plumbing systems, including hot water tanks and bathroom fixtures; air conditioning units, and heating systems. Rain coming in a door or window and leakage from the roof would be covered. Exclusions may include the sprinkler system, floods, blocked sewers, or seepage in a basement floor or walls.

Since leakage from sprinkler systems is an exclusion in the above policy, it is wise for the owner to protect himself with sprinkler leakage insurance. Coverage under this policy will include leakage, accidental discharge, and accidents to the system's water tank.

GLASS INSURANCE

The glass insurance policy will cover all damage to glass, except that glass damage caused by fire which would normally be covered under the fire insurance policy. Rates will vary depending upon the type of glass used, the occupancy of the premises, and the location.

Comprehensive general liability insurance

This policy is offered to provide comprehensive coverage to the insured who may wish to have all his liability covered under a single policy and not several individual policy contracts. The insurance company, in a survey, will determine and recommend the types of coverage needed by the prospective client. These hazards are described in the policy and the premium will be based upon the liabilities to be covered.

Boiler and machinery insurance

Basically, this form of insurance covers explosion, breakdown of steam boilers, engines, electrical motors, generators, and machinery of various types. It includes damage caused by an accident, cost of repairing, bodily injury, loss to a third person's property, and any loss that may be covered by special endorsement. Limitations and exclusions are set forth in the insurance contract.

Rent insurance

This is a form of business interruption insurance for the lessor or landlord. It covers loss of rental income, and the loss of use or rental value of the owner-occupied portion of the building. This may be by endorsement to the fire insurance policy. The maximum loss of rent paid will be set forth in the insurance contract, but in no case will a loss be paid greater than the amount of actual loss in the event there was no damage to the property.

Leasehold interest insurance

Leasehold interest insurance protects the tenant against an increase in or a possible cancellation of his lease, and may also cover subleasees, losses of advance rents paid, and those who have an investment in the improvements, such as a tenant under a ground lease.

Demolition endorsement

This type of insurance is an endorsement to the fire insurance policy and is designed to protect the individual against increased costs to repair buildings damaged by fire if the increased cost is due to legal requirements, such as buildings codes. While such codes are not retroactive for existing buildings, if a building does burn down or is materially damaged by fire, such new codes will be enforced.

Workman's compensation

Statutes adopting workman's compensation have been developed in all states. These statutes provide that an employee may recover damages for injuries or death resulting within the scope of the employee's work, and from risks involved in that work. Since the adoption of such statutes, recoveries have been widened until today almost all injuries are included.

Because of the wide scope of recoveries allowed, and because negligence is not a valid defense, an employer must protect himself with *workman's compensation insurance*. In some states two plans are available. One is a state plan and the other a private insurance plan. Rates will be based upon the type of occupation and an estimate of the employer's payroll. Such estimates are subject to audit.

The length of time the employee will receive payments will depend upon whether the injury constitutes total disability, partial disability, or death, in which case benefits may also go to certain designated relatives of the deceased employee.

Review questions

1. Define the insurance contract and state how one may have an insurable interest in property.
2. Name the common risks covered by insurance pertaining to real estate and liabilities associated with property.
3. Distinguish between risks that are capable of being assumed and those that are excluded from a normal insurance risk.
4. What is meant by the terms "short rate" and "coinsurance clause" of policy of insurance?
5. Name at least five kinds of special insurance coverage policies, and explain the use of each in the ownership of real property.

14

The Real Estate Agent

In the early history of our nation, almost all persons were able to represent themselves in business transactions. Today, society and the economy have become so complex that it is impossible for the individual to make all of his own business transactions. Thus, the agent has come into existence. A majority of businessmen in our society today are agents for someone else.

Definition of terms

Agent. An agent is one who represents another (called a principal) in dealings with third parties. The agent may be employed to sell, give advice, purchase, and a variety of other things related to modern business transactions. In every agency three parties are involved: (1) the person represented, called the principal, (2) the agent who represents the principal, and (3) the third party with whom the agent deals on behalf of his principal.

Principal. Any person capable of contracting and conducting his own business transactions may appoint an agent. The transactions which are exceptions to the rule are voting, the execution of a will, and the taking of an oath. The principal must be mentally competent, and of legal age. A minor may not appoint an agent; however, the agent may be a minor.

Employer–Employee. An employer–employee relationship exists when, by agreement, expressed or implied, one person, called the employee, undertakes personal services for another called the employer, under the employer's supervision and control. A person may be both an agent and an employee, depending upon the scope of his authority. For example, the secretary may be an employee of the business firm, but when she delivers documents to another firm, she may become an agent. This distinction may be an important one particularly in the area of *tort liability*. (A tort is any civil wrong.)

Independent contractor. The independent contractor is one who is responsible to his employer for the final results of his work. He is independent in his occupation, he exercises his own judgment on the job that he is doing, and he is responsible for all of his own acts. Because an independent contractor relationship exists, the employer has no right to control the method of doing the work under contract. For example, Adam contracts with Brown, an independent contractor, to build a house. Adam is interested only in the final product. Adam does not tell Brown whom he must hire, where he must buy his materials, and so forth. Adam is concerned only that the house meets the plans and specifications set forth under the contract. Brown, as an independent contractor, is responsible for all of his own acts.

Special and general agents

Agents may be classified according to the scope of their authority. A *special agent* is one who is employed to perform a particular act or business transaction. Adam employs Brown, a licensed real estate broker, to sell his home, and a valid listing agreement is signed. Brown sells the home, completing the particular function for which he was employed. The *general agent* includes all others. The general agent is authorized to do anything and everything that his principal can do. The contracts performed may be of both a personal and business nature. Adam employs Brown as his general agent to conduct all of his business and personal affairs. Adam, as the principal, is responsible for all acts of the general agent.

BROKERS AND SALESMEN

Real estate brokers and salesmen may be classified as general agents or special agents, although they normally fall under the latter classification. In a majority of cases the real estate broker is employed to negotiate the purchase, sale, or leasing of real property. While the broker may or may not have possession of the property, he does not take title thereto. In most states, real estate salesmen are classified as employees of the broker. Most such statutes provide that the broker exercise reasonable supervision over the salesmen's activities.

It is highly desirable that the real estate broker enter into a working agreement with his sales personnel. An agreement, in writing, will eliminate misunderstandings between the parties. A suggested contract of employment form is included as Fig. 12; however, each individual broker may have special provisions he may wish to include.

Creation of the agency relationship

The agency relationship is created in four principal ways: (1) precedent authorization or by express appointment, (2) subsequent ratification, (3) estoppel, and (4) necessity.

Most agency agreements are voluntary in nature and are formed by prior authorization, either oral or written, expressed or implied. A listing agreement signed by both principal and agent prior to the agent fulfilling his function as a special agent would be an example of an agency formed by precedent authorization or by express appointment.

When a person attempts to act for another without his permission, expressed or implied, and said person's acts are approved by the principal, the principal is bound, and an agency by subsequent ratification has been formed. When a principal learns of unauthorized representations made by another proposing to be his agent, the principal may repudiate the acts, ratify them, or imply approval by his conduct.

In either of the above cases, an *actual agency* is said to exist; that is, one formed by authorization or subsequent ratification.

An agency is created by *estoppel* (called an ostensible agency) when the principal causes a third person to believe another to be his agent who is not in fact employed by him. This may have been intentional on the part of the principal or by want of ordinary care. This is an involuntary agency relationship created by law to prevent an injustice. The elements necessary to create an ostensible agency are: (1) conduct on the part of the principal which indicates the agent's apparent authority, and (2) the third party's reliance upon such apparent authority.

Another type of involuntary agency by necessity may be created by law without the actual consent of the principal on the grounds of public policy. A wife, for example, has the authority to pledge her husband's credit for the necessities of life. The law may confer certain authority upon the employee or agent who must act in the best interests of his em-

Broker-Salesman Contract

(Employee)

CALIFORNIA REAL ESTATE ASSOCIATION STANDARD FORM

1 This agreement entered into this _____ day of _____ 19____ by and between

_____ hereinafter called Broker and _____

_____ hereinafter called Salesman, hereby agree, subject to termination at will by either party, to the following conditions and details of their relationship:

BROKER

2 Broker is defined as the operator of a real estate firm or business, licensed as a broker under the laws of the State of California by the Real Estate Commissioner, to sell or otherwise deal in real estate, and who employs one or more salesmen.

SALESMAN

3 Salesman is defined as: (a) A person duly licensed under the laws of the State of California by the Real Estate Commissioner as a salesman and employed by Broker. (b) A person duly licensed under the laws of the State of California by the Real Estate Commissioner as a broker and employed by Broker as a real estate salesman.

GENERAL CONDITIONS

4 Salesman shall read and be governed by the Code of Ethics of the National Association of Real Estate Boards, the real estate law of the State of California and the by-laws of the local real estate board, and any future modifications or additions thereto. A copy of the code of ethics and of the local Board by-laws are attached hereto.

BROKER OBLIGATIONS

5 Broker maintains offices adequately and properly equipped with furnishings, equipment and facilities reasonable and adequate for the proper operation of a general real estate brokerage business, staffed with trained employees engaged in serving the public as a real estate broker.

6 As a part of these facilities, Broker procures and maintains listings for sale, lease and rental of real estate as well as purchasers, lessees and renters thereof, and has for some time and does now enjoy the good will and reputation for fair dealing with the public generally.

7 Broker is duly and regularly licensed as a real estate broker under license issued by the Real Estate Commissioner of the State of California and maintains memberships in the local real estate board, the California Real Estate Association and the National Association of Real Estate Boards.

8 Broker agrees to make available to Salesman all current listings in the office except such as Broker may find expedient to place exclusively in the possession of some other salesman.

9 Salesman has no authority, either express or implied, to represent anything to a prospective purchaser unless it is in the listing agreement or unless he receives specific written instructions from Broker.

10 Broker shall provide, within limitations herein set forth, Salesman with advertising and with necessary office equipment, including space, desk, telephone, telegrams, signs, business cards, stationery, escrow assistance, legal advice and supervisory assistance and cooperation with salesman in connection with his work.

11 All advertising shall be approved and placed by Broker.

12 Broker must first approve the ordering of all title searches and the opening of all escrows.

13 In the event any transaction in which Salesman is involved results in a dispute, litigation or legal expense. Salesman shall cooperate fully with Broker and Broker and Salesman shall share all expense connected therewith, in the same proportion as they would normally share the commission resulting from such transaction if there were no dispute or litigation. In any event, the salesman shall not be financially responsible for any expenses that are in excess of the amount that he would have normally received as his share of the commission had there been no dispute or litigation. It is the policy to avoid litigation wherever possible and Broker reserves the right to determine whether or not any litigation or dispute shall be prosecuted, defended, compromised or settled. and the terms and conditions of any compromise or settlement or whether or not legal expense shall be incurred.

14 Salesman shall not make any long distance calls or send any telegrams without prior approval of Broker. All telephone calls and telegrams over $1.00, including tax, shall be paid one-half by Salesman for whose benefit the cost was incurred, and one-half by Broker.

15 All Salesmen shall receive an equal amount of floor time.

16 All Salesmen shall be allowed to purchase a home from among the firm's listings, providing the Broker is paid the normal share of commission due Broker as Broker's share of commission. Said purchase of a home shall be for the Salesman's own use and occupancy. If another Salesman is involved through having obtained the listing. said Salesman shall receive his normal listing fee in the same manner as if a sale had been made to someone not connected with the office.

17 No salesman shall be required to work an average of more than six days a week.

18 Broker shall close his office and his open houses on the following legal holidays: Fourth of July, Thanksgiving Day, Christmas Day and Easter Sunday.

COMMISSIONS

19 Broker agrees to pay Salesman as and for Salesman's compensation for services rendered on a commission basis for all work done by Salesman in accordance with fee schedule adopted by Broker's office, a copy of which is attached hereto and shall be considered a part of this agreement. No commission shall be considered earned or payable to Salesman until the transaction has been completed and the commission collected by the Broker. Commissions

earned shall be payable twice each month, on the _____ and _____ day of each month.

Figure 12 Sample employment form

20   The schedule of commissions and divisions thereof as attached hereto shall be used in every transaction, and any variation therefrom shall first be approved by Broker. Any arrangement for division of commission with other brokers shall be first approved by Broker. In the event two or more salesmen employed by Broker participate in a commission on the same transaction, it shall be divided between the participating salesmen according to prior agreement or by arbitration.

21   Any expense incurred in negotiating the sale, including travel expense, hotels, meals, maps, special services employed, listing fees, multiple listing commissions, etc., shall first be deducted from the gross commission received.

SALESMEN'S OBLIGATIONS

22   Salesman agrees to conduct his activities and regulate his habits so as to maintain and to increase, rather than diminish the good will and reputation of Broker.

23   Salesman shall furnish his own automobile and pay all expenses thereof and shall carry liability and property damage insurance satisfactory to the Broker, name Broker as co-insured and deliver copy of endorsement to Broker.

24   Salesman shall remain continuously licensed by the State of California to sell real estate and shall pay the required renewal fee.

25   Salesman shall not obligate Broker for materials or service or the purchase of real property or anything or in any other way, without first obtaining consent of Broker, verbally or in writing.

26   Salesman shall use only real estate forms approved by Broker.

27   Broker reserves the right to reject any exclusive listing deemed unsatisfactory, and to return said listing to the owner.

28   Salesman acknowledges that he is an employee of Broker and that he will abide by all written rules and regulations now in force or subsequently adopted by Broker. Broker agrees to carry compensation insurance for all employees.

29   All letters received, and a copy of all letters written by Salesmen pertaining to the business of Broker shall be the property of Broker, and be turned over to Broker for Broker's records. All letters written by Salesmen shall be approved by Broker before mailing or delivering.

30   All money, documents or property received by Salesman in connection with any transaction of Broker shall be delivered to Broker immediately. All checks or money orders shall be made payable to either Broker, to a title company or to another Broker-approved escrow holder. In the event that all or any portion of the deposit is forfeited, and the seller has received his share of the funds, a division of the remainder of such deposit shall be made between Broker and Salesman in the same proportion as though the amount received was a commission received in connection with the transaction.

31   In connection with any transaction, if it becomes necessary or desirable to receive all or part of the commission in property other than cash, then approval of Broker shall first be obtained. In such event, Broker and Salesman may agree as follows:
  a. To divide such property between Broker and Salesman in kind, in the same proportion as their respective interests in the commission involved; or
  b. Broker may pay Salesman his full share of the commission in cash, in which event Broker shall have the full ownership of the property so received; or
  c. To retain such property in the names of Broker and Salesman and thereafter to dispose of the same at such time at such price and on such terms as Broker and Salesman shall agree. Any profit or loss or any carrying charges or other expenses with respect to such property, shall be shared between Broker and Salesman in the same proportion as their respective interests in the commission involved.

32   This agreement for division of commission shall not apply to subdivision sales or acreage for subdivisions or large or unusual transactions which require special time and services on the part of Broker. Commissions received and paid on such transactions will be subject to special written agreement.

ARBITRATION

33   In the event of disagreement or dispute between Salesmen in the office or between Broker and Salesman arising out of or connected with this agreement, which cannot be adjusted by and between the parties involved, such questions shall be submitted to the local real estate Board committee governing such disputes or if this is not agreed upon, the problem must be submitted to a temporary Board of Arbitration for final adjustment. Such board shall be selected in the following manner: Each of the parties to the disagreement or dispute shall select one member who shall be a licensed broker or licensed salesman. Such selection shall be made within five days from the time notice is given in writing by either party to the other, that arbitration is desired. The two arbitrators thus selected, in case they cannot reach a decision after a single conference or adjustment thereof, shall name a third arbitrator who shall be a person not licensed by the Real Estate Commissioner. Such arbitration may follow the provisions of Sections 1280 through 1293 of the Code of Civil Procedure for the State of California.

TERMINATION OF CONTRACT

34   This contract and the association created hereby may be terminated by either party hereto, at any time, upon notice to the other, said notice to be in writing; but the rights of the parties to any commission which accrued prior to said notice shall not be divested by the termination of the contract.

35   When this agreement has been terminated for any reason, any deals Salesman has made that are not closed shall be considered his property and upon closing of said deals, full Salesman's share of commission shall be paid to him; and Salesman shall receive agreed listing commissions on his listings if sold within the life of such listings, and commission received by Broker. This shall not apply to any extension of the said listings beyond the original listing period.

36   In the event salesman leaves and has deals or listings pending that require further services normally rendered by Salesman, the Salesman and Broker, or Broker alone, shall make arrangements with another Salesman in the organization to perform the required services, and the Salesman assigned shall be compensated for taking care of pending deals or listings.

37   Broker and Salesman agree to all the foregoing terms and conditions and to use their skill, efforts and abilities in cooperating to carry out the terms of this agreement for the mutual benefit of Broker and Salesman.

38   In Witness Whereof, the parties hereto have set their hands this day and year first above written.

BROKER

SALESMAN

This contract prepared by California
Real Estate Association as a suggested
guide for members and their attorneys.

Figure 12 (continued)

ployer and yet is unable to consult with his principal or employer. In an emergency, a store employee may call a physician to attend to a customer who has received an injury in the store.

An *attorney-in-fact* is a person who has been given a power of attorney. Such a person need not be a lawyer. Adam, by power of attorney, appoints Brown to act for him. Brown would be an attorney-in-fact. In most states a power of attorney dealing with real property must be recorded in the county where the property is located to be effective. Thus to eliminate the power of attorney, a revocation of such must also be recorded.

A *dual agency* exists when the same person represents more than one principal in the same transaction. Under the code of ethics of the National Association of Real Estate Boards, and most state statutes, the real estate agent may not represent two principals in the same transaction unless he informs them and has their consent. The broker may, however, collect a commission from both, providing each principal understands that the broker is collecting a commission from the other. Frequently, in the exchange of properties, a broker will represent both parties. Failure to make this fact known to both principals may mean suspension or revocation of the broker's license.

Agency agreements

An agency agreement is a contract between the principal and the agent. Since it is a contract, the agreement must contain all of the essential elements thereof. There must be mutual assent, the parties must be capable of contracting, and the agreement must be for a lawful object. The one possible exception is consideration. To be enforceable, an agency agreement for the sale or purchase of real property must be in writing.

As stated above, *consideration* is not essential to the creation of an agency agreement; that is, the agent may act gratuitously. Adam leaves Brown, a friend, in charge of his store while getting a haircut. Brown drops a box on a customer and is joined as a codefendant in an action brought by the customer. Brown cannot deny that he was, in fact, Adam's agent, even though he acted without remuneration. Brown is liable for his own torts.

Agency agreements may take the form of a unilateral contract; however, in some states, agreements of this nature may not be enforceable. Therefore, most form listing agreements provide the following clause: "In consideration of the execution of the foregoing, the undersigned Broker agrees to use diligence in procuring a purchaser." The listing or agency agreement now becomes a bilateral contract, that is, a promise for a promise. The property owner promises to sell under the terms and conditions of the listing agreement and the broker promises to use due diligence in finding a purchaser for the property.

If the statute of frauds requires that a certain contract be in writing to be enforceable, the agency agreement relating thereto must also be in writing. This is known as the equal dignities rule.

When an agent enters into a contract for compensation or a commission in the sale of real property, some memorandum thereof must be in writing and subscribed to by the party to be charged if the agreement is to be valid. Adam verbally employs Brown, a licensed broker, to sell his real property under certain terms and conditions and promises to pay Brown a 6 percent commission in the event the property is sold. Brown sells the property for Adam, who then refuses to pay the commission as agreed. Brown may not enforce his contract because there was no written memorandum relating to his employment. (Note: Exceptions to this rule occur when the agent or broker acts in the immediate presence of his principal and executes instruments under the direction of his principal.)

Agent's scope of authority

A real estate broker's authority is governed by the terms of his agency contract. Generally, such authority may be classified into three categories: (1) express, (2) incidental, and (3) customary.

An agreement to sell or purchase real property will set forth the terms of the agency agreement. *Express authority* may also be by conduct of the parties, or implied authority, when the agent informs the principal of his intentions and the principal says or does nothing.

Incidental authority is authority that is reasonably necessary to carry out and execute the agreement. For example, the advertising of the principal's real property would be incidental to the authority granted in the agreement.

Customary authority might be used by the professional property manager in the collection of rents from tenants, or the eviction of said tenants in the event that such rents are not paid as provided in the lease agreement.

In most cases, a contract merely authorizes the broker or his salesman to find a purchaser for the real property. Unless the agreement provides for accepting a deposit, the broker or his salesman is not authorized to collect same. If he does so, he will do so as agent of the buyer rather than as an agent of the principal. However, most form listing agreements do authorize the agent to accept a deposit.

Delegation of power by an agent

The general rule is that an agent may not delegate authority granted
to him in the agency agreement except when: (1) the act is purely mechanical in nature, (2) it is a well-known custom to do so, (3) a necessity
or sudden emergency exists, or (4) subagents are contemplated.

An artist is employed to paint a portrait because of his skill in painting; therefore, he may not delegate his work to another. A secretary,
however, may do the typing on a form agreement for her employer because it is purely mechanical.

A real estate broker may, as a rule, fill in a form contract, but he may
not draw or create a new contract. The actual drawing of a contract
must be done by an attorney licensed to practice law. It is also customary
to delegate certain authority to the escrow officer in closing a transaction.

In an emergency, it may be necessary for the agent to delegate authority to protect his principal's interest. Thus, the agent may delegate
to another his call for a medical doctor, in case of injury to someone on
the principal's property.

When a home is listed by the broker, and said agreement provides that
the property will be placed on the multiple listing interchange, subagents
are contemplated.

Duties of the principal and agent

Certain duties and responsibilities rest with both the principal and
the agent:

1. Both the principal and agent must act in good faith and in fair-
   ness to each other. The agent may have no personal interest in conflict with that of his principal.
2. An agent may act for two parties only when he has the consent of
   both.
3. The agent may make no secret profit at the expense of his principal. If he does so, he is liable to the principal. The same relationship exists between principal and agent as between a trustee and
   the beneficiary of an estate.
4. The agent must inform the principal of all material facts in a transaction.
5. The agent must be both obedient and responsible to his principal.
   He must obey lawful instructions. If he does not, he is liable for
   damages to his principal.
6. The principal must compensate the agent for his services, as well
   as for expenses incurred in his work.

7. An agent, for purpose of effecting the agency agreement, must do everything necessary and usual in the ordinary course of business.

8. An agent may make actual representations to fulfill the agency agreement if he knows they are true. He must act in the name of his principal and not in his own, unless it is the usual course of business to do so.

9. In an emergency, the agent's power is broadened, and he may disobey instructions if it should be in the best interest of his principal.

10. An agent is liable for his own torts. Since the principal reaps the benefits of those acts performed by his agent, he may also be responsible for torts caused by his agent to third persons, if such torts are caused within the scope of the agency.

Third persons

The duties and responsibilities of third persons are summarized in the following:

1. Third persons should take reasonable steps to determine the extent of the agent's authority. As a general rule, a third party cannot rely upon the agent's statements alone, and if he has reason to doubt the agent's authority, he should check with the principal.

2. When the third person has reason to believe that the agent may be dealing adversely with his principal, such third person should realize that he deals at his own peril.

3. A third person cannot, generally, rely upon the agent's statements concerning the occurrence of a future event.

4. As a general rule, the third person may hold a disclosed principal liable to a contract in which his agent is acting within the scope of his authority or apparent authority. When there is neither apparent authority nor actual authority, the principal may not be bound.

5. When the agent acts for an undisclosed principal, and the third party enters into such a contract, the third party may generally enforce a contract against the agent. When the third party learns of the undisclosed principal, he may hold either the agent or the principal liable. Until relief is obtained from one, a right of action against the other is not barred. Therefore, if the agent wishes to avoid liability, he should disclose his principal.

6. As a general rule of law, the agent is liable for his own torts, negligent acts, or fraudulent acts, against third persons; in most agency agreements, the principal is liable also for those torts of his agent committed within the scope of the employment. The possible exception is that concerning the real estate broker who, en route to show property, is involved in an automobile accident. However, when the property owner connives with the agent to misrepresent, both may be liable. For example, during the showing of a home, the customer asks if the house is wired for an electric stove. The agent points to a 220 plug and says "there is a 220 plug." The owner present says or does nothing. Both may be liable in this case, if the customer assumes that this information answers his question.

Termination of the agency agreement

The agency relationship may be terminated in any one of the following ways: (1) mutual agreement, (2) expiration of term, (3) extinction of subject matter, (4) death of either principal or agent, and (5) operation of law.

The parties to an agency agreement may terminate it by mutual agreement. Thus, when the real estate agent and the property owner agree to cancel the listing agreement, they may do so. However, should the agent or principal renounce the agreement, the principal may be liable for breach of contract and any damages suffered by the other party. For example, when the principal renounces the agreement during the time it is valid and the broker furnishes a buyer ready, willing, and able to purchase on the terms and conditions of the contract, the broker usually may maintain a valid suit for his commission.

If the subject matter of the agency agreement becomes extinct, the agreement is terminated. When the property subject to the agency agreement is materially damaged or totally destroyed by fire, the listing agreement will be terminated, unless the damaged improvements thereon are incidental to the sale of the land.

The death of either the principal or the agent will terminate the agency agreement. Adam, a broker, has a file of listings on numerous properties in Chicago. When he dies, his son Bill takes over the business as the new broker. Adam's death terminated the agency agreements. Bill must now secure new agency agreements from each of the property owners.

The general rule is that an agency agreement will be terminated by operation of law, as in the case of bankruptcy. As discussed earlier in the text, when bankruptcy occurs, all assets are placed in the hands of a receiver appointed by the court that has jurisdiction.

Broker's commission

The real estate broker's commission is fixed by custom rather than by law. It is a matter of agreement between the principal and agent.

The broker has earned his real estate commission when he has found a buyer ready, willing, and able to purchase the property at the listed price, on the exact terms and within the life of the listing agreement or any extension thereof. It matters not how little or how much effort has been extended by the broker. He is entitled to his commission if he gets the desired results.

When brokers cooperate in the sale of land or other properties, they may agree on the method of dividing fees and commissions. Binding agreements between brokers are effective. Such agreements may be made orally, and may be enforced just like any other contract that is not required to be in writing. As a matter of practice, however, to save disagreement at a later date, brokers normally exchange letters as to the division of commissions.

In common practice, the client or the principal employs the broker to to sell his property; however, it is not unusual for a buyer to employ a broker to find property for him, in which case the buyer may agree to pay the broker a commission or a finder's fee. The broker could, under these circumstances, collect a commission from both the customer and the principal, but if he does so, he must inform both that he is collecting a commission from each.

Licensing real estate brokers and salesmen

A majority of the states today have statutes regulating the licensing and activities of real estate brokers and salesmen. The purpose of these statutes is to protect the land-buying public from fraudulent acts on the part of a few unscrupulous or incompetent individuals. Basically, there are two parts to most of the laws governing real estate in the various states: (1) the statutes enacted by the state legislatures, and (2) the rules and regulations of the real estate commissioner, administrator, or executive secretary who is charged with the enforcement of the statute. Such rules and regulations, called *administrative law*, once made in accordance with the statutes of that state, have the same force and effect as the law itself.

REGULATING BODY

Each state will have, as noted above, a regulating body and a public official charged with the enforcement of the real estate statute. A number of states, including California, Florida, Georgia, Kansas, and Pennsylvania, have real estate commissions. The number of persons serving on these commissions will vary from three to six. Usually the state official charged with enforcing the real estate statute will act as chairman of the commission or other regulating body. Usually appointments are made to the commission by the governor or other designated official on a four-year basis, but this may vary in the different states.

Some of the duties of the regulating body might include inquiring into the needs of licensees, deciding upon business policy of the regulating agency, and conferring with and advising the governor and other state officials concerning the real estate business in the state.

LICENSEE QUALIFICATION AND EXAMINATION

The requirements for a real estate broker or salesman will vary from state to state; however, a person engaged in any of the following activities for compensation, or in expectation of compensation, generally will need to be licensed:

1. Selling or offering to sell
2. Buying or offering to buy
3. Soliciting or obtaining listings
4. Negotiating the purchase, sale or exchanging of property
5. Leasing, renting, or offering to lease or rent, or collecting advance fees
6. Assisting or offering to assist persons in filing applications for the purchase or lease of federal or state lands
7. Soliciting offers or lenders, or negotiating loans, or collecting payments
8. Selling, buying or negotiating the purchase, sale, or exchange of promissory notes secured by liens on real property

A real estate salesman is a person employed by a real estate broker who works for compensation, or in expectation of compensation, for performing any of the acts set forth above.

The educational requirements will also vary, depending upon the various statutes. In California, for example, current legislation requires the broker to complete two three-semester unit courses or the equivalent thereof in an approved academic institution of higher learning before taking the examination. These required courses include real estate practice and legal aspects of real estate. The current examination for the broker is divided into three sessions—(1) a full day general examination that all applicants are required to take; (2) a one and one-half-hour session on real estate finance; and (3) a one and one-half-hour session on real estate appraisal. If the applicant has succcessfully completed a three-semester unit course or the equivalent thereof in an academic institution of higher learning in either or both of these subjects, the real estate commissioner may waive that portion of the examination. In January 1972, both real estate finance and real estate appraisal will be courses required prior to taking the examination for a license.

Additional requirements for licensing might include residency for a certain length of time, legal age, and so forth. All applicants for a license are usually required to furnish proof of their honesty and good reputation.

There is no standard format, statewise, for examinations, but it is likely that a good knowledge of the following will be required of most applicants:

1. The English language, its reading, writing, spelling, and basic arithmetic
2. The basic principles of real estate conveyance, purposes and legal effects of deeds, mortgages, leases and land contracts of sale, land economics, and appraisal
3. The obligations of principal and agent, of real estate practice, business ethics, and so on

PERSONS EXEMPT FROM LICENSING REQUIREMENTS

Anyone dealing with his own property (property owned in fee simple) is usually exempt from the license requirement.

Persons acting under a duly executed power of attorney (attorney-in-fact) are also exempt. An attorney at law, in most states, performing his duties as an attorney may be exempt from license requirements. If the attorney enters the real estate business, coming within the definition of a real estate broker, he must take the broker's examination and secure a license. Finally, a receiver, or a trustee selling under a deed of trust, is exempted.

DISCIPLINARY ACTION

The public official charged with the duty of enforcing the real estate statutes in any state may, upon his own motion or upon receiving a written complaint from a person, investigate the actions of the licensee. His power, in most cases, is limited to a suspension or revocation of a license. While the statutes may provide fines and prison terms, such penalties are left to a court of law. The more common grounds for suspension or revocation of a license include:

1. Making any substantial misrepresentation
2. Making false promises likely to influence, persuade or induce
3. Acting for more than one party to a transaction without the knowledge or consent of all parties
4. Commingling business or personal money with the property of others which is received and held by him in trust
5. Claiming a secret profit without the knowledge of the principal
6. When a combined listing option agreement is used by the real estate

broker before exercising option to purchase, failing to reveal to the purchaser, in writing, the full amount of his profit and, further, to obtain the written approval of the principal before the taking of such a profit

7. Making false promises through real estate agents or salesmen and pursuing a continued and flagrant course of misrepresentation of property

8. Any other conduct that could constitute fraud or dishonest dealing

Review questions

1. Define *agency* as it exists in the real estate business.
2. Contrast the employer–employee relationship with the status of an independent contractor.
3. In what four ways may an agency relationship be created?
4. Name and explain three classifications of the authority of an agent.
5. List and explain five of the principal duties of principal and agent.
6. Summarize the duties and responsibilities of third persons in real estate transactions.
7. In what ways may an agency agreement be terminated?
8. When has a broker earned his commission on a sale?
9. What is the usual method, in most states, of licensing real estate brokers and salesmen?
10. What is meant by the term "realtor," and what are the regulations common to the use of this name?

Multiple-choice questions

1. The power of attorney may be terminated: (a) by the attorney, (b) by revocation by written communication to attorney-in-fact, (c) only by a recorded notice, (d) only by court order, (e) by none of the foregoing.
2. "Agency" is the relationship created by: (a) steamship companies, (b) one who is apointed to act for another, (c) an optionee and an optionor, (d) none of these, (e) all of these.
3. The commission a broker receives if he finds a buyer ready, willing and able is due him because it is: (a) the law, (b) regulated by the real estate commission, (c) part of the agreed contract, (d) the custom in most states, (e) none of these.
4. In order to collect a commission through court action, a broker must, in most states, prove he was licensed at: (a) the time the commission was earned, (b) the time the escrow closed, (c) the time the down payment was submitted, (d) the time the deed was received, (e) none of the foregoing.
5. Most license laws prohibit anyone licensed as a broker or salesman from: (a) participating in a real estate transaction as a principal, (b) taking options, (c) taking combined listings and options, (d) none of these, (e) all of these.

6. A position of trust exists between the agent and his principal. This relationship is known as: (a) beneficial, (b) fiduciary, (c) mandatory, (d) estoppel, (e) all of these.

7. An agent is one who: (a) represents another to third persons, (b) always acts as an independent contractor, (c) must always be an ostensible agent, (d) operates only under a power of attorney, (e) none of the foregoing.

8. A real estate salesman is an agent: (a) for the principal directly, (b) for his employing broker, (c) for the third party, (d) none of these, (e) all of these.

9. Which of the following is free to accomplish an end result as he sees fit? (a) agent, (b) independent contractor, (c) employee, (d) none of these, (e) all of these.

10. Broker Jones, knowing that Smith wants a certain parcel of land, contacts the owner to purchase it and does so without authority from Smith. Smith ratifies Broker Jones's action. This agency was formed by: (a) prior agreement, (b) ratification, (c) estoppel, (d) none of these, (e) all of these.

15

The Real Estate Office

The real estate office is the focal point of all activities—some highly specialized in nature—and, therefore, it is of paramount importance that it be efficiently run on a businesslike basis. Furthermore, the successful operation of a business is associated with good leadership. The qualities of good leadership will be discussed later in this chapter.

The efficiently run real estate operation will have a guide, commonly referred to as a *policy manual*, setting forth the philosophy, rules and regulations under which the business is to operate. This manual should be "tailor made" to suit each particular business and the personality and philosophy of the broker-executive of the firm. A well-developed policy manual will further aid in personnel training and planning, thus eliminating a possible high turnover of sales personnel and staff.

The real estate executive, his sales personnel, and staff will create an image of the office, favorable or unfavorable, in the eyes of the public. The image of the real estate office is important and will create a lasting impression on the public. An unfavorable impression made by one member of the firm will reflect on all personnel and operations therein. A favorable image is created, in part at least, by a well-planned and organized office.

Organization and forms of ownership

The broker is the head of his business enterprise and must select the form of business ownership under which the business will operate. The success of his business will depend upon his company policies and the decisions he makes.

INDIVIDUAL PROPRIETORSHIP

It is estimated that approximately 90 percent of the real estate broker-age firms in the United States are individually owned. The increased real estate market activity in recent years has convinced a large number of people that anyone can succeed in the real estate business. This is not necessarily true, because risks common to other small businesses also pertain to the real estate business. The independent broker must have a positive mental attitude and be willing to risk his own efforts and time for business success. He should have enough capital to carry him for a minimum period of one year in his basic business operations. He is, further, a catalyst who must rely upon his own diplomacy, skill, and tact for bringing the seller and purchaser together.

The advantages of the single proprietorship are the opportunity for the independent, and the reaping of financial rewards commensurate to the efforts put forth in the business by the owner. If the owner has capital, he does not have to seek outside financing, and he can operate without consulting with anyone on policy matters. The ease of organization, too, is an advantage of the single proprietorship.

On the other hand, a greater demand on the time and energy of the owner will be made, particularly during the formative stages of the business. The broker-executive operating a single proprietorship must solve problems without consultation with others, and, therefore, he is limited to his own skill and knowledge. The broker-executive, in case of business failure, will be totally responsible for all of his business losses because the remaining assets of the business may not cover the debts and expenses incurred. Thus, to act independently, one must be willing to accept responsibility and work long hours, giving careful attention to the office operation.

PARTNERSHIP

A partnership is a voluntary association of two or more individuals joined together as co-owners to operate a business for a profit. Real estate brokers and others planning to enter into co-ownership of a business are wise to consult an attorney. As a general rule, a partnership may be formed by an oral agreement—unless a provision in the statute of frauds declares otherwise—but it is not good business procedure to do so. Minds become clouded and misunderstandings may result concerning the duties and responsibilities in the participation of each partner. Properly drawn articles of copartnership will eliminate the majority of such disagreements. These articles will set forth, among other things, the names of the partners, the purpose for which the partnership is formed, and the duties and responsibilities of each. The articles, when recorded, will give notice to "the whole world" of the existence of the partnership and of the rights and interest of each partner. The laws of each state govern the relation of partnerships toward the public, and, in the absence of articles of co-partnership, will govern the rights and duties of partners.

Partnerships may be classified as *general, special,* and *limited* partnerships. It is the general partnership which is of primary concern.

A general partnership may be formed by real estate brokers to conduct a real estate office. In certain states a salesman may not be a general partner. Unless otherwise agreed, all partners share equally in the management, profits, and losses of the business.

The advantages of a partnership include the pooling of the capital, skill, and experience of all partners, with the division of responsibility for efficient management. While the partnership as such must file an information return for income tax purposes, it does not pay income tax. Each individual partner pays federal and state income tax based upon his share of profits or losses; thus this is an advantage over the corporation.

The advantages of a partnership may easily become disadvantages. As a general rule, each partner binds the partnership when he acts within the scope of the business. Unless each partner is thoroughly familiar with the personality, skill, and experience of the other partners, disagreements may result. All partners are, further, jointly and severally liable for the debts of the general partnership. If insolvency results, creditors will take action against the personal assets of each or all of the partners. Death, of course, dissolves a partnership.

A special partnership is formed for a single transaction, such as the development of a subdivision or the purchasing of a building. The same rules of law outlined above apply.

The limited partnership is composed of one or more general partners and one or more limited partners. The general partners are liable jointly and severally for the partnership, while the limited partners are liable for their investment only. The limited partner may lose his status, however, if he enters into management decisions. The advantages include: (1) the raising of large sums of capital without relinquishing management for it, and (2) the relative ease of dissolution when the business venture is completed. The profits are shared in proportion to the division of duties and amount of capital investment in the partnership. A limited partnership, like a general partnership, is taxed on individual income. This agreement should be written, and an attorney should be consulted.

CORPORATION

A corporation is a legal entity, created by law, that receives its authority from the government. As a general rule, a state may grant to a corporation any powers the state chooses, except those limited or placed on it by the federal or state constitution. Like an individual, a corporation may sue or be sued, and may own property in its own name. The study of corporate law is a complete field in itself:

Advantages of the corporation include:

1. Limited liability of stockholders, for their investment only
2. Continuation of existence in case of death or disability of a stockholder or officer
3. Ease of obtaining sums of capital in the sale of stock
4. Salability of shares of stock
5. Paid management with experience and ability in the business operation

Disadvantages include:

1. Dual taxation, first on corporation earnings and then on dividends distributed to the stockholders
2. Cost and expense of incorporating
3. Obtaining credit because of the limited liability status

An attorney should be consulted in the formation of a corporation because all laws must be strictly observed.

SYNDICATES

Syndicates may be used for purposes of financing, developing, and purchasing large income properties. Laws governing syndicates will vary from state to state, and the real estate practitioner is advised to familiarize himself with those laws.

For the real estate practitioner, particularly those in commercial and investment properties, large sums of capital can be raised for the purchase of properties by combining many small investors of $1,000 or more. This enables the small investor to diversify, and creates for the practitioner additional sales that would otherwise be lost.

The syndicate may take many forms, including the general partnership, special partnership, limited partnership, and joint venture.

PROBLEMS OF ORGANIZING AND
OPENING THE REAL ESTATE OFFICE

The prime person for opening a real estate brokerage office is the successful real estate salesman. He may be motivated by the fact that he has acquired sufficient knowledge in the industry and is contributing more than his share for the compensation he is receiving. Although the successful salesman has passed a broker's license test and has some capital saved up, an investigation of why small businesses fail should be in order.

The broker-executive must have proven business experience and a specialized knowledge of office and personnel administration; otherwise, the decision-making process will become a "trial and error" situation.

The basic qualifications of a successful broker are twofold. First, he must have had successful *experience* in the real estate business and its organization and operation; second, he must have the ability to manage the complex problems of *supervision* and cost control of the organizational activities. Successful experience as an office manager is valuable training for the broker before opening his own office. Other alternatives open are employment with a small firm where there is an opportunity to become a partner, or with a large firm that might provide the opportunity to become specialized in the field of office management. In addition, in institutions of higher learning educational opportunities are available that provide academic courses where the individual is deficient in knowledge.

DEPARTMENTS AND AREAS OF SPECIALIZATION

A specialist, preferably one with several years of experience, should be selected to head the specialized areas included in the operation of the real estate office. Because of the complexity of the business, it is impossible for an individual broker to be an expert at all things. It is for this reason that most of the small brokerage firms confine their activity to the sale of residential housing. This area alone is highly specialized, and the competition is stiff.

Specialization in the areas of business outlined above does permit the large real estate firm to provide a complete service for its clients.

SELECTING THE OFFICE LOCATION

The most important factor in business is the selection of the proper location. The location will largely be decided upon according to the type of clients to be served. In a residential housing office, the majority of listings and sales will be within a one- to two-mile radius of the office, in a highly populated area. Therefore, the office location should be in the property area with which the firm wishes to deal. As a general rule, the higher the density of population, the smaller the sphere of operation.

A feasibility study should be conducted to determine the type of neighborhood desired, customers to be served and their income levels, and the potential volume of sales. Neighborhood shopping centers are especially good for residential housing operations. Firms specializing in large-income properties, such as commercial and industrial, may be located in a downtown professional building. Regional shopping centers may also be desirable for developers and property management firms. In some cases, the property management firm may have served as the leasing agent for the center.

The exterior of the real estate office should be well designed and in good architectural taste, reflecting the personality of the broker and his firm. A long-term lease will assure the broker that he can continue in operation in his chosen location.

The office location must be easily accessible for automobile and foot traffic alike. A conveniently located building will help the broker get his share of "walk-in" business. Adequate and attractive window space, for advertising the office and its listings, should be available. Pictures of homes sold and homes for sale have excellent drawing power.

The office sign should be easy to read, day and night, to provide the best institutional advertising possible. The broker must keep his name before the public, and a well-designed sign can, at least in part, accomplish this function.

OFFICE LAYOUT

First impressions are important, and the impression made on a member of the public entering the real estate office will be good if the furnishings are of uniform type, design, and in good taste. Furnishings should be adequate and comfortable to make the customer feel at ease, and yet allow the broker or salesman to retain the attention of the customer. Overly comfortable furnishings may mean a loss of this desired attention.

The customer's first impression of the real estate office will usually be that of the receptionist and reception room, although in a small business operation, this person may be the broker or the salesman on floor duty. Embarrassment may occur if the customer enters the office and all eyes focus on him, or if everyone in the office is busy and he receives no attention. A comfortable reception room and a warm receptionist should make the customer feel at ease.

Salesmen's desks should be of uniform size, and a good grade will prove inexpensive in the long run. The desk size should be adequate to allow the salesman to spread out maps, pictures, or other pertinent data on a parcel of property. Approximately 125 to 150 square feet per desk should be allowed, with sufficient passing room to speed the flow of work between the various departments. Name plates should be on each salesman's desk. Desks should be clean, and the salesman should not have more than one piece of work on his desk at a time. The salesman on floor duty should occupy the front desk.

The ideal office provides for a conference or closing room, located close to the broker's desk for careful supervision and administration. Two smaller rooms with a movable divider may serve as a sales meeting room as well. Where space does not permit a closing room, the broker's private office may be used. The broker should have his own private office to discuss personnel matters with his staff. Space is usually rented on a square foot basis, so the proper utilization of it will save the company dollar.

THE OFFICE BUDGET

Management (in any business) consists of those individuals who direct and control the business enterprise; in the real estate brokerage business, it is the broker. The broker-administrator must plan and control his enterprise. To plan is to set up objectives to be attained, and to control is to insure that procedures of operation conform with the established objectives. A budget is expressed in financial terms and figures, and may be called a plan for the future. It is based on past experience, and, through this past experience, projections are made for the future.

Budgets are normally made for a fiscal year; the usual fiscal year is January 1 to December 31. Budgets should be constantly reviewed, however, during shorter periods—quarterly, or semi-annually.

Poor and improper accounting records, and failure to budget the company dollar, have been major causes of small business failures in the United States. The broker, particularly the new broker, is advised to consult his accountant.

Selection of staff and sales personnel

The number of staff and sales positions in a real estate firm will vary with the desired size of the firm. In the selection of all personnel, staff or sales, carefully drawn job descriptions will aid the employer, and will help the employee to know what will be expected of him if he is hired. A few of the qualities to consider in the selection of personnel are set forth below.

In most real estate offices, the secretary will also act as receptionist. The impression she makes, on the telephone or in person, may give the customer his first image of the firm. The qualities affecting this impression are voice, personal appearance, posture, and poise. The secretary-receptionist must learn to control her voice and diction, and speak in a soft, pleasant voice with a tone of helpfulness. Her personal appearance should be neat and attractive at all times, and in good business taste. Her attitude should be one of readiness to serve.

The secretary-receptionist must like people and appreciate the material product with which real estate people work—real property. She can create an atmosphere of friendliness, for both customers and sales staff, without being intimate. She should never discuss the transactions of her employer with members of a competitive firm.

Duties of the secretary-receptionist include receiving customers, answering the telephone, typing, filing, relieving salesmen of as much detail work as time permits, assisting her broker-executive, and keeping the office in a tidy condition. However, salesmen are usually expected to tidy their own desks. She must not perform any duties that may require a state real estate license.

In many business offices today the janitorial service is included in the office rent, but when it is not, a janitorial service firm should be contracted. In most firms, it is not economically feasible to hire a full-time custodian, and salesmen should not be expected to act as janitors.

A sales or office manager is usually employed when the sales staff numbers between eight and ten. His employment allows the broker-executive more time for his own transactions and for the other administrative responsibilities of the business.

The sales manager must not only like people, but must also be able to gain their respect and confidence. He must, further, be available to sales personnel when he is needed, in the morning, afternoon, or evening. Particularly with new personnel, patience and understanding are a must. A person who does not like detail work will generally not make a good manager. He is friendly to all personnel but, at the same time, is firm in enforcing policies—he must be impartial.

The sales manager may receive a small salary plus an override on the sales commissions of the firm. He creates his own sales and does not take floor time or office calls if he is permitted to sell. The sales manager should set an example for all sales personnel, and his integrity should be above reproach.

SALES PERSONNEL

Successful real estate salesmen—men and women alike—enjoy people, and like to help these people solve their real estate problems. In order to serve the needs of homeowners, the person in real estate should possess the following qualifications:

1. He must be an energetic person who enjoys work.
2. He must be a person who is not interested in being chained to a desk.
3. He must be interested in studying and gaining knowledge of the community in which he is working.
4. He must be enthusiastic about his job.
5. He must have a knowledge of contracts, financing, and appraising of property value, and he must avail himself of every opportunity to know his product.
6. He must be interested in the real estate business as a career, not as a hobby.
7. He must be willing to cooperate and get along with his fellow man.
8. He must be a consistent sales producer and have unquestioned integrity.
9. He must have the understanding and cooperation of his family.
10. The professional salesman (or broker) supports his local, state, and national trade associations.

The selection of sales personnel is sometimes handled in a haphazard manner. The proper use of an application form and an oral interview with both the applicant and spouse may well prevent some of the turnover of sales personnel. The broker-executive or sales manager should speak with former employers, and check the accuracy of the information on the application form.

The salesman should have a clear understanding of what is expected of him once he is employed, and should be required to be familiar with the office procedures outlined in the firm's policy manual. When employed he should be introduced to each member of the staff.

MEN VS. WOMEN

The real estate sales person, man or woman, must be seriously interested in the real estate business. Women, particularly those with small children, may find it difficult to devote their full time to listing and sales activity. In full- or part-time employment, both men and women should have the cooperation of their spouse.

Women are particularly adept at selling homes. Because the homemaker spends a good deal of time in the home, the saleswoman may be able to overcome the objections of a woman better than could a man.

As a general rule, women do not have technical knowledge of financing, economic trends, and building construction, but these deficiencies may be made up through self-education and courses of study at colleges and universities.

COMPENSATION

The real estate broker will normally receive a sales commission of 5 to 6 percent on the selling price of property; however, this percentage may be as high as 10 percent in the sale of land and recreational properties. The salesman usually receives one half of the commission, and the broker, the other half.

To encourage listings, brokers will usually pay a percentage of the commission to the listing salesman. The listing commission may vary from 10 percent on an open listing to 20 percent on an exclusive listing. The listing commission is based upon the amount of sales commission received.

Compensation procedures should be clearly outlined in the office policies and procedures handbook.

THE OFFICE SALES MEETING

A weekly sales meeting may help both new and experienced salesmen in the organization. Each sales meeting should accomplish specific objectives and be well planned in advance. Guest speakers from outside the office can be used when appropriate. Subjects covered may include the proper use of the telephone, listing and selling techniques, showing of property, and financing.

Professional real estate organizations

All business or professional groups seek public recognition. Each would like to attain the professional status held by teachers, attorneys, doctors, ministers, engineers, and so forth. As a profession, each of these groups tends to supervise its own members. Professional status can be attained in the real estate business if competency, integrity, and outstanding business service are included in defining its goals.

There is a great body of knowledge which all members of the profession must possess if they are to qualify as "competent." The broker or salesman should take every opportunity to avail himself of knowledge pertaining to real estate so that he may better serve his principal and customer. "Integrity" must be understood as honesty and impartiality in dealing with clients. *The Code of Ethics of the National Association of Real Estate Boards* is included in Chapter 16.

Two things have been evident in groups attaining a professional status: education, and the support of local, state, and national organizations.

NATIONAL ASSOCIATION OF REAL ESTATE BOARDS

The National Association of Real Estate Boards (NAREB) sponsors a national convention each year with outstanding speakers. It further cooperates with state associations and local boards with an exchange of speakers. Its many committees include: education, legislation, and publishing. Two major NAREB distinctions are its code of ethics, adopted by all real estate boards in the United States, and its trademark name and insignia, embroidered with the term "Realtor."

A realtor is a licensed real estate broker who is a member of a local board of realtors, or an individual member of the National Association of Real Estate Boards. The realtor is subject to NAREB's rules and regulations, observes its standards of conduct, and is, therefore, entitled to its benefits. The term "Realtor" was coined by Charles N. Chadbourn, a member of the Minneapolis Real Estate Board. It was presented to NAREB in 1916 and was adopted by the association.

OTHER REAL ESTATE ORGANIZATIONS

As the real estate business has become more complex and specialized, various groups have organized within the framework of the National Association of Real Estate Boards. A few of these groups include the American Institute of Real Estate Appraisers, the Institute of Farm Brokers, the Institute of Real Estate Management, the National Institute of Real Estate Brokers, the Real Estate Boards Secretary's Council, the Council of State Representatives, the Society of Industrial Realtors, the Urban Land Institute, the American Society of Real Estate Counselors, and the Women's Council.

The real estate broker works with many related associations, such as the National Association of Home Builders, the Building Owners and Managers Association, the Prefabricated Home Manufacturers Institute, and so forth.

In the field of finance, the real estate broker or salesman should be conversant with the United States Savings and Loan League, the American Savings and Loan Institute, the Society of Residential Appraisers, the National Association of Mutual Savings Banks, and the Mortgage Bankers Association.

Real estate education

In some states, colleges and universities have developed real estate curriculums leading to an associate of arts, bachelor's, or graduate degree.

In California, for example, a complete uniform real estate curriculum has been established in over 80 community colleges. Basic courses include real estate principles, practice, legal aspects of real estate, finance, appraisal, and economics. Among the advanced courses are property management, tax factors affecting real estate, and commercial and investment properties.

Review questions

1. Explain in what ways the policy manual is a necessary guide to any well-operated real estate office.
2. List the organizational forms of business ownership which a real estate office has available according to its individual needs.
3. Why are the office layout and office furnishings so important to success in the real estate business?
4. How does the broker control his business enterprise, in terms of present and future financial needs?
5. How would you as a broker select your office staff and sales personnel to avoid the trial and error method of operation?
6. What points must you consider concerning an applicant for a sales position?
7. Give the advantages and disadvantages of full-time employment, and contrast these to those of part-time employment.

8. How is the real estate broker and salesman normally paid under his agency contracts? Under commission split in the broker's office?
9. What benefits are derived from membership in professional real estate organizations, state, national, and local?
10. Define the objectives of the NAREB code of ethics. How does its observance assist the real estate broker in his community?

16

The Real Estate Transaction: Listing, Selling, and Closing

Listings and valuation of listing

The various types of listing agreements were discussed in Chapter 6, and the fiduciary relationship of agent to principal in Chapter 14. The Code of Ethics of the National Association of Real Estate Boards, Part II, Articles 11 and 15 state:

Article II. In accepting employment as an agent, the Realtor pledges himself to protect and promote the interests of the client. This obligation of absolute fidelity to the client's interest is primary, and does not relieve the Realtor from the obligation of dealing fairly with all parties to the transaction.

Article 15. The exclusive listing of property should be urged and practiced by the Realtor as a means of preventing dissension and misunderstanding and of assuring better service to the owner.

This chapter is concerned with the day to day activities of the real estate broker and salesman in the actual listing, selling, and closing process of the real estate transaction.

THE LISTING PROCESS

The multiple listing agreement, based on the exclusive authorization and right-to-sell contract, should be encouraged, as pointed out in Article 15 of the code. Multiple listing associations are conducted by a group of brokers, usually the local real estate board, organized to present a service to property owners. The multiple listing gives the widest exposure possible for the property owner, and provides the broker with a selling tool proven many times over. The listing broker continues to maintain control over his listing, even though he shares it with other subagents, the members of the multiple listing association.

In order for any sales organization to exist, it must have salable merchandise, and nothing is more basic to the real estate broker than salable listings. The real estate practitioner who is enthusiastic, energetic, aggressive, knowledgeable, and has the ability to obtain such listings, will enjoy success and financial independence.

The public relations policy developed by the real estate brokerage firm will directly affect the success of that firm in the industry. The firm must gain the respect and confidence of the community. The purpose of a good public relations program is to develop the personality image of the business and to have this image well-liked in the community. The more personal friends and contacts a person can develop, the more listings and sales the brokerage office will have.

SOURCES OF SALABLE LISTINGS

Each salesman is a public relations officer, and comes in contact in his everyday activities with many potential customers who wish to buy or sell their property. Sources of listings include:

1. Referral and follow-up program. The broker who has developed a good public relations program and has a record of sales will always have owners who want to list their property. Satisfied customers result from a superior business service and the integrity of the brokerage firm.

2. Canvassing door-to-door. While this method is not considered professional by some in the industry of real estate, it has developed salesmen who have been some of the highest producers in the sales field. It is an excellent method of meeting people, but it requires good manners, grooming, patience, and an optimistic point of view.

3. "For sale by owner" signs and ads. When the salesman sees a sign or ad of this nature, he knows the property is for sale. He must persuade the property owner, however, that the sale should be handled by a professional.

4. Expired listings. There is usually a reason why a listing has expired with the property remaining unsold. The property may have been over-priced, or not properly serviced. It is not ethical for a firm to solicit a listing before it has expired, but after the expiration date, it is open territory. The salesman should properly analyze the listing to determine why it did not sell, and approach the owner with a fresh point of view. At no time should the salesman say anything detrimental about his competitor.

5. Newspaper articles. The local newspaper will have articles concern-

ing business promotions and transfers, births, marriages, and so on. These items may be clipped from the paper and sent to the individuals along with a short letter of congratulation.

6. Telephone solicitation. For this method, good telephone manners are a must, and the broker should train his staff in the proper telephone techniques. The salesman who is a consistent user of the reverse telephone directory and consistently makes six to seven calls a day will produce many fine listings for his office. Remember, the salesman does not take a listing on the telephone, but sets himself up for a personal interview to take the listing. A positive mental attitude is important for this technique.

7. Office location. The general brokerage office will do approximately 85 percent of its business within a radius of one to two miles of the office location. It is important to keep the firm name in front of the public; thus, an attractive office with a sign that can be easily read on a busy street will draw clients into the office.

8. Financial institutions, trust departments, and attorneys. When a person wants to buy or sell his property, he will often consult his financial advisors. A well-established broker who has gained the confidence of bankers, savings and loan executives, or attorneys will have a built-in source of listings.

9. Building contractors. The contractor of homes, whether he is a speculative builder or a large tract builder, is a busy specialist who may welcome the services of an enthusiastic, energetic, and aggressive real estate firm. The aggressive brokerage office will find a lucrative source of listings by cultivating confidence in some of the leading building contractors.

10. Personnel directors in industry. Executives and other key personnel in the local industry are often transferred to new company locations. The transferee will want to sell his home as quickly as possible, obtaining the fair market value for it. The alert broker and salesman with a successful record can help solve this problem.

11. "Sold" signs on property. The owner wishing to sell wants action and a "sold" sign in front of a property just sold by a real estate firm shows that action has resulted through the efforts of that firm. Others in the neighborhood wishing to sell will want to ride with this success.

12. Classified advertising for properties needed. Prospective buyers will sometimes be looking for a special type of property not presently listed by the firm. A classified ad may fulfill this request. The advertisement should be honest and not just an attempt to get another listing.

13. Direct mail. Direct mail may be used effectively in gaining new listings or in the selling of property. It must be used consistently, however, to keep the firm name in front of the prospect. This medium may take the form of a personalized letter, post card, folder or brochure. Remember that any piece of advertising must accomplish four things: *attention, interest, desire,* and *action.*

14. Membership in service clubs, civic organizations, and so on. The

more personal friends and contacts a person can develop, the more listings and sales the brokerage office will have. Everyone knows something about real estate and the salesman who belongs to various types of organizations will have an opportunity to discuss his services with others.

15. Garage sales and furniture ads. Prospective sellers will often dispose of surplus items prior to putting their home on the market; therefore, a regular check of this classified section of the newspaper may produce good listings.

16. Supermarket bulletin boards. A world of information is readily available for the alert salesman who will take the time to read this important advertising medium. Usually the seller is not knowledgeable about the merchandising of his home, and needs the professional assistance of the broker and salesman.

TAKING THE LISTING

The serious seller, one with a strong motive for selling, will provide the salesman with complete information necessary for merchandising his property. Adequate time should be given the seller by the salesman to collect information concerning the owner's deed, mortgage, and other documents. This may save everyone's time; otherwise, these important documents may be in the owner's bank box and not available.

The salesman can provide the professional counseling that the prospective seller needs. The seller will have many questions, which should be answered in a tactful, forthright manner. The salesman should not "bluff." If he does not know the answer to a question, a simple "I do not have the answer to your question, but I will be happy to get the information for you" will suffice.

It may be necessary for the salesman to overcome certain obstacles or objections in taking the listing. These objections, if handled properly, may be turned into selling points for the office. The salesman should be prepared to answer to any of the following:

1. We want to sell by ourselves and save the real estate commission.
2. The valuation you quote is too low. Mrs. Jones obtained $30,000 for her home, and ours is worth more.
3. If I wait long enough, I will get my price.
4. I won't have to pay the FHA points as my own seller.
5. Broker X will list my home at a higher figure.
6. I don't want a sign on my property.
7. We will sleep on it.
8. We will only give a 30-day listing.
9. We will give you an open listing.

10. It would be better for me to rent my home when interest rates are so high.

The salesman must be prepared to answer to any of these objections or ones similar to them. Naturally, a seller wants to receive top price for his property and, in the process of selling, wants to save every dollar he can, but it is up to the salesman to convince the prospective seller that he can honestly do both. The salesman is in a position to quote actual sales prices from a competitive market analysis of such properties.

A list of all possible objections may be long; however, if the salesman knows the market, and is familiar with what his firm can do for the client, each objection can be turned to a reason in favor of the seller's decision to list with your firm.

PROSPECTING FOR BUYERS

Prospecting starts by making a thorough analysis of the listing agreement. In taking the listing, as pointed out above, complete information concerning the property should be obtained. Pertinent information includes: (1) proximity to transportation, public, and parochial schools, (2) data concerning the general neighborhood of the property, (3) present zoning and possibilities for zone change, (4) physical condition of the property, such as size and deferred maintenance; and (5) price and terms of sale.

Although prospective customers can be found among the broker's or salesman's daily contacts, they are obtained largely from (1) neighbors, (2) tenants (in the case of income properties), (3) advertising in newspapers and trade magazines, (4) signs placed on properties, (5) direct mail, (6) open houses, (7) office files on current prospects, (8) office drop-ins, (9) developers and subdividers, and (10) investors or speculators.

Selling process—negotiating between buyer and seller

The successful real estate broker is skilled in bringing about a true meeting of the minds between buyer and seller. If the seller has a strong motive for selling and the property is priced correctly in comparison with other like properties, the property should sell. A property well-listed is a property half-sold.

The selling process involves four steps: (1) listing the property, (2) prospecting, (3) negotiating between buyer and seller, and (4) closing. The first two steps have already been discussed.

Selling begins when the prospect and the salesman meet, whether it be through a telephone conversation or a face-to-face meeting. The first impression is an important one because the prospect will tend to evaluate the office and sales staff by the impression the salesman makes. The primary interest of the salesman should be to provide a service for the customer, and not only to sell.

The salesman must learn to analyze the prospective customer's present and future needs. He must take ample time to get acquainted with these needs and to determine how much the customer can afford to pay for the property, particularly residential property. The salesman will need to know things such as family size, school needs, husband's occupation, family hobbies, and forms of recreation enjoyed by the family. In the case of commercial and investment properties, similar facts must be obtained. The real needs of the customer are not always apparent at the first meeting.

Each customer has real problems and basic needs, and he comes to the professional real estate office or firm to obtain the answers to these problems and to have his needs fulfilled. Basically the customer has a need for confidence, information, professional counseling, and financing. If the salesman can fulfill these needs, the real estate commission will tend to take care of itself.

The basic needs of the customer can be fulfilled by the salesman if he has accurate data to justify the price of the property, data concerning the neighborhood, and all other pertinent material facts concerning the property. In addition, the salesman should be fully informed about current market conditions, including the mortgage money market, and should readily recognize situations in which the customer should seek the advice of an attorney or tax expert.

The salesman should know not only the important selling features of the property, but also the possible objections. If the alert salesman has recognized both prior to showing the property, he will be able to give the customer truthful and direct answers.

The salesman must be a person with a sincere interest in the needs of the customer. He must, further, be able to arouse curiosity and interest, be a good listener, have imagination, and unquestioned integrity.

The use of a sales kit will aid the salesman in taking a listing and in selling the properties listed by his real estate firm. It should contain current materials and be well-organized. Items in the sales kit might include appointment or daily planning manual, multiple listing book, brochures on the firm and the services it performs, checks and promissory notes, listing agreements, sales contracts, office and lockbox keys, street maps showing schools, churches, and highways; 50-foot steel tape, flashlight, and any other information that might be important to the area. The make-up of the sales kit may vary depending upon the area of specialization. IM-PORTANT—keep the sales kit up-to-date.

Closing the real estate transaction

The closing of a real estate transaction must involve at least two persons, the buyer and seller. Since the real estate firm may be representing both parties thereto, care should be taken to make sure that both understand fully the transaction to eliminate any future misunderstandings. If the salesman has fulfilled the basic needs of both, this will eliminate "buyer's panic" and "seller's remorse."

The sales contract or deposit receipt was discussed in Chapter 6, Law of Contracts (Real Property), and the reader is urged to review this chapter carefully. It should be remembered that the sales contract is the first binding agreement between buyer and seller, for which if either defaults he may be liable for breach of contract.

The salesman should explain each part of the contract provisions carefully, step by step, making sure that the customer understands each part. If legal counsel is needed, the customer should seek it.

The offer to purchase is signed by the customer, then presented to the sellers for their approval. As a general rule, offers should not be presented over the telephone, but rather at an appointment set up at which both the husband and wife are present. Again, each provision should be gone over carefully with the sellers. Remember, a counter-offer, discussed in Chapter 6, requires the approval of both buyer and seller.

After all parties have agreed to the sales contract, they ready to proceed to the final closing through escrow, or another qualified firm, such as a law firm or a financial institution. The reader may wish to review at this point Chapter 12, Title Search, Examination, and Closing.

A broker has earned his commission when he has furnished a buyer ready, willing, and able to purchase the listed property on the terms and conditions of the listing contract. A professional broker or salesman knows that service must be provided after the sales contract has been completed. The professional will cooperate with the financial institution in closing any new real estate loan or the assumption of an existing one. He should, further, cooperate with the escrow agent or firm handling the final closing of the transaction; this may include helping to prepare instructions and in some cases, after the transaction has been closed, explaining the closing statements to the buyer and seller. In some states, the law may place the responsibility on the real estate broker for informing all parties to the transaction of the terms and conditions thereof. In a few states, the law permits the licensed real estate broker to escrow transactions.

Real estate ethics

Ethics has a different meaning to different persons, but in general ethics is a standard of conduct by which to live and conduct business operations. Not only does the real estate broker have a fiduciary relationship to his principal; he is also in a position of trust in relation to his fellow licensees and to the customer. He may not use this position of confidence and trust to the detriment of his principal, fellow licensees, or customers.

The realtor pledges to observe the Code of Ethics and Standards of Conduct set forth by the National Association of Real Estate Boards:

THE REALTOR'S PLEDGE

I pledge myself . . .

To protect the individual right of real estate ownership, and to widen the opportunity to enjoy it;

To be honorable and honest in all dealings;

To seek better to represent my clients by building my knowledge and competence;

To act fairly towards all in the spirit of the Golden Rule;

To serve well my community and through it my country;

To observe the realtor's Code of Ethics and conform my conduct to its lofty ideals.

CODE OF PRACTICES

The (name of Board of Realtors) subscribes to the policy that a favorable public attitude for equal opportunity in the acquisition of housing can best be accomplished through leadership, example, education, and the mutual cooperation of the real estate industry and the public.

The following is hereby stated as the Code of Practices of this Board:

1. It is the responsibility of a Realtor to offer equal service to all clients without regard to race, color, religion, or national origin in the sale, purchase, exchange, rental, or lease of real property.

   a. A Realtor should stand ready to show property to any member of any racial, creedal, or ethnic group.

   b. A Realtor has a legal and ethical responsibility to receive all offers and to communicate them to the property owner. The Realtor being but an agent, the right of decision must be with the property owner.

   c. A Realtor should exert his best efforts to conclude the transaction.

2. Realtors, individually and collectively, in performing their agency functions have no right or responsibility to determine the racial, creedal, or ethnic composition of any neighborhood or any part thereof.

   a. A Realtor shall not advise property owners to incorporate in a listing of property an exclusion of sale to any such group.

   b. A Realtor may take a listing which insists upon such exclusion, but only if it is lawfully done at the property owner's insistence without any influence whatsoever by the agent.

3. Any attempt by a Realtor to solicit or procure the sale or other disposition in residential areas by conduct intended to implant fears in property owners based upon the actual or anticipated introduction of a minority group into an area shall subject the Realtor to disciplinary action. Any technique that induces panic selling is a violation of ethics and must be strongly condemned.

4. Each Realtor should feel completely free to enter into a broker–client relationship with persons of any race, creed, or ethnic group. Any conduct inhibiting said relationship is a specific violation of the rules and regulatons of this board, and shall subject the violating Realtor to disciplinary action.

CODE OF ETHICS[1]
NATIONAL ASSOCIATION OF REAL ESTATE BOARDS

Preamble

Under all is the land. Upon its wise utilization and widely allocated ownership depend the survival and growth of free institutions and of our civilization. The Realtor is the instrumentality through which the land resource of the nation reaches its highest use and through which land ownership attains its widest distribution. He is the creator of homes, a builder of cities, a developer of industries and productive farms.

Such functions impose obligations beyond those of ordinary commerce. They impose grave social responsibility and a patriotic duty to which the Realtor should dedicate himself, and for which he should be diligent in preparing himself. The Realtor, therefore, is zealous to maintain and improve the standards of his calling and shares with his fellow Realtors a common responsibility for its integrity and honor.

In the interpretation of his obligations, he can take no safer guide than that which has been handed down through twenty centuries, embodied in the Golden Rule:

---

[1]Adopted by the NAREB in 1913, amended in 1924, 1928, 1950, 1951, 1955, 1956, and 1961.

"Whatsoever ye would that men should do to you, do ye even so to them."

Accepting this standard as his own, every Realtor pledges himself to observe its spirit in all his activities and to conduct his business in accordance with the following Code of Ethics:

Part I: Relation to the Public

Article 1. The Realtor should keep himself informed as to movements affecting real estate in his community, state, and the nation, so that he may be able to contribute to public thinking on matters of taxation, legislation, land use, city planning, and other questions affecting property interests.

Article 2. It is the duty of the Realtor to be well informed on current market conditions in order to be in a position to advise his clients as to the fair market price.

Article 3. It is the duty of the Realtor to protect the public against fraud, misrepresentation or unethical practices in the real estate field. He should endeavor to eliminate in his community any practices which could be damaging to the public or to the dignity and integrity of the real estate profession. The Realtor should assist the board or commission charged with regulating the practices of brokers and salesmen in his state.

Article 4. The Realtor should ascertain all pertinent facts concerning every property for which he accepts the agency, so that he may fulfill his obligation to avoid error, exaggeration, misrepresentation, or concealment of pertinent facts.

Article 5. The Realtor should not be instrumental in introducing into a neighborhood a character of property or use which will clearly be detrimental to property values in that neighborhood.

Article 6. The Realtor should not be a party to the naming of a false consideration in any document, unless it be the naming of an obviously nominal consideration.

Article 7. The Realtor should not engage in activities that constitute the practice of law and should recommend that title be examined and legal counsel be obtained when the interest of either party requires it.

Article 8. The Realtor should keep in a special bank account, separated from his own funds, monies coming into his possession in trust for other persons, such as escrows, trust funds, client's monies and other like items.

Article 9. The Realtor in his advertising should be especially careful to present a true picture and should neither advertise without disclosing his name, nor permit his salesmen to use individual names or telephone numbers, unless the salesman's connection with the Realtor is obvious in the advertisement.

Article 10. The Realtor, for the protection of all parties with whom he deals, should see that financial obligations and commitments regarding real estate transactions are in writing, expressing the exact agreement of the parties; and that copies of such agreements, at the time they are executed, are placed in the hands of all parties involved.

Part II: Relations to the Client

Article 11. In accepting employment as an agent, the Realtor pledges himself to protect and promote the interests of the client. This obligation of absolute fidelity to the client's interest is primary, but it does not relieve the Realtor from the obligation of dealing fairly with all parties to the transaction.

Article 12. In justice to those who place their interests in his care, the Realtor should endeavor always to be informed regarding laws, proposed legislation, governmental orders, and other essential information and public policies which affect those interests.

Article 13. Since the Realtor is representing one or another party to a transaction, he should not accept compensation from more than one party without the full knowledge of all parties to the transaction.

Article 14. The Realtor should not acquire an interest in or buy for himself, any member of his immediate family, his firm or any member thereof, or any entity in which he has a substantial ownership interest, property listed with him, or his firm, without making the true position known to the listing owner, and in selling property owned by him, or in which he has such interest, the fact should be revealed to the purchaser.

Article 15. The exclusive listing of property should be urged and practiced by the Realtor as a means of preventing dissension and misunderstanding and of assuring better service to the owner.

Article 16. When acting as agent in the management of property, the Realtor should not accept any commission, rebate or profit on expenditures made for an owner, without the owner's knowledge and consent.

Article 17. The Realtor should not undertake to make an appraisal that is outside the field of his experience unless he obtains the assistance of an authority on such types of property, or unless the facts are fully disclosed to the clients. In such circumstances the authority so engaged should be so identified and his contribution to the assignment should be clearly set forth.

Article 18. When asked to make a formal appraisal of real property, the Realtor should not render an opinion without careful and thorough analysis and interpretation of all factors affecting the value of the property. His counsel constitutes a professional service. The Realtor should not undertake to make an appraisal or render an opinion of value on any property where he has a present or contemplated interest unless such interest is specifically disclosed in the appraisal report. Under no circumstances should he undertake to make a formal appraisal when his employment or fee is contingent upon the amount of his appraisal.

Article 19. The Realtor should not submit or advertise property without authority and in any offering, the price quoted should not be other than that agreed upon with the owners as the offering price.

Article 20. In the event that more than one formal written offer on a specific property is made before the owner has accepted an offer, any other formal written offer presented to the Realtor, whether by a prospective purchaser or another broker, should be transmitted to the owner for his decision.

Part III: Relations to His Fellow-Realtor

Article 21. The Realtor should seek no unfair advantage over his fellow-Realtors and should willingly share with them the lessons of his experience and study.

Article 22. The Realtor should so conduct his business as to avoid controversies with his fellow-Realtors. In the event of a controversy between Realtors who are members of the same local board, such controversy should be arbitrated in accordance with regulations of their board rather than litigated.

Article 23. Controversies between Realtors who are not members of the same local board should be submitted to an arbitration board consisting of one arbitrator chosen by each Realtor from the real estate board to which he belongs or chosen in accordance with the regulations of the respective boards. One other member, or a sufficient number of members to make an odd number, should be selected by the arbitrators thus chosen.

Article 24. When the Realtor is charged with unethical practice, he should place all pertinent facts before the proper tribunal of the member board of which he is a member, for investigation and judgment.

Article 25. The Realtor should not voluntarily disparage the business practice of a competitor, nor volunteer an opinion of a competitor's transaction. If his opinion is sought it should be rendered with strict professional integrity and courtesy.

Article 26. The agency of a Realtor who holds an exclusive listing should be respected. A Realtor cooperating with a listing broker should not invite the cooperation of a third broker without the consent of the listing broker.

Article 27. Negotiations concerning property listed exclusively with one broker should be carried on with the listing broker, not with the owner, except with the consent of the listing broker.

Article 28. The Realtor should not solicit the services of an employee or salesman in the organization of a fellow-Realtor without the knowledge of the employer.

Article 29. Signs giving notice of property for sale, rent, lease or exchange should not be placed on any property by more than one Realtor, and then only if authorized by the owner, except as the property is listed with and authorization given to more than one Realtor.

Article 30. In the best interest of society, of his associates and of his own business, the Realtor should be loyal to the real estate board of his community and active in its work.

Conclusion

The term "realtor" has come to connote competence, fair dealing, and high integrity resulting from adherence to a lofty ideal of moral conduct in business relations. No inducement of profit and no instructions from clients can ever justify departure from this ideal, or from the injunctions of the code.

OPEN HOUSING LAWS

The Federal Open Housing Law is administered by the Department of Housing and Urban Development commonly known as HUD. If a state or local fair housing law is substantially equivalent to the federal laws, HUD must turn the case over to local enforcement officials. In such cases, the person who complains cannot sue in the federal courts.

HUD regulations clearly explain which state and local fair housing laws are "substantially equivalent" to the federal law. More than 23 states and more than 100 cities have passed fair housing laws or ordinances covering private housing.

In addition to these enforcement procedures, the U.S. Attorney General can bring action in cases where there is a general pattern of discrimination or an issue of general public importance.

SUMMARY OF FEDERAL OPEN HOUSING LAW

All those connected with residential real estate—brokers, builders, lenders, buyers, sellers, and investors—are subject to the Open Housing Law. The law bans discrimination in the sale, rental, or financing of a dwelling. More specifically, the law (1) bans discrimination in the sale or rental of housing insured or guaranteed by the federal government, or located in a federally assisted urban renewal or slum clearance project; (2) applies to all dwelling units, no matter how financed, if they are sold or rented through a real estate broker or his agent; however, the owner is permitted to choose any buyer he wishes if he sells or rents the house himself (the owner may lose his exemption if his advertising of the home for sale or rent has any discriminatory words or references). Two exceptions are: (a) single-family homes, provided the owner does not own more than three single-family homes at one time and that if the owner is a nonoccupant of a single-family home he sells, he gets the exemption for only a 24-month period; (b) one- to four-family dwellings, if the owner occupies one of the units.

Vacant land is covered if it is offered for sale or lease for the construction of a dwelling. This, of course, may be difficult to determine in some cases, but if the land is zoned exclusively for residential purposes, its sale or rental would be covered.

Generally, commercial property is not covered, but this problem arises: Suppose a building contains a store on the ground floor and a residence on the second. On its face, the law would cover such a building. "Dwelling" is defined as "any building, structure, or portion thereof which is occupied as . . . a residence by one or more families. . . ." Forthcoming regulations may clarify this problem.

Subleases are covered under the law. The term "to rent" includes: to rent, to sublease, to let, and otherwise to grant for a consideration the right to occupy premises not owned by the occupant.

Cooperative apartments and condominium units may be covered. This question is really one of whether or not the single-family exemption applies to such units. The law does not give the answer, which must await issuance of regulations. In many cases, such units have the characteristics of both apartment units and single-family homes. Some are more like single-family homes than others; for instance, there are condominiums consisting of separate single-family homes (with the land owned jointly), some townhouse condominiums, and some condominiums in apartment buildings.

Builders and brokers have to keep records under the law. While there are no record keeping requirements specified by the law, the regulations which will be issued may well require special records. In any event, the law does give the government the right to inspect the records of anyone charged with discrimination.

The law applies to any person who believes he has been discriminated against, and he must file a written complaint with HUD, which will then try to settle the matter by conciliation and persuasion. If the matter is not settled in this way, the person making the complaint can file suit in a federal district court, unless the local law is substantially equivalent to the federal law, in which case it must be turned over to local enforcement officials.

1968 Supreme Court decision (Law 1866)

The Supreme Court's recent decision on racial discrimination raises countless questions. Most legal experts agree it has the effect of wiping out the exemptions of the 1968 open occupancy law without negating the measure itself. The decision declares "All citizens of the United States shall have the same right, in every state and territory, as is enjoyed by white citizens thereof to inherit, purchase, lease, sell, hold, and convey real and personal property." In its ruling, the Court, on the basis that this is a valid exercise of the power of Congress to enforce the 13th Amendment, held that this law "bars all racial discrimination, private as well as public, in the sale or rental of a property." The decision involved a case arising in St. Louis—*Jones* v. *Mayer*—in which a couple had sought to purchase a home in a subdivision and was refused on the basis of the race of the husband. The action of the subdivider had been upheld in the lower courts, and the Supreme Court reversed it on appeal.

The decision is the "most far-reaching action of the Court in our times," and "is to create an open housing law throughout the country, and to bring under it all property of every type and description. Any documents relating to transactions in property should not now restrict on racial grounds. This does not mean, however, that persons other than 'white citizens' cannot be rejected as buyers or renters of property on the same basis that a 'white citizen' would be rejected, such as credit or other detrimental personal record that would apply equally to any individual. But the rejection cannot be made on the basis of race."

The Negro in America is a free man. If there is any impediment to that freedom in the future, the court has noted the means by which it will be struck down. This is the message that every realtor should know and understand; every citizen—whatever his attitude toward racial prejudice—must recognize this decision.

Review questions

1. In the listing process are two basic kinds of listings preferred by the listing brokers. What are these listings and how do they serve both principal and agent?
2. List ten of the more common sources of listings, and comment on the desirability of each.
3. What objections should a salesman expect to encounter in taking a listing?
4. Give the four steps of the selling process with comment on each.
5. What should be included in the salesman's sales kit, and how is it used in his daily routine?
6. Trace the steps in the closing of the real estate transaction that should be observed carefully by the salesman in order to eliminate doubt in the mind of the buyer.
7. State the "Golden Rule," and in your own words give your interpretation of it.

8. What is the objective of Open Housing Laws, and how does the recent Supreme Court decision affect the Open Housing Law's enforcement?
9. Explain what the "Code of Practices" states, giving the four main sections or divisions of the code.
10. Summarize some of the more important duties of the broker when listing and selling property to properly serve the client.

17

The Appraisal Process

Definition of appraisal

An appraisal is an estimate or opinion of value as of a given date. It is usually a written statement by a qualified appraiser of the market value or loan value of property, after his analysis of many facts. This analysis is affected by the appraiser's ability to assemble pertinent data and his experience and judgment. Professional appraisers have long worked together to standardize their methods and techniques.

It is not expected that real estate brokers and salesmen should qualify as expert appraisers, but they should be familiar with the theoretical concepts of value, the forces that influence value, and the methods by which such values can be derived. This knowledge is essential in arriving at the highest and best use or the most profitable use of property. A prime corner location with an apartment house on it may very well be worth $175,000, but put to the highest and best use, by substituting a commercial building, the value may be increased by as much as 50 percent.

Property values

Property values may be classified as *utility value* or *market value.* Utility value is the value in use to an owner-occupant and is sometimes referred to as subjective value. It will include the many amenities that attach to property. Amenities are such extra comforts as trees, location, view, design, and materials. Market value, sometimes referred to as objective value, is the price at which a willing seller would sell, and a willing buyer would buy, both being fully informed as to market conditions, neither being under abnormal pressure to buy or sell. The market value of property may change with economic conditions in the community, state, or nation. We may expand our definition of market value and say that it is the highest price in terms of money which a property will bring if exposed in the open market a reasonable length of time to find a buyer ready, willing, and able to purchase the property with full knowledge of its use and capabilities.

Other types of value include the following: assessed value, book value, capital value, cash value, commercial value, exchange value, fair value, improved value, insurable value, liquidation value, loan value, nuisance value, plottage value, rental value, replacement value, sales value, and salvage value. For a complete definition of these terms, the student is referred to the glossary at the back of the book. The value of property is at best an estimate of the combined portions of all present and anticipated enjoyment or profit.

A distinction between *cost* and *price* should be made. Cost is a measure of expenditures of labor, materials, or other sacrifices of some nature. Price, on the other hand, is the sum paid for something.

Characteristics of values

The purpose for which an appraisal report is being made will usually dictate the evaluation methods employed and influence the estimate of value. The concept of value employed may be assessed value, condemnation value, liquidated value, cash value, mortgage loan value, or fire insurance value. For example, the value placed on property by a fire insurance company will be based upon the replacement of the improvements alone and will not include the value of the land. The assessed value, however, will include the value of both land and building. The law states that the tax assessor will assess at full cash value, in some states, 100 percent; in others the rate of assessment is approximately 25 percent of the full cash value; in Michigan, the rate is 50 percent of full cash value.

There are four essential elements of value: *utility, scarcity, demand* and *transferability*. Utility refers to use by an owner-user. An item may be scarce, but if it has no use, there will be no demand for it. Utility, the use to which property can be put, creates demand, but demand, to be effective, must be implemented by purchasing power. A tract of homes in an overbuilt area may have utility, but since there is an oversupply of homes, demand will not be present.

Value is based upon the principle of "highest and best use." *Highest and best use* may be defined as that use which is most likely to produce the highest net return over a given period of time.

Forces influencing values

Three principal forces influence real estate values:

1. *Social ideals and standards,* such as marriage rates, population growth and decline, birth rates, attitudes toward education, divorce, and so on.
2. *Economic adjustments,* such as industrial and commercial growth or decline trends, wage levels within the community, natural resources, employment trends, availability of credit and mortgage monies, interest rates, price rates, and taxes.
3. *Governmental regulations,* such as building codes, zoning laws, FHA and VA loans, credit controls, stock market controls, and health measures.

Directional Growth of the City. The appraiser or real estate broker or salesman should be aware of the growth trends of the community. Properties located in the direction of growth will usually maintain their values or appreciate, if the growth is rapid and steady.

Location. Location of property cannot be overemphasized. Factors to consider include ingress, egress, traffic patterns and counts, easements, and rights-of-way or alleys. A piece of land may have excellent location but may not have access to the street and, therefore, would lose some of its value.

Utility. The highest and best use to which the property can be put should be considered. Factors affecting the utility of the property will include zoning ordinances, building codes, and private and public deed restrictions.

Size. The width and depth of property will determine to a large extent the uses to which a parcel of land can be put. Commercial property may front on an excellent boulevard, and yet the depth of the property may not be sufficient to permit its development. A 50-foot lot may lose much of its value for a residence, since many of our home designs now require a wider frontage.

Shape. A parcel of land ordinarily cannot be developed to its best advantage if it is irregular in shape. For example: A twenty-acre parcel of land, measuring 660 x 1320 feet but lacking a lot 150 x 150 feet in one corner will lose some of its advantage to a real estate developer, because it prohibits maximum yield in lots.

Thoroughfare Conditions. The condition of streets, their widths, and traffic patterns will affect properties with street frontage. Value of lots in a residential subdivision, for example, will be affected by a main thoroughfare going through the subdivision. If the traffic is slowed down by curved streets, the value of the lots will normally increase.

Social Atmosphere in Residential Districts. Many residential areas will be affected by prestige value. Lots in such desirable areas command a higher price than similar lots in other areas with less prestige.

Plottage. Plottage occurs when several parcels of land are brought under a single ownership to command a higher utility than could be found for smaller parcels. An older residential neighborhood may contain a substandard subdivision of lots 25 or 50 feet in width. Such lots singly command the lowest value, but by being brought under one ownership they will increase in value.

Conspicuousness. This refers to the publicity or advertising value of property. An oil company will put a service station only on a corner where it is conspicuous and has access to traffic.

Grades. The topography of the land will affect value. Value will vary from level land, rolling hills, and hillside properties to steep mountainous land.

Obsolescence. Obsolescence may be caused by architectural design, construction, layout of rooms (in the case of residential properties), or outdated equipment. Changes in the use of neighborhood properties may also contribute to such obsolescence.

Appreciation. Appreciation of property may be caused by city growth and increased costs in land. It may also result in rising labor costs and materials. In all cases, it must be more rapid than physical and economical obsolescence to maintain value on the market.

Building Restrictions and Zoning. Restrictions and zoning may increase value or be detrimental to value. Assume that an area is zoned for R-1 (single-family residence) use, but across the street, the property is *rezoned* to light manufacturing use. This change may be detrimental to the value of residences in the R-1 zone. Property zoned R-1 may sell for $10,000 an acre, but rezoned to R-4, it may increase in value to $20,000 an acre.

Residential Property. In arriving at an estimate of the value for residential property, consideration is given to the lot and the present value of the building, allowing for depreciation, neighborhood analysis, and other factors such as assessed valuation and recent sales in the neighborhood. The value of the improvement may be estimated at the cost per square foot for replacing the building (allowing an adequate amount for depreciation). Consideration should be given to items such as the condition of the building, fixtures, workmanship, interior decorating, plumbing, heating, condition and type of the roof, lawn, shrubbery, and foundation. Raw land zoned for residential use is usually sold by the net acre.

Industrial Property. Industrial property is usually sold by the square foot or by the acre. An industrial firm coming into the area normally will not want to buy more land than necessary to construct a building and provide adequate parking. In comparing industrial property sites, consideration may be given to the cost per square foot. Other factors to be considered are the topography of the land and type of subsoil. Rock or other types of subsoil may make a site impossible to develop, or the ground may contain quicksand. Improper drainage could be an important factor. A chemical plant, for example, would give consideration to the last item in considering a site.

Plottage value is important to the industrial developer. Consideration must be given to possible expansion; if the site is too small it could be detrimental to future growth. By the same token, an area of unusual size will have a lesser unit of value. The assistance of a competent engineer to plan the tract and plant layout is an advantage to the industrialist, for improper planning could well cost his firm a considerable amount of capital.

Agricultural or Farm Land. In the evaluation of such properties, consideration should be given to the long-term trend of prices for crops grown or expected to be grown on the lands. Factors to be considered will be the suitability of soil for crops, water supply (and the cost of producing such water), the location of markets, the labor supply, and climate conditions. Agricultural or farm land is usually priced per gross acre.

Methods of appraisal

Three principal methods are used in appraising real property: (1) comparative analysis or market data, (2) replacement cost, and (3) capitalization or income. The skilled appraiser will consider all three methods, then select the one most appropriate for purposes of appraisal.

COMPARATIVE ANALYSIS OR MARKET DATA METHOD

The comparative analysis or market data approach, particularly applicable to residential property, is the simplest method of appraisal and the one most likely to be used by real estate brokers and salesmen. It is an excellent check against the other two methods of appraising. This method is based on the assumption that a willing buyer should pay no more for a property than the cost of acquiring a comparable substitute property. A comparison is made between the subject property and similar properties as to time of sale, location, utility, and the physical characteristics of the improvement.

The basic information needed will be actual sales and listings, or offerings of similar or substitute properties. In each instance, consideration should be given to the date of sale, for it may be necessary for the appraiser to project an outdated price, using as criteria the age, style, and size of the property. He must also give consideration to possible amenities. The conditions under which the sale was made are also important. If the sale was a depressed one, the sale price may not reflect market value, for market value is reflected by a willing buyer and a willing seller, both being informed as to market conditions and neither being under pressure to buy or sell. When the sale was financed with a very low down payment and a large second deed of trust, the sale price of the property may be inflated, and adjustments may be necessary in order to arrive at the market value as distinguished from market price. A further distinction should be made between listings for sale and actual sale transactions. When listings are used, they tend to reflect the upper limits of value, while offers to purchase tend to reflect the lower limits of value. Therefore, the appraiser should use caution in dealing with such figures.

The county assessor's office will disclose sales of property which have been recorded. Such information will include the date of recording, the legal description, and the amount of county revenue stamps placed on the grant deed. The county revenue stamps will give a hint of the sales price. The state law allows that documentary stamps, in the amount of $.55 for each $500 or fraction thereof of the owner's equity, be placed on the grant deed. These stamps represent the total sale price, less the amount of any existing loan that is assumed. (State revenue stamps were discussed in Chapter 12.) The appraiser should use caution, however, because excess stamps may have been placed on the deed to mislead individuals as to the sale price. The California Real Estate Association provides an excellent form for a comparative analysis of substitute properties.

REPRODUCTION OR REPLACEMENT COST METHOD

Reproduction cost is interpreted by most authorities to mean the cost involved to reproduce an exact duplicate of the building under construction with no changes or additions. If a building has existed for a number of years, it would be impractical to reproduce the same structure, same fixtures, and so forth. Therefore, this method might be more appropriately termed the *replacement cost* method.

The cost approach is an estimate of the sum required to replace a property in its present condition. It tends to reflect the upper limits of value, since people would not normally be willing to pay more than it would cost to reproduce the property or more than their ability to obtain an equally satisfactory property. The following four steps are involved in the cost approach to appraisal of property:

1. An estimate is made of the value of land.
2. The replacement cost of all improvements is arrived at by one of the methods described below.
3. Existing depreciation is substracted.
4. The depreciated cost of the building is added to the value of the land.

An independent estimate must be made of the value of land. This would normally be the highest and best use to which the property could be put. The value of the land should always be the current market value based upon the market data approach.

The replacement cost of the improvements may be figured by one of several methods. These methods include a quantity survey analysis, units-in-place, segregated cost, or the square-foot cost method.

The *quantitative survey analysis* method should be used by experienced appraisers. Under this method, the building is broken down into its original materials, excavation of the site, and so on. All materials are then priced, including the builder's overhead and profit.

Under the *unit-in-place* method, the cost to erect or install a single portion of a structure is calculated. For example, the cost of a square foot of brick wall, a square foot of floor covering, a board foot of lumber, or a cubic foot of concrete in place is determined. These costs will include the costs of labor, overhead, and, usually, the builder's profit. The unit-in-place cost method is not a complete appraisal system and it is not recommended for use in such appraisals.

The *segregated* cost method provides for separate consideration of each of the major component parts of a building, but does not require excessive measuring. Usually the total floor area and the linear feet of exterior walls are the only quantities required.

The *square foot* and *cubic foot* methods are used by most appraisers and are considered the simplest short-cut methods. (In California it is customary to use the square foot method for residences, and to use the cubic foot method for warehouses, or loft buildings used for storage.)

Under the square foot method, a cost index supplied by a professional appraising firm such as Marshall and Stevens Company (Los Angeles) is applied to the overall square footage of the improvement. The cost per square foot is based upon the quality of construction. It is usually graded very good, good, fair, and poor. Actual cost figures are also obtainable from local contractors in the area; however, building costs will vary considerably from one area to another.

The third step required in the cost approach method is to determine the existing *depreciation* of the improvement. This amount is deducted from the replacement cost of the building to determine the present value (or book value). Difficulties are sometimes encountered in estimating correctly the depreciation on older properties. These estimates require much skill, and experience, as well as good judgment on the part of the appraiser.

The final step is to add the depreciated value of the improvement to the value of the land.

CAPITALIZATION OR INCOME METHOD

Under the capitalization or income method, the market value is determined on the basis of the income that a property will produce. This method is particularly applicable to income producing properties such as apartment houses and commercial buildings. The capitalization rate will depend upon interest rates in general for properties of a comparable degree of risk, and also on financing currently available in the money market. In determining the value of income producing property, the progressive steps are:

1. The net annual income of the property is determined by making proper allowance for vacancies, collection losses, taxes, insurance, maintenance and management, a reserve for replacement of equipment and furnishings, prior to the end of their estimated economic life.

2. An appropriate capitalization rate or present worth factor is selected. The rate selected will actually be the rate that investors demand to be attracted to such an investment, and will also depend upon the mortgage money market and interest rates in general.

3. The final step is to divide the net income by the capitalization rate. The following example may be helpful in understanding this process:

EXAMPLE

8-unit apartment house—5 years old. Each apartment leased for $100 per month.

$8 \times \$100 = \$800.00$ per month or $\$800 \times 12 = \$9600$ per year

10% vacancy factor $= \$960$ per year

$9600.00	Gross income
−960.00	Proven vacancy factor
$8640.00	Gross income (adjusted for vacancy factor)

Annual expenses*	Management	$ 960.00
	Taxes	640.00
	Utilities	180.00
	Insurance	175.00
		$1955.00

$8640.00	Gross income
−1955.00	Expenses
$6685.00	Net income

$$\text{Capitalization Rate: } 8\% = \frac{\$6685}{.08} = \$83,562.50 \quad \text{Valuation}$$

GROSS MULTIPLIERS

Many of our real estate transactions deal with the selling of older or middle-aged residential property. Therefore, the real estate broker or salesman should understand the gross multiplier method. This method of appraising is based upon the relationship between rental value and sale price of comparable properties. This is a "rule-of-thumb" method whereby we say that a certain type of property is worth 100 to 130 times its gross monthly income. (To make a valid comparison of older residential property to income property, a comparison of *like kind* must be selected on the rental market.)

Gross multipliers may also be used to compare income producing properties. The gross multiplier in such cases is determined by dividing the gross monthly income into the actual sale price of income producing units that have sold. The table on page 244 will point out the value of this method.

The appraisal process is divided into five steps:

1. Definition of the problem
2. Preliminary survey
3. Collection of data
4. Analysis of data
5. Writing the report

---

*In addition to the above, other items for deductions may occur legally such as reserves for replacement, depreciation, and so forth.

Property	Sold at		Gross Monthly Income		Gross Multiplier
A	$175,000	÷	$1750	=	100
B	$190,000	÷	$2000	=	95
C	$165,000	÷	$1700	=	97
D	$159,000	÷	$1390	=	114
			$6840		406

$$1710 \qquad\qquad 101.5$$
$$4\overline{)6840} \qquad\qquad 4\overline{)406}$$

Gross Monthly Income $1710 × 101.5 = $173,565 or $173,600

DEFINITION OF PROBLEM

The real property to be appraised should be properly identified. The mailing address of the property including the city and the state should be given. A formal appraisal report will also include the complete legal description, whether it be a lot and block, tract, metes and bounds, or a government survey description. The description will include the county wherein the property is recorded.

The purpose of the appraisal should be clearly stated. Is the property to be appraised a vacant lot? A single-family residence? A multiple-family residence? What interests are to be appraised? (In appraising property, the rights of ownership are appraised and not merely the physical land itself or the improvements.) Is a fee simple ownership being appraised with an easement across the property? Is the realtor asked to determine the lessor's or lessee's interest?

In identifying the property, the purpose and function of the valuation will determine the types of information needed in the appraisal process. Is the realtor appraising a home for its market value, or for mortgage loan purposes? An appraiser may be asked to appraise property for insurance purposes or for condemnation proceedings, among other reasons. If the appraisal is being made for insurance purposes, only the improvements on the land would be considered; thus, the insured value will be quite different from the market value, which would include both improvements and land.

PRELIMINARY SURVEY

The preliminary survey will include the highest and best use to which the property may be put. The appraiser should give consideration to the present improvement on the site. Is it a proper improvement? In making a neighborhood analysis, the appraiser may discover that the highest and best use for the subject property under consideration is not single-family residential income use. If the property being appraised is a single-family unit, emphasis will be placed on the comparative analysis market data approach. In a multiple-family unit, major emphasis will be placed upon the capitalization or income approach.

COLLECTION OF DATA

The value of property will depend upon utility, supply and demand, coupled with the purchasing power of a given community. Data needed by the real estate appraiser will include population trends, income levels, and employment opportunities. General data may be obtained from various governmental publications, newspapers, and magazines. Regional data may be obtained from governmental agencies and regional commissions. Some of the larger banks publish monthly reports on business conditions which are valuable, such as the *Federal Reserve Bulletins.* Much community data may be obtained from local chambers of commerce, planning commissions, city councils, lending institutions, and boards of realtors. Neighborhood data, on the other hand, may be obtained from personal inspection and from realtors and builders active in the area. Important data will include growth trends in the community, percentage of increase in population, the age and appearance of the neighborhood, planned developments, and the proximity of the subject property to schools, churches, businesses, recreation, and the like. Data concerning substitute properties may be obtained from reports on sales and listings. These will be available to the appraiser or realtor from the assessor's records and the county recorder's office, property owners in the neighborhood, multiple listing associations, and title insurance companies.

ANALYSIS OF DATA ACCORDING TO SELECTED VALUE

The data so collected are now put to use and analyzed according to the approach to value the appraiser has selected.

THE APPRAISAL REPORT

When the appraiser arrives at his final opinion of value from the data collected, his reasons for reaching his conclusions are reported. The form of report used will depend upon the type of property and the needs and desires of the client.

Depreciation

Depreciation may be defined as the loss of value from any cause. Loss of value is brought about by physical deterioration, and functional or economic obsolescence of the structure. Depreciation occurs on the improvement itself and not on the land. The principal forces or influences are often grouped under three major headings, as follows:

1. Physical deterioration, which may result from:
   a. Wear and tear from use of improvements
   b. Deferred maintenance or neglected care
   c. Dry rot, termites or fungus
2. Functional obsolescence, which may result from:
   a. Utility loss, which is inherent in the property itself
   b. Poor architectural design such as high ceilings and under-sized garage, inadequate number of bathrooms and the like
   c. Inadequate number of modern facilities or lack of modern facilities
   d. Out-of-date equipment
3. Economic or social obsolescence, which may result from:
   a. Misplacement of improvements, improper zoning, or legislative restrictions
   b. Lack of supply or demand
   c. Change of locational demand

It has been said that everything that man creates moves toward its "deterioration year" from the first day of its creation. Certain depreciation that takes place, however, may be deferred. The owner may repaint, remodel, replace component parts of the building (such as the roof), and thereby defer some of the depreciation.

Accrued depreciation, the property loss in value that has already occurred, is considered in the cost approach to value. *Accrual depreciation*, the property loss in value which will occur at some time in the future, is considered in the income approach to value.

ACCRUED DEPRECIATION

Let us now turn to methods of estimating accrued depreciation. The first such method is referred to as the *straight line method*. This method is based on depreciation tables that have been developed to reflect age, life experience, and the depreciation of improvements, assuming average care and maintenance.

For example, if a building has a total economic life of 40 years, it would take 2.5 percent depreciation per year to depreciate the building completely. If, to replace the building, it would cost $50,000 and the estimated economic life was 40 years or 2.5 percent per year, $1250 would be charged for each year of actual age of the building. This is sometimes referred to as chronological age (the actual number of years that the building has been in existence). The straight line method of depreciation has been used by the Internal Revenue Service, and it is perhaps the most easily understood by laymen. It is by far the easiest to calculate of the various methods used. This method does not take into account the actual physical condition of the building. Neither does it consider economic conditions affecting the property such as zoning or legislative actions. In actual practice, as is true with an automobile, a building does not depreciate at a given percentage each year. The highest percentage of depreciation occurs during the early life of the building.

A second method used to calculate depreciation is called the *observed condition method*. The accrued depreciation is determined by establishing the cost of making all needed repairs to correct curable physical deterioration and functional obsolescence, plus the estimated loss in value due to any curable physical deterioration and functional, or economic obsolescence. The observed deficiencies inside and outside the structure are observed and their cost to cure is calculated. The cost to cure is the actual amount of accrued depreciation which had taken place. Certain functional obsolescence, however, may not be cured; for example, such items as poor room arrangement or outdated construction materials. Such functional obsolescence is measured by calculating the loss in rental value due to the condition of the property. Functional obsolescence due to outdated plumbing fixtures, lighting fixtures, or kitchen equipment is determined and assigned a dollar value.

A third method for estimating accrued depreciation is called the *building residual method*. This is a technical approach used by professional appraisers. Under this approach, the land is valued separately and its annual net return is deducted from the estimated annual net return of the property, including land and building. The balance of the income is then attributed to the building. This amount is divided by the capitalization rate. The depreciation figure is the difference between the residual value of the building and that of a new structure of similar type.

ACCRUAL DEPRECIATION

Accrual depreciation or future depreciation is a loss of value to a building that has not yet occurred but that will occur sometime in the future. Accrual depreciation occurs annually throughout the economic life of the improvements. It is a deduction from annual income. This annual amount set aside must provide for the return of the value of the entire capital investment over the remaining economic life of the building. Accrual depreciation may be measured by three different methods.

Under the *straight line method* of depreciation, a percentage is deducted each year of the estimated economic life of the improvement to fully replace the capital investment.

Sometimes referred to as the reinvestment method, the *sinking fund method* assures the recapture of the investment in the improvement by setting aside an annual amount each year and investing it in a sinking fund or in an account which accumulates compound interest.

At the end of the economic life of the improvement, the fund will then equal the total amount of capital invested. Amortization tables are available to the appraiser to determine the amount that must be set aside each year to reach a given dollar amount at the end of any given period of time; under this method one deals with the present value of dollars.

Under the *declining balance method,* a fixed rate of depreciation is subtracted annually from the cost of the improvement to the investor and the selected rate is applied only to the remaining balances.[1]

200% Declining Balance (4%)		*150% Declining Balance (3%)*	
$100,000		$100,000	
− 4,000	1st year	− 3,000	1st year
96,000		97,000	
− 3,840	2nd year	− 2,910	2nd year
92,160		94,090	
− 3,686	3rd year	− 2,823	3rd year
$ 88,474	Book value at end of third year	$ 91,267	Book value at end of third year

Another method sometimes used by accountants and appraisers in calculating depreciation is referred to as the *sum-of-the-years* method.[2] This

---

[1]Under the new tax bill only new or first users may apply the 200 percent declining balance, and it is limited to new apartment buildings only. The 150 percent declining balance may be applicable to first investors or to any new improvement, and 125 percent applies to old residential units with 20 years of useful life.

[2]This method of depreciation is cited only by way of complete reference to depreciation methods possible. For further description of this method, the reader should refer to current textbooks on appraising.

method is available to new users only. Under this method, the appraiser estimates the economic life of the structure and totals the number of years. The following example illustrates this method:

$$n + 1 \frac{(n)}{2} = 50 + 1 \frac{(50)}{2} = 1275$$

$$\frac{59}{1275} \times 100,000 =$$

$$\frac{49}{1275} \times 100,000 =$$

$$\frac{48}{1275} \times 100,000 =$$

Book value at the end of three years:
$100,000.00
$- 11,528.63$
$\overline{\$\ 88,471.37}$

Accelerated depreciation of real property

For owners of residential construction (buildings which generate 80 percent or more of their gross rental income from the leasing of dwelling space) there is no change for first users, under the current tax law. All three methods of accelerated depreciation are still available.

The depreciation rate for second and subsequent owners of residential construction will depend upon the remaining economic life of the structure. If the economic life of the structure is less than 20 years, the owner is limited to the straight line method. If the economic life is more than 20 years, the owner may depreciate the improvement at the rate of 125 percent of the straight line rate on the declining balance.

For commercial and industrial properties (other than residential), developers (first users) are limited to 150 percent method of depreciation on the declining balance. The sum-of-the-years-digits and the double declining balance methods are no longer available. These depreciation rates apply generally to all buildings acquired after July 24, 1969.

Depreciation recaptured as ordinary income

"Recapture" is a term used to describe depreciation allowances which are recovered at the time of sale. For example, if an improvement (exclusive of land) cost $500,000 and was depreciated during the ownership period by $50,000, the cost basis of the improvement is reduced to $450,-000. If it is sold for $550,000, there is a gain of $100,000, but $50,000 of this gain represents recaptured depreciation.

Prior to December 31, 1969, the amount of depreciation taken over the straight line rate was subject to recapture as ordinary income (to the extent of gain) at a recapture rate of 100 percent, minus 1 percent for each full month the property was held over 20 months from the date the property was placed in service. Thus at the end of the tenth year there was no recapture and the profit would generally be a capital gain.

Under the current tax law there is a holding period during which all excess depreciation taken over the straight line rate is subject to recapture as ordinary income (to the extent of gain), at a recapture rate of 100 percent, minus 1 percent for each full month the property was held over 100 months from the date the property was placed in service. If accelerated methods of depreciation are now used, full capital gain treatments are not available until after $16\frac{2}{3}$ years of ownership.

The professional accountant or attorney specializing in taxation should always be consulted when questions concerning taxes arise.

Review questions

1. Give the accepted definition of an appraisal.
2. What characteristics influence value, and what are the principal forces influencing real estate value?
3. List the three principal methods of appraising real property.
4. How are these methods used in residential appraisal?
5. What do we mean by capitalization or income method? Contrast with the gross multiplier method.
6. Distinguish between depreciation and accrued depreciation.

Multiple-choice questions

1. Stability of income on investment properties depends primarily on: (a) modernization of the building, (b) qualifying of tenant, (c) competitive buildings in area, (d) increase in taxes, (e) none of these.
2. Demand as it applies to real estate is: (a) conspicuous, (b) objective, (c) subjective, (d) amenable, (e) none of these.
3. Which of the following is best used to describe market value? (a) willing seller–willing buyer concept, (b) market price, (c) cost concept, (d) directional growth, (e) none of these
4. Which of the following best describes appraisal? (a) opinion of the value of a property, (b) assessed value, (c) loan evaluation, (d) listing price, (e) exchange value

5. Which of the following is the best way to evaluate a neighborhood? (a) schools, (b) transportation, (c) people in the neighborhood, (d) none of these, (e) all of these

6. Which of the following *is not* an example of economic obsolescence? (a) rezoning, (b) industry moving out, (c) misplaced improvements, (d) outdated kitchen, (e) all of these

7. One method of appraising real estate is: (a) capitalization of net income, (b) replacement cost, (c) comparative analysis, (d) all of the foregoing, (e) none of these.

8. The replacement cost method of appraisal is most useful in appraising: (a) income properties, (b) vacant land, (c) single-family residences, (d) service properties (schools or public buildings), (e) none of these.

9. Which of the following is not a proper charge in determining net income for capitalization purposes? (a) vacancy and collection losses, (b) mortgage interest, (c) management fees, (d) maintenance expenses, (e) none of these

10. Loss in value of property because it is out of date or out of style is said to be: (a) economic or social obsolescence, (b) functional obsolescence, (c) physical deterioration, (d) deferred maintenance, (e) none of these.

18

Property Management

The professional property management business constitutes a special segment of the real estate industry, and represents another area in which real estate brokers participate. This is particularly true of brokerage firms that manage the one- and two-family dwelling, the small apartment house, the office building, and the neighborhood shopping center. While the average brokerage office will not be involved on a full-time basis in managing large apartment complexes, huge office buildings, and regional shopping centers, a knowledge of agency, contracts, rental agreements, and leasehold agreements is very important. The legal aspects of these subjects were discussed in previous chapters.

The professional property manager should have a thorough knowledge not only of the legal aspects of real estate, but also of such subjects as accounting, advertising, business administration, business law, mathematics, credits and collections, human relations in business, maintenance and repairs, purchasing, and taxation. The amount of knowledge needed will vary with the scope of business operations.

History of property management

Property management is of comparatively recent origin; it developed into a highly specialized field within the last two decades, as a result of three principal causes:

1. Urbanization
2. Technological advancements in the construction industry
3. Absentee ownership

The concentration of population in urban areas, caused principally by the industrial revolution, has created a need for the professional property manager. The assembly line and highly developed technological methods in manufacturing industries have brought people in ever increasing numbers to cities, creating a large demand for rental units. As the mass population moved to the city, needs were created for professional services such as doctors, attorneys, and real estate brokers. These professional people required adequate office facilities. Thus, not only have existing cities grown, but entire new cities have developed. All of these buildings require competent and professional management.

As the cities grew, so did the technological advancements in the construction industry. Two- or three-story buildings, that were adequate before the industrial revolution, were so no longer. With the use of the steel frame building and modern elevators, height was no longer a major problem in creating structures. Construction is now limited only by man's imagination and ingenuity. In answer to the problems of urbanization, the construction industry moved to the large tract developments, providing suitable housing to meet the ever growing demands at low cost. Techniques were developed to forecast population growth, trends, and neighborhood patterns.

Absentee owners need the professional property manager. The real wealth of the nation, indeed two-thirds of it, lies in real property. Real estate has always proven to be a good hedge against inflation. In addition to appreciating in value over the years, property represents a good tax shelter for the investor. Large insurance firms and various other investment firms have found that real estate rounds out their investment portfolios. The purchase-leaseback agreement, used in recent years, has been profitable for some. In addition, real estate brokerage firms have entered into various syndicated activities providing large sums of money for the purchase of investments. An absentee owner needs someone to look after his property; thus, such owners look today to the professional property manager.

Today, almost every type of property improvement might be managed by the property manager, including single- and multi-family dwellings, large scale public housing, factories, hotels, motels, all types of commercial buildings, churches, hospitals, industrial parks, and parking lots. A few colleges and universities in the country now offer programs in property management, including hotel and restaurant management. More of these programs leading to a degree will undoubtedly develop.

Institute of Real Estate Management

The Institute of Real Estate Management was founded in 1933 under the auspices of the National Association of Real Estate Boards. Among other things, it provides its members with up-to-date management data. Membership is restricted to individual realtor members who specialize in real estate management. The bylaws of the institute state that "the Governing Council may elect to membership any individual who:[1]

1. Has been accepted as a Candidate for membership in the Institute;
2. Has paid all application and service fees as prescribed in these By-laws;
3. Files official forms as required by the Institute, giving the detailed information requested there in full, and signs an irrevocable waiver of claim against this Institute, any of its members, employees or agents for any act in connection with the business of this Institute, and particularly as to its acts in electing or failing to elect, or disciplining him as a member;
4. Has been recommended for active membership by the Admissions Committee as to having met all necessary qualifications for the CPM designation as provided in the Regulations;
5. Has been actively engaged in a responsible capacity in the administrative operation of real property for three years and has had at least two additional years of experience in property management, or applicable educational or allied practical experience in the field of real estate, acceptable to the Institute;
6. Holds some form of membership in a member board of, or an individual membership in, the National Association of Real Estate Boards;
7. Satisfactorily passed examinations given or approved by the Institute as prescribed in the Regulations;
8. Subscribes to the Bylaws, Regulations, Code of Ethics, and the official pledge of the Institute.

Functions of the property manager

A distinction should be made at this point between the various types of property managers, because the function of each varies. The property manager is a member of a real estate firm and will manage large numbers of properties for many owners. The individual manager is employed by the property manager or directly by the owner, usually on a salary basis. The resident manager is an employee who lives on the property and is expected to perform the duties outlined by the managing agent or the owner. The building superintendent is a supervisor, and is usually responsible for the maintenance of the building.

As indicated earlier in the chapter, the professional property manager

---

[1]James C. Downs, *Principles of Real Estate Management*, 8th ed. (Institute of Real Estate Management), pp. 3–4.

should be an expert in many areas, including merchandising, leasing, maintenance, repairs, accounting, human relations, insurance, and taxes. The manager also has a fiduciary obligation to the owner to provide for his owner the highest possible net return from the property based on its highest and best use. Ideally, the property manager should be employed before construction of the improvement starts, and the manager should even be consulted in the planning stages. As a result of his many years of experience, the manager will be able to offer suggestions that may save operating dollars later.

It is the property manager who must also satisfy the needs of the tenant, who is interested in getting the maximum value from his rental dollar. As a professional, the manager knows what specific tenants will be looking for in renting space.

The professional manager is also interested in his community. He should be a leader in that community providing professional assistance in the development of codes for the general welfare of all.

Specific duties of the property manager[2]

Among the property manager's general functions are a few specific duties which he must perform:

1. Establish the rental schedule
2. Merchandise the space and collect the rents
3. Create and supervise maintenance schedules and repairs
4. Supervise all purchasing
5. Develop a tenant relations policy
6. Develop employee policies, and supervise their operations
7. Maintain proper records and make regular reports to the owner
8. Qualify and investigate tenants' credit
9. Prepare and execute leases
10. Prepare decorating specifications and secure estimates
11. Hire, instruct, and maintain satisfactory personnel to staff the building(s)
12. Audit and pay bills
13. Advertise and publicize vacancies through selected media and broker lists
14. Plan alterations and modernizing programs
15. Inspect vacant space frequently
16. Keep abreast of the times and posted on competitive market conditions
17. Pay insurance premiums and taxes, and recommend tax appeals when warranted

---

[2] *Reference Book*, Department of Real Estate, State of California, 1970 ed., p. 383.

Developing the rental schedule and collecting rents

The professional property manager in the community or regional area of operation will know what is the fair rental value of the units he is managing from the data in his files. The fair rental value of a property will depend upon many factors, including supply and demand, neighborhood, and the income level of the families within the community.

A firm collection policy established by the property manager will eliminate much of the difficulty encountered in the collection of rents. Many owners and managers run credit checks and take applications from prospective tenants.

When rents are past due, the follow-up system established by the firm should be enforced. If the rent continues to be delinquent for 30 days, legal proceedings may be necessary.

Property maintenance

The owners of an investment expect the property manager to be a "guardian angel" over the investment. The manager, an expert in maintenance requirements, will develop a regular maintenance schedule. He knows that operating on a regular schedule will tend to make tenants happy. When the property is properly maintained, the tenant will normally respect the property and not abuse it. If there are complaints from the tenants, the manager should answer them promptly.

Regular inspection of all utility services such as air conditioners and heating systems should be conducted. In very large management firms, full-time employees may be hired to do these tasks. Management firms in some areas of the country have also found it profitable to contract with pool maintenance firms for care of their swimming pools.

Purchasing

The property manager is an expert in the field of purchasing. Since he may manage hundreds of units, office complexes, and the like, he can save his owners' dollars through volume purchasing. Certain sundry items, for example, paper, light bulbs, brooms, and waxes, may be purchased in large quantities at special prices and kept in storage until needed.

Purchasing for major repairs may be done by an outside contractor or by employees of the management firm. The management firm, for example, may purchase carpeting in large quantities and have employees install it. How ever it is done, costs must be controlled.

Employment procedures

Any business firm is only as successful as the executives and employees of that firm. In many ways, the employee represents the owner and his firm to the tenant, even though an employer–employee relationship may exist. Therefore, a careful procedure for the selection and training of employees should be developed.

Each employee's qualifications should match the job he is seeking, and he should have a sincere interest in it. He should know what will be expected of him; therefore, job descriptions carefully developed and drawn by the employer will aid in the selection of personnel and will further aid the employee in knowing what will be expected of him.

Owner and property management contract

A written contract between the owner and property manager setting forth all conditions and responsibilities of each party thereto is essential, to eliminate misunderstandings that may occur in the future. Such a contract may be drawn by an attorney; however, standard form contracts are available.

SEPARATE RECORD FOR EACH PROPERTY MANAGED								

Owner		Deposit	
Address		Monthly Rent	
Property		Commission:	
Tenant's Name		Leases	
Units		Collection	
Remarks		Management	

Date	Received From or Paid To	Description	Receipt Or Check Number	Amount Received	Date Deposited	Amount Disbursed	Balance

Figure 13

Accounting records

The professional property manager must render and interpret financial statements to the owner of the property; therefore, it is mandatory that records be kept on each building (Fig. 13). It is also necessary that a separate bank account be kept for each, and that a trust account be established at a bank in which to handle all the client's money (Fig. 14).

SEPARATE RECORD FOR EACH BENEFICIARY OR TRANSACTION FOR CLIENT'S FUND PLACED IN TRUST FUND BANK ACCOUNT						
	Discharge of Trust Accountability For Funds Paid Out			Trust Accountability For Funds Received		
Description	Date of Check	Check Number	Amount	Date of Deposit	Amount	Account Balance

Figure 14

In establishing such records, it is advisable to consult an accountant. The accounting system should be reviewed from time to time by the accountant to make certain it is meeting the needs of the property management firm and the owners of the property.

Earnings

The professional property manager usually operates on a percentage of the gross income from the investment. The percentage obtained, from 1 to 10 percent, will depend upon the amount of gross income. Large property complexes may pay as low as 1 or 2 percent, while single-family dwellings may be as high as 10 percent of the gross income. The average today on apartment dwellings will be from 5 to 10 percent of the gross income.

Review questions

1. What special knowledge and training must a property manager have to be successful in property management?
2. Name the three main causes of the need for property management, and give a brief comment on each.
3. Who can belong to the Institute of Real Estate Management and what does it provide for members of the organization?
4. Give the most important functions of the property manager, and list ten specific duties of a property manager.
5. List the types of records for which a property manager is held responsible to an owner.
6. In what way is the property manager's knowledge in purchasing of benefit to the owner?
7. How do proper maintenance schedules help to hold tenants longer in rentals?
8. Upon what factors will the establishment of fair rental schedules depend to be in line with the community rental markets?
9. Should the property manager be employed by the owner before, during, or after the building is built?
10. How can a resident manager on the property assist the management agent? How do his obligations and duties differ from those of the agent manager?

19

City Planning, Zoning, and Land Development

While evidence of community planning may be found dating from the middle ages, the orderly planning of counties and cities did not start in the United States until the 20th century. The rapid growth of urban population, caused by the industrial revolution, strides made in transportation, and housing laws (federal and state), has created a need for more effective use of land resources.

In addition, rapid growth of urban areas has created enormous problems which are a concern of the federal, state, county, and city governments. These problems include air pollution, water pollution, mass transportation facilities, sewage facilities, slums, and blight. A proper balance must be developed for single- and multi-family dwellings, and commercial, industrial, and recreational land use. To help accomplish this end, regional planning commissions have been established in some states. A continuing effort must be made to solve not only existing problems but also future problems.

Policies and policy planning

Planning policies made by city or county officials are developed after meeting with various civic organizations and interested citizens. As a result of these meetings, there should be a better understanding and appreciation of problems, existing and future, their solutions, and the policies upon which there is agreement.

Policies are courses of action adopted and followed by governments in their attempts to meet the many-faceted land use problems associated with city and county growth. They should be statements of ways these governments will act to achieve their goals. Policies should provide a consistent framework for decision making on a day-to-day basis and for the distant future.

The identification of policy is an important phase of planning. Before policy is established, a consensus on the major issues and "agreement in principle" should be established without the distraction of detail. These details make it difficult to focus on the general but very basic issues. At later dates the agreed-upon policies will be the basis for a general plan. This will be a more detailed guide for development—an interpretation in concrete form of agreed-upon policies.

Police power

Police power may be defined as the sovereign power of the state, usually delegated to the city and county, to safeguard the public health, morals, and safety, and to promote the interests of the public at large. Perhaps the most important use of police power is in zoning laws. The zoning laws, building codes, and related regulations have far-reaching effects on almost every phase of real property.

Planning legislation

During the 19th century, and prior to the passage of the "enabling acts," any change from the city or county plan needed the consent of the state legislature through a special act. As the rapid growth in urban centers began to take place in the early years of the 20th century, the state legislatures were induced to pass enabling acts which authorized cities and counties to embark on comprehensive planning.

Planning commission

The enabling acts gave the cities and counties the necessary power to appoint a planning board or commission, and to hire qualified staff to implement a comprehensive plan.

The commission is usually appointed by the city manager or mayor with the approval of the city council. The county planning commission is usually appointed by the county board of supervisors. The city or county planner, sometimes called the *planning technician*, is usually a full-time employee of the governmental unit, except in very small communities.

The powers of the planning commission may vary widely between cities and counties in the states. In some cases they work in advisory capacity only, preparing the plan and presenting it to the appropriate legislative body. In other areas they may develop the plan and actually implement it, subject to the veto power of the legislative body. All matters relating to planning must be referred to the planning commission.

Organizations that supply information about planning include the American Planning and Civic Association, Washington, D. C.; American Society of Planning Officials, Chicago; and the American City Planning Institute, Cambridge, Massachusetts.

Objectives of the city plan

Any city or county plan must be flexible in order to provide for orderly expansion, which may go even beyond the present limits of the city. Land in the county today may be annexed to the city. The plan must also provide for sudden internal growth and the future correction of existing urban structures. The planning commission should stimulate interest in community problems by coordinating civic and community developments, and help to stabilize property values through orderly city growth.

Issues in planning

Here follow some issues that must be faced by planning commissions, legislative bodies, and the citizens of a community, before a master plan can unfold.

RESIDENTIAL HOUSING ISSUES

1. In considering residential zoning, is it desirable or possible to tailor the amount of available residential land and construction to the actual market needs? Should market analysis studies be required, as they often are for commercial rezoning?
2. How can minority and low income groups be afforded a full range of low-cost housing opportunities in all parts of the city (or county)?
3. How can many personal aspirations be translated into a variety of housing types in a variety of locations?
4. What residential patterns will best satisfy the collective goals of the city? The county, in planning, must take the goals of each community into consideration.

PUBLIC FACILITIES ISSUE

1. In anticipating the need, land acquisition, and growth rate of population, how many additional schools, fire houses, libraries, and so forth, will be needed for the years projected in the master plan? In addition, how many miles of highways, sewers, storm drains, water lines, and administrative and special buildings will be needed?
2. In projecting the needs of the community, how can any existing or future problems of jurisdictional boundaries be solved?
3. What sources of revenue can be anticipated to be available for the capital improvement program?
4. Is a professional feasibility study by an outside firm required to help solve the public utilities issues?

THE COMMERCIAL LAND ISSUES

1. How much land should be zoned commercial; exactly enough to satisfy the needs of the consumers, or as much as speculators and developers demand?
2. Where should commercially zoned lands be located? Where they will best serve a trade area, and where are they desired by property owners?
3. In considering the approval for commercial uses, should free-flowing traffic be a consideration? Should safe and convenient access be a consideration?
4. What should be the character of new shopping areas? Can attractive, balanced complexes be obtained?
5. What should be the role of older shopping areas? So that they are not allowed to deteriorate—victims of competition—how should active steps be taken to ensure that they will once more become significant and healthy parts of the city's or county's future?
6. Can past mistakes be corrected? Should there be instituted private and public renewal to refurbish and revitalize existing decayed areas?

TRANSPORTATION ISSUES

1. How can the problems of high costs in providing improved expressways, highways, and streets be solved? Do they reach capacity soon after they are built, or even before they are completed?
2. Should rapid transit facilities be studied and instituted to relieve expressways and highways?
3. Are current air facilities adequate for present and future needs?
4. Are current railroad facilities adequate to meet the present and future needs of industry?

INDUSTRIAL ISSUES

1. How much land should be zoned for industrial purposes? Should emphasis be placed on industrial parks?
2. What forms of industry are desirable for the community—heavy, medium, or light? Should any kind of industry be permitted to locate in the community if it desires to do so?
3. Where should the industrial land be located? How much land should be permitted to be zoned for industry, now, and in the future; exactly enough to satisfy the needs of industry, or as much as speculators and developers demand?

Developing the master plan

The Standard City Planning Enabling Act of 1928, section seven, has this to say concerning the master plan:

> The plan shall be made with the general purpose of guiding and accomplishing a coordinated, adjusted, and harmonious development of the municipality and its environs which will, in accordance with present and future needs, best promote health, safety, morals, order, convenience, property, and general welfare, as well as efficiency and economy in the process of development; including among other things adequate provisions for traffic, the promotion of safety from fire and other damages, adequate provision for light and air, the promotion of the healthful and convenient distribution of the population, the promotion of good civic design and arrangement, wise and efficient expenditure of public funds, and the adequate possession of public utilities and other public requirements.

The purpose, then, of the master plan, is to serve as a guide for arriving at decisions, public and private, which, hopefully, will result in a constantly improving urban environment. A master plan can only be developed after sufficient information has been obtained through surveys to determine present and future needs. Information obtained should include population growth, age groups, breakdown of the labor force, economic activity, traffic on main arteries, building trends, and the like.

A master plan does not implement itself. It is a guide to be actively used, but must be flexible enough to meet the ever-changing needs of the urban environment. The plan should be reviewed at least once each year, up-dating any sections that require change.

Zoning

Both cities and counties have zoning laws. The latter exercise their powers in the unincorporated areas, and the cities within their jurisdictional limits. Cities and counties must work closely together for harmonious land use and development.

A zoning ordinance governs the use of land. The purpose of the ordinance is to legally and specifically define and provide for implementation of the master plan. Zoning ordinances determine the type of use, density of population, essential facilities required (such as parking standards), and whether areas will be used for single- or multi-family dwellings; for commercial purposes (light, medium, or heavy); or for industrial purposes (light, medium, or heavy).

Zoning protects against nuisances and physical hazards, and protects the safety, health, morals, and welfare of the citizens.

NONCONFORMING USE

When a new zoning ordinance is passed, any existing lawful uses are usually permitted to remain until that use is discontinued, or until the destruction of the building occurs. This is primarily because of hardship for owners or unusual difficulties. The courts might also declare such an ordinance unconstitutional if it eliminated present uses immediately.

CONDITIONAL USE PERMIT

Zoning ordinances sometimes authorize the planning commission to grant a conditional use permit if the facts presented by the applicant justify the permit and if the permitted use seems desirable for public convenience. Land zoned for industrial purposes will usually permit a limited number of commercial facilities, such as a service station, to serve the people working in the industrial area. When the commission turns down the request, the applicant may appeal to the city council or the county board of supervisors.

VARIANCES OR EXCEPTIONS

A variance or exception based upon hardship or exceptional circumstances is designed to give some degree of flexibility to zoning administration. The administrative body granting the variance may attach conditions to it, to conform with the purpose of the master plan. A variance (or exception) is an approved deviation from the plan.

SPOT ZONING

Spot zoning represents an amendment to the general zoning ordinance. To spot zone is to zone a specified parcel of land differently from neighboring property. Generally, cities and counties are reluctant to set up such zoning because it tends to create islands.

Each state will have laws setting forth certain minimum standards of construction for buildings. In addition to the state laws, counties and cities may have their own local building codes that will supplement and strengthen the state laws. The local building inspector enforces the building code. The construction industry or owner of property must always comply with the more stringent of the two laws.

The Federal Housing Administration and Veterans Administration have indirectly influenced local building standards through their financing programs. Their requirements may, in some cases, be more restrictive than those of either the state or the local code.

Land development

Government at the federal, state, and local levels is involved in nearly every phase of the real estate business. Not only do government units buy, own, and sell real estate, but they are also involved in other fields, such as real estate finance, the regulation of real estate agents, and land subdivisions. The federal government is involved in subdivisions particularly through the Federal Housing Authority (FHA) and Veterans Administration (VA) financing programs; the states are involved, through regulations imposed by the legislatures for the prevention of fraud, and misrepresentation in the sale of subdivisions, including advertising; and the cities and counties are involved through the layout of streets, lot sizes, and improvements required such as road surfacing, gutters, sidewalks, drainage, water mains, and sewage disposal facilities.

Types of subdivisions

Subdivisions are of various types and may include any of the following:

1. Lot and residential subdivisions.
2. FHA-insured subdivisions. Under an FHA-insured cooperative subdivision, an association of members is usually formed, each issued one share of stock, and each given the right to occupy a particular part of any improvements erected. When all monies have been paid and the entire subdivision has been sold, a deed is usually delivered to the buyer of the property.
3. Community apartment houses. Community apartment houses are also

known as cooperatives or are sometimes referred to as "own your own" apartments. Under such an arrangement, a board of directors is usually formed and the users of the various apartments make their payments directly to the board of directors who, in turn, apply the amount so paid to one mortgage payment. The same would be true of taxes, assessments, and the like. If an owner desires to remodel, or repaint, he is usually required to obtain permission from the board of directors. As a rule the directors reserve the right to approve all sales of individual units.

4. Condominium. Under a condominium, the buyer actually holds a fee title to his individual apartment unit. He further owns an undivided interest in the common areas and facilities of the building, including an undivided interest in the land. Under a condominium, the individual owner secures and pays his own mortgage, his own taxes, and so forth. For all practical purposes, he is the sole owner.

5. Mineral, oil, and gas subdivisions.

6. Resort-type subdivisions. When resort property is subdivided, all local regulations must be observed, including those pertaining to water and sewage.

7. Commercial subdivisions. Commercial shopping centers have been growing in almost all areas of the nation, particularly since World War II. While ownership may be held in fee simple by a corporation or other individual owner, the centers are held to be subdivisions because of the subdivided space through leasing.

Definition of subdivision

In general, a subdivision may be defined as improved or unimproved lands divided into lots or parcels (usually five or more) for the purpose of sale, lease, or financing, whether immediate or in the future. For study or compliance purposes, however, the reader should check the definition and laws concerning subdivisions in his own state.

The process of land development

The first logical step in a subdivision for the real estate developer or owner is to make a real estate market analysis. In actual practice this will be based on judgment and opinion, rather than a complete feasibility study. Such an analysis is necessary to determine if a market exists for the type of subdivision under consideration. Whether the venture will be successful or not is dependent largely upon the accuracy and scope of the market analysis.

The developer or subdivider should give close attention to the location of the subdivision. A critical analysis should be made of proximity to employment, shopping, and whether or not the subdivision will be harmonious with others in the surrounding area and with any existing improvements. Photographs taken from the air will show the relationship of the proposed subdivision to shopping centers, schools, existing tracts of homes, and so on.

Careful analysis must be made of all costs that go to make up the purchase price of the property. Included in these costs are interest to be paid on the encumbrance during the development of the property, real estate points, development costs, and prepayment penalties on the encumbrance or mortgage. After the cost analysis is completed, a thorough investigation of the requirements of governmental bodies should be made. This will include close cooperation with such administrative offices as the city or county planning commission, city council or county board of supervisors, sanitation control, state official in charge of subdivision activity, flood control engineers, county road department, city engineers, and planning technicians. Fig. 15 shows the procedures and steps that a subdivider goes through.

Information requirements

Certain documents and information must usually be filed with the state, city, or county before lots are sold or leased in a subdivision. These may include all or any part of the following:

1. Abstract of title or title report. This report should show the owner of record and all liens and encumbrances against the property, and should be issued after the final subdivision map is recorded in the county recorder's office.

2. Final subdivision recorded map. The final subdivision map requires the approval of all city or county officials, as well as of the planning commission or board and the city council or county board of supervisors. It is filed in the county recorder's office of the county in which the property is located. Copies are usually retained by the city or county, and a copy must be filed with the state official in charge of subdivisions.

3. Sale documents. The developers usually file with the appropriate state officials all preliminary and final sale contracts proposed for use prior to the sale of any lots in the subdivision. These may include deeds, mortgages, leases or option agreements, or contracts to sell. The purpose of such filing is the prevention of fraud, misrepresentation, and deceit.

4. Covenants, conditions, and restrictions. The laws of most states require that a copy of all covenants, conditions, and restrictions be presented to the potential buyer of a lot. These must also be filed with the appropriate governmental officials.

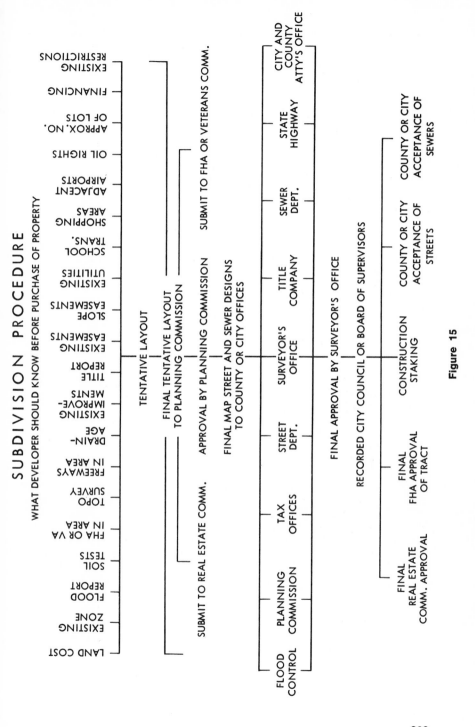

SUBDIVISION PROCEDURE

WHAT DEVELOPER SHOULD KNOW BEFORE PURCHASE OF PROPERTY

LAND COST
EXISTING ZONE
FLOOD REPORT
SOIL TESTS
FHA OR VA IN AREA
TOPO SURVEY
FREEWAYS IN AREA
DRAIN-AGE
EXISTING IMPROVE-MENTS
TITLE REPORT
EXISTING EASEMENTS
SLOPE EASEMENTS
EXISTING UTILITIES
SCHOOL TRANS.
SHOPPING AREAS
ADJACENT AIRPORTS
OIL RIGHTS
APPROX. NO. OF LOTS
FINANCING
EXISTING RESTRICTIONS

SUBMIT TO REAL ESTATE COMM.

TENTATIVE LAYOUT

FINAL TENTATIVE LAYOUT TO PLANNING COMMISSION

APPROVAL BY PLANNING COMMISSION

SUBMIT TO FHA OR VETERANS COMM.

FINAL MAP STREET AND SEWER DESIGNS TO COUNTY OR CITY OFFICES

FLOOD CONTROL
PLANNING COMMISSION
TAX OFFICES
STREET DEPT.
SURVEYOR'S OFFICE
TITLE COMPANY
SEWER DEPT.
STATE HIGHWAY
CITY AND COUNTY ATTY'S OFFICE

FINAL APPROVAL BY SURVEYOR'S OFFICE

RECORDED CITY COUNCIL OR BOARD OF SUPERVISORS

FINAL REAL ESTATE COMM. APPROVAL
FINAL FHA APPROVAL OF TRACT
CONSTRUCTION STAKING
COUNTY OR CITY ACCEPTANCE OF STREETS
COUNTY OR CITY ACCEPTANCE OF SEWERS

Figure 15

269

5. Water supply provisions. All subdivisions for the sale or lease of lots must have definite provisions concerning water facilities. These must meet all local health standards. If water facilities do not exist or if exceptions or reservations are made by the water company, a full disclosure must be made to the prospective purchaser.

6. Health permit. A health permit must be obtained from the appropriate health department. This permit should show the sewage disposal plans, if public sewers are not available. If septic tanks or cesspools are to be used in the tract, permission must be obtained from the appropriate health officers.

7. Fire protection letter. If fire protection is available, a letter should be obtained from the fire department or fire district, stating that protection will be furnished. When no such protection is to be given, the subdivider, owner, or his agent must so state.

8. Flood and drainage. The owner, subdivider, or his agent must obtain from the flood control engineers (county or city), a letter stating that proper provisions have been made for flood and drainage problems. In some states, counties, or cities, it may be necessary for the developer to furnish these reports at his own expense, if jurisdictional health officials are not available.

9. Fill report. When filled ground is involved in the subdivision, the developer must show an engineer's filled ground report. This report should contain the number of lots filled, the depth of the fill, the method of filling, the amount of compaction and an opinion from the engineer on the ability of the fill to sustain construction loads.

10. Private road cost estimate. Where roads are other than public dedicated roads, the developer is usually required to submit to the appropriate governmental officials an estimate from an engineer showing the cost per linear foot to construct roads to county standards, and the estimated cost per linear foot for maintaining such roads. Ordinances sometimes place limitations on the length, width, and use of private roads.

Financing the subdivision

Before the property is actually purchased for subdivision purposes, the subdivider must not only check out the feasibility of subdividing but must also check the availability of financing. When FHA or VA financing is contemplated, he should check with the local lending agencies, or with the district FHA or VA office, to determine their requirements and specification.

The subdivider may take one of three courses of action in determining the above:

1. Purchase the property for cash
2. Option the property
3. Enter into a conditional escrow

The first is not practical, because if the subdivision proves unfeasible, he will not want the land. The option agreement or conditional escrow, however, should allow him enough time to make his feasibility study, have a tentative map prepared, and receive a firm commitment on his financing, both for the purchase of the property and for development. The time allowed should be a minimum period of six months; one year is desirable. If the land does not prove suitable for a subdivision, or if financing cannot be obtained, the subdivider is released from his contract. He may, however, lose his option money. If the above is a condition of the escrow, deposit moneys will usually be returned to the subdivider.

DISPOSITION OF MONEYS

A blanket mortgage or deed of trust covers an entire parcel of land. It is unlawful for the developer, owner, or subdivider to sell or lease lots within a subdivision, unless these lots can be released free and clear from the blanket encumbrance. A parcel release clause provides that a stipulated parcel within a subdivision may be released after a certain sum of money has been paid on the lot to the holder of the blanket encumbrance. When no parcel release clause exists, the laws of each state must be observed.

Review questions

1. Give at least three issues in planning that usually must be faced by planning commission or board. Discuss each.
2. What is the purpose of a "master plan"? Obtain a copy of the master plan of your community. What objectives were set up in developing the plan?
3. Define the following: (a) nonconforming use, (b) conditional use permit, (c) spot zoning.
4. Explain the major differences between community apartment houses and condominiums.
5. Describe the process that a subdivider might go through in the development of a subdivision.

Definition
of Words and Phrases

A. L. T. A. Title Policy: A type of title insurance policy issued by title insurance companies which expands the risks normally insured against under the standard type policy to include unrecorded mechanic's liens, unrecorded physical easements, facts a physical survey would show, water and mineral rights, and rights of parties in possession, such as tenants and buyers under unrecorded instruments.

Abatement of Nuisance: Extinction or termination of a nuisance.

Abstract of Judgment: A condensation of the essential provisions of a court judgment.

Abstract of Title: A summary of the conveyances, transfers, and any other facts relied upon as evidence of title, together with any other elements of record that may impair the title.

Acceleration Clause: Clause in trust deed or mortgage giving lender right to call all sums owing him to be immediately due and payable upon the happening of a certain event.

Acceptance: When the seller or agent's principal agrees to the terms of the agreement of sale, approves the negotiation on the part of the agent, and acknowledges receipt of the deposit in subscribing to the agreement of sale, that act is termed an acceptance.

Access Right: The right of an owner to have ingress and egress to and from his property.

Accretion: An addition to land from natural causes as, for example, from gradual action of the ocean or river waters.

Accrued Depreciation: The difference between the cost of replacement new, as of the date of the appraisal, and the present appraised value.

Definitions and phrases as set forth in the Real Estate Commissioner's *Reference Book*, 1970 ed. (Department of Real Estate, State of California), pp. 477–96. Reprinted by permission.

Acknowledgment: A formal declaration before a duly authorized officer, by a person who has executed an instrument, that such execution is his act and deed.

Acoustical tile: Blocks of fiber, mineral or metal, with small holes or rough-textured surface to absorb sound, used as covering for interior walls and ceilings.

Acquisition: The act or process by which a person procures property.

Acre: A measure of land equaling 160 square rods, or 4,840 square yards, or 43,560 square feet, or a tract about 208.71 feet square.

Administrator: A person appointed by the probate court to administer the estate of a person deceased.

Ad Valorem: According to valuation.

Adverse Possession: The open and notorious possession and occupancy under an evident claim or right, in denial or opposition to the title of another claimant.

Affidavit: A statement or declaration reduced to writing, sworn to or affirmed before some officer who has authority to administer an oath or affirmation.

Affirm: To confirm, to aver, to ratify, to verify.

Agency: The relationship between principal and agent that arises out of a contract, either expressed or implied, written or oral, wherein the agent is employed by the principal to do certain acts dealing with a third party.

Agent: One who represents another from whom he has derived authority.

Agreement of Sale: A written agreement or contract between seller and purchaser in which they reach a meeting of minds on the terms and conditions of the sale.

Alienation: The transferring of property to another; the transfer of property and possession of lands, or other things, from one person to another.

Alluvion: (Alluvium) Soil deposited by accretion. Increase of earth on a shore or bank of a river.

Amenities: Satisfaction of enjoyable living to be derived from a home; conditions of agreeable living or a beneficial influence arising from the location or improvements.

Amortization: The liquidation of a financial obligation on an installment basis; also, recovery, over a period, of cost or value.

Appraisal: An estimate and opinion of value; a conclusion resulting from the analysis of facts.

Appraiser: One qualified by education, training and experience who is hired to estimate the value of real and personal property based on experience, judgment, facts, and use of formal appraisal processes.

Appurtenance: Something annexed to another thing, which may be transferred incident to it. That which belongs to another thing, as a barn, dwelling, garage, or orchard, is incident to the land to which it is attached.

Assessed Valuation: A valuation placed upon property by a public officer or board, as a basis for taxation.

Assessed Value: Value placed on property as a basis for taxation.

Assessment: The valuation of property for the purpose of levying a tax, or the amount of the tax levied.

Assessor: The official who has the responsibility of determining assessed values.

Assignment: A transfer or making over to another of the whole of any property, real or personal, in possession or in action, or of any estate or right therein.

Assignor: One who assigns or transfers property.

Assigns; Assignees: Those to whom property shall be transferred.

Assumption Agreement: An undertaking of a debt or obligation, primarily resting upon another person.

Assumption of Mortgage: The taking of title to property by a grantee, wherein he assumes liability for payment of an existing note secured by a mortgage or deed of trust against the property, becoming a coguarantor for the payment of a mortgage or deed of trust note.

Attachment: Seizure of property by court order, usually done to have it available in event a certain judgment is obtained in a pending suit.

Attest: To affirm to be true or genuine; an official act establishing authenticity.

Attorney in Fact: One who is authorized to perform certain acts for another under a power of attorney; power of attorney may be limited to a specific act or acts, or be general.

Avulsion: The sudden tearing away or removal of land by action of water flowing through it.

Backfill: The replacement of excavated earth into a hole or against a structure.

Balloon Payment: When the final installment payment on a note is greater than the preceding installment payments and it pays the note in full, such final installment is termed a balloon payment.

Baseboard: A board placed against the wall next to the floor around a room.

Base and Meridian: Imaginary lines used by surveyors to find and describe the location of private or public lands.

Base Molding: Molding used at top of baseboard.

Base Shoe: Molding used at junction of baseboard and floor. Commonly called a carpet strip.

Batten: Narrow strips of wood or metal used to cover joints, interiorly or exteriorly; also used for decorative effect.

Beam: A structural member transversely supporting a load.

Bearing Wall or Partition: A wall or partition supporting any vertical load, in addition to its own weight.

Bench Marks: A location indicated on a durable marker by surveyors.

Beneficiary: (1) One entitled to the benefit of a trust; (2) One who receives profit from an estate, the title of which is vested in a trustee; (3) The lender on the security of a note and deed of trust.

Bequeath: To give or hand down, by will; to leave by will.

Bequest: That which is given by the terms of a will.

Betterment: An improvement upon property that increases the property value and is considered as a capital asset, as distinguished from repairs or replacements where the original character or cost is unchanged.

Bill of Sale: A written instrument given to pass title of personal property from vendor to the vendee.

Blacktop: Asphalt paving used in streets and driveways.

Blanket Mortgage: A single mortgage that covers more than one piece of real property.

Blighted Area: A declining area in which real property values are seriously affected by destructive economic forces, such as encroaching inharmonious property usages, infiltration of lower social and economic classes of inhabitants, or rapidly depreciating buildings.

Board Foot: A unit of measurement of lumber; one foot wide, one foot long, one inch thick; 144 cubic inches.

Bona Fide: In good faith, without fraud.

Bracing: Framing lumber nailed at an angle in order to provide rigidity.

Breach: The breaking of a law, or failure of duty, either by omission or commission.

Breezeway: A covered porch or passage, open on two sides, connecting house and garage or two parts of the house.

Bridging: Small wood or metal pieces used to brace floor joists.

B.T.U.: British thermal unit. The quantity of heat required to raise the temperature of one pound of water one degree Fahrenheit.

Building Line: A line set by law a certain distance from a street line in front of which an owner cannot build on his lot (a setback line).

Building Paper: A heavy waterproofed paper used as sheathing in wall or roof construction as a protection against air passage and moisture.

Built-in: Cabinets or similar features built as part of the house.

Bundle of Rights: Beneficial interests or rights.

Capital Assets: Assets of a permanent nature used in the production of an income, such as: land, buildings, machinery, and equipment. Under income tax law, it is usually distinguishable from "inventory," which comprises assets held for sale to customers in ordinary course of the taxpayer's trade or business.

Capitalization: In appraising, determining value of property by considering net income and percentage of reasonable return on the investment.

Capitalization Rate: The rate of interest that is considered a reasonable return on the investment, and used in the process of determining value based upon net income.

Casement Window: Frames of wood or metal, which swing outward.

Caveat Emptor: Let the buyer beware. The buyer must examine the goods or property and buy at his own risk.

Chain of Title: A history of conveyances and encumbrances affecting the title from the time the original patent was granted, or as far back as records are available.

Chattel Mortgage: A personal property mortgage. (See definition of *Security Agreement* and *Security Interest*.)

Chattel Real: An estate related to real estate, such as a lease on real property.

Chattels: Goods or every species of property movable or immovable which are not real property.

Circuit Breaker: An electrical device which automatically interrupts an electric circuit when an overload occurs; may be used instead of a fuse to protect each circuit and can be reset.

Clapboard: Boards, usually thicker at one edge, used for siding.

Cloud on the Title: Any conditions revealed by a title search that affect the title to property, usually relatively unimportant items, but which cannot be removed without a quitclaim deed or court action.

Codicil: In law, an addition to a will, to change or explain some provision or to add new ones. An appendix or supplement.

Collar Beam: A beam that connects the pairs of opposite roof rafters above the attic floor.

Collateral: The property subject to the security interest. (See definition of *Security Interest.*)

Collateral Security: A separate obligation attached to contract to guarantee its performance; the transfer of property or of other contracts, or valuables, to insure the performance of a principal agreement.

Collusion: An agreement between two or more persons to defraud another of his rights by the forms of law, or to obtain an object forbidden by law.

Color of Title: That which appears to be good title but which is not title in fact.

Combed Plywood: A grooved building material used primarily for interior finish.

Commercial Acre: A term applied to the remainder of an acre of newly subdivided land after the area devoted to streets, sidewalks and curbs, and so on, has been deducted from the acre.

Commercial Paper: Bills of exchange used in commercial trade.

Commission: An agent's compensation for performing the duties of his agency; in real estate practice, a percentage of the selling price of property, or percentage of rentals.

Commitment: A pledge, promise, or firm agreement.

Common Law: The body of law that grew from customs and practices developed and used in England "since the memory of man runneth not to the contrary."

Community Property: Property accumulated through joint efforts of husband and wife.

Compaction: Whenever extra soil is added to a lot to fill in low places or to raise the level of the lot, the added soil is often too loose and soft to sustain the weight of buildings. Therefore, it is necessary to compact the added soil so that it will carry the weight of buildings without the danger of their tilting, settling or cracking.

Competent: Legally qualified.

Compound Interest: Interest paid on original principal, and also on the accrued and unpaid interest which has accumulated.

Condemnation: The act of taking private property for public use by a political subdivision; declaration that a structure is unfit for use.

Conditional Commitment: A commitment of a definite loan amount for some future unknown purchaser of satisfactory credit standing.

Conditional Sale Contract: A contract for the sale of property stating that delivery is to be made to the buyer, title to remain vested in the seller until the conditions of the contract have been fulfilled. (See definition of *Security Interest*.)

Condominium: A system of individual fee ownership of units in a multi-family structure, combined with joint ownership of common areas of the structure and the land. (Sometimes referred to as a vertical subdivision.)

Conduit: A metal pipe in which electrical wiring is installed.

Confession of Judgment: An entry of judgment upon the debtor's voluntary admission or confession.

Confirmation of Sale: A court approval of the sale of property by an executor, administrator, guardian or conservator.

Consideration: Anything of value given to induce entering into a contract; it may be money, personal services, or even love and affection.

Constructive Notice: Notice given by the public records.

Contract: An agreement, either written or oral, to do or not to do certain things.

Consumer Goods: Goods used or bought for use primarily for personal, family or household purposes.

Conversion: Change from one character or use to another.

Conveyance: The transfer of the title of land from one to another. It denotes an instrument that carries from one person to another an interest in land.

Corporation: A group of persons established and treated by law as an individual or unit with rights and liabilities, or both, distinct from those of the persons composing it.

A corporation is a creature of law with certain powers and duties of a natural person. Created by law, it may continue for any length of time the law prescribes.

Counterflashing: Flashing used on chimneys at roofline to cover shingle flashing and to prevent moisture entry.

Covenant: Agreements written into deeds and other instruments promising performance or nonperformance of certain acts, or stipulating certain uses or nonuses of the property.

C.P.M.: Certified Property Manager; a member of the Institute of Real Property Management of the National Association of Real Estate Boards.

Crawl Hole: Exterior or interior opening permitting access underneath building, as required by building codes.

C.R.E.A.: California Real Estate Association.

Curtail Schedule: A listing of the amounts by which the principal sum of an obligation is to be reduced by partial payments, and of the dates when each payment will become payable.

Curtesy: The right that a husband has in a wife's estate at her death.

Damages: The indemnity recoverable by a person who has sustained an injury, either in his person, property, or relative rights, through the act or default of another.

Debtor: This is the party who "owns" the property which is subject to the security interest. Previously he was known as the *mortgagor* or the *pledgor*.

Deciduous Trees: Lose their leaves in the autumn and winter.

Deck: Usually an open porch on the roof of a ground or lower floor, porch, or wing.

Dedication: An appropriation of land by its owner for some public use, accepted for such use by authorized public officials on behalf of the public.

Deed: Written instrument which, when properly executed and delivered, conveys title.

Default: Failure to fulfill a duty or promise or to discharge an obligation; omission or failure to perform any act.

Defeasance Clause: The clause in a mortgage that gives the mortgagor the right to redeem his property upon the payment of his obligations to the mortgagee.

Deferred Maintenance: Existing but unfulfilled requirements for repairs and rehabilitation.

Deficiency Judgment: A judgment given when the security pledge for a loan does not satisfy the debt upon its default.

Depreciation: Loss of value in real property brought about by age, physical deterioration, or functional or economic obsolescence. Broadly, a loss in value from any cause.

Desist and Refrain Order: The Real Estate Commissioner is empowered by law to issue an order directing a person to desist and refrain from committing an act in violation of the real estate law.

Deterioration: Impairment of condition. One of the causes of depreciation and reflecting the loss in value brought about by wear and tear, disintegration, use in service, and the action of the elements.

Devisee: One who receives a bequest made by will.

Devisor: One who bequeaths by will.

Directional Growth: The location or direction toward which the residential sections of a city are destined or determined to grow.

Donee: A person to whom a gift is made.

Donor: A person who makes a gift.

Dower: The right which a wife has in her husband's estate at his death.

Duress: Unlawful constraint exercised upon a person whereby he is forced to do some act against his will.

Easement: Created by grant or agreement for a specific purpose, an easement is the right, privilege or interest that one party has in the land of another (example: right of way).

Eaves: The lower part of a roof projecting over the wall.

Economic Life: The period over which a property will yield a return on the investment, over and above the economic or ground rent due to land.

Eminent Domain: The right of the government to acquire property for necessary public or quasi-public use, by condemnation; the owner must be fairly compensated.

Encroachment: Trespass; the building of a structure or construction of any improvements, partly or wholly on the property of another.

Encumbrance: Anything which affects or limits the fee simple title to property, such as mortgages, easements or restrictions of any kind. Liens are special encumbrances that make the property security for the payment of a debt or obligation, such as mortgages and taxes.

Equity: The interest or value which an owner has in real estate over and above the liens against it; branch of remedial justice by and through which relief is afforded to suitors in courts of equity.

Equity of Redemption: The right to redeem property during the foreclosure period, such as a mortgagor's right to redeem within a year after foreclosure sale.

Erosion: The wearing away of land by the action of water, wind or glacial ice.

Escalator Clause: A clause in a contract providing for the upward or downward adjustment of certain items to cover specified contingencies.

Escheat: The reverting of property to the state when there are no heirs capable of inheriting.

Escrow: The deposit of instruments and funds with instructions to a third neutral party to carry out the provisions of an agreement or contract; when everything is deposited for carrying out the instructions, it is called a complete or perfect escrow.

Estate: As applied to the real estate practice, the term signifies the quantity of interest, share, right, equity, of which riches or fortune may consist, in real property; the degree, quantity, nature, and extent of interest which a person has in real property.

Estate for Life: A freehold estate, not of inheritance, but which is held by the tenant for his own life or the life or lives of one or more other persons, or for an indefinite period that may extend for the life or lives of persons in being, and beyond the period of life.

Estate for Years: An interest in lands by virtue of a contract for the possession of them for a definite and limited period of time. A lease may be said to be an estate for years.

Estate of Inheritance: An estate which may descend to heirs. All freehold estates are estates of inheritance, except estates for life.

Estate of Will: The occupation of lands and tenements by a tenant for an indefinite period, terminable by one or both parties.

Estoppel: A doctrine which bars one from asserting rights that are inconsistent with a previous position or representation.

Ethics: That branch of moral science, idealism, and justness that treats of the duties that a member of a profession or craft owes to the public, to his clients or patron, and to his professional brethren or members.

Exclusive Agency Listing: A written instrument giving one agent the right to sell property for a specified time but reserving the right of the owner to sell the property himself without the payment of a commission.

Exclusive-Right-to-Sell Listing: A written agreement between owner and agent giving agent the right to collect a commission if the property is sold by anyone during the term of his agreement.

Execute: To complete, to make, to perform, to do, to follow out; to execute a deed, to make a deed, especially including signing, sealing, and delivery; to execute a contract is to perform the contract, to follow out to the end, to complete.

Executor: A person named in a will to carry out its provisions concerning the disposition of the estate of a person deceased.

Expansible House: Home designed for further expansion and additions in the future.

Expansion Joint: A bituminous fiber strip used to separate units of concrete to prevent cracking because of expansion as a result of temperature changes.

Facade: Front of a building.

Fee: An estate of inheritance in real property.

Fee Simple: In modern estates, the terms "fee" and "fee simple" are substantially synonymous. The term "fee" is of Old English derivation. "Fee simple absolute" is an estate in real property, by which the owner has the greatest power over the title which it is possible to have; an absolute estate. In modern use it expressly establishes the title of real property in the owner, without limitation or end. He may dispose of it by sale, or trade, or will, as he chooses.

Fiduciary: A person in a position of trust and confidence, as principal and broker: broker as fiduciary owes certain loyalty which cannot be breached under rules of agency.

Financing Statement: This is the instrument that is filed in order to give public notice of the security interest, and thereby protect the interest of the secured parties in the collateral. See definitions of *Security Interest and Secured Party.*

Finish Floor: Finish floor strips are applied over wood joists, deadening felt, and diagonal subflooring before finish floor is installed; finish floor is the final covering on the floor: wood, linoleum, cork, tile, or carpet.

Fire Stop: A solid, tight closure of a concealed space, placed to prevent the spread of fire and smoke through such a space.

Fixtures: Appurtenances attached to the land, or improvements, that usually cannot be removed without agreement, as they are real property; examples: plumbing fixtures, store fixtures built into the property, and the like.

Flashing: Sheet metal or other material used to protect a building from seepage of water.

Footing: The base or bottom of a foundation wall, pier, or column.

Foreclosure: Procedure whereby property pledged as security for a debt is sold to pay the debt in event of default in payments or terms.

Forfeiture: Loss of money or anything of value, due to failure to perform.

Foundation: The supporting portion of a structure below the first floor construction, or below grade, including the footings.

Fraud: The intentional and successful employment of any cunning, deception, collusion, or artifice, used to circumvent, cheat or deceive another person, whereby that person acts upon it to the loss of his property and to his legal injury.

Front Foot: Property measurement for sale or valuation purposes; the property measures by the front foot on its street line—each front foot extending the depth of the lot.

Frostline: The depth of frost penetration in the soil. Varies in different parts of the country. Footings should be placed below this depth to prevent movement.

Furring: Strips of wood or metal applied to a wall or other surface to even it, to form an air space, or to give the wall an appearance of greater thickness.

Gable Roof: A pitched roof with sloping sides.

Gambrel Roof: A curb roof, having a steep lower slope with a flatter upper slope above.

Gift Deed: A deed for which the consideration is love and affection and where there is no material consideration.

Girder: A large beam used to support beams, joists and partitions.

Grade: Ground level at the foundation.

Graduated Lease: Lease that provides for a varying rental rate, often based upon future determination; sometimes, rent is based upon result of periodical appraisals; used largely in long-term leases.

Grant: A technical term made use of in deeds of conveyance of lands to import a transfer.

Grantee: The purchaser; a person to whom a grant is made.

Grantor: Seller of property; one who signs a deed.

Grid: A chart used in rating the borrower risk, property, and the neighborhood.

Gross Income: Total income from property before any expenses are deducted.

Ground Lease: An agreement for the use of the land only, sometimes secured by improvements placed on the land by the user.

Ground Rent: Earnings of improved property credited to earnings of the ground itself after allowance is made for earnings of improvements; often termed *economic rent.*

Header: A beam placed perpendicular to joists and to which joists are nailed in framing for chimney, stairway, or other opening.

Highest and Best Use: An appraisal phrase meaning that use which, at the time of an appraisal, is most likely to produce the greatest net return to the land or buildings over a given period of time; that use which will produce the greatest amount of amenities or profit. This is the starting point for appraisal.

Hip Roof: A pitched roof with sloping sides and ends.

Holder in Due Course: One who has taken a note, check or bill of exchange in due course:

(1) Before it was overdue;

(2) In good faith and for value;

(3) Without knowledge that it has been previously dishonored and without notice of any defect at the time it was negotiated.

Homestead: A home upon which the owner or owners have recorded a Declaration of Homestead, as provided by state statutes; protects home against judgments up to specified amounts.

Hundred Percent Location: A city retail business location which is considered the best available for attracting business.

Hypothecate: To give a thing as security without giving up possession of it.

Incompetent: One who is mentally incapable; any person who, though not insane, is, by reason of old age, disease, weakness of mind, or any other cause, unable, unassisted, to properly manage and take care of himself or his property, and by reason thereof would be likely to be deceived or imposed upon by artful or designing persons.

Increment: An increase. Most frequently used to refer to the increase of value of land that accompanies population growth and increasing wealth in the community. The term "unearned increment" is used in this connection, since values are supposed to have increased without effort on the part of the owner.

Indirect Lighting: The light is reflected from the ceiling or other object external to the fixture.

Indorsement: The act of signing one's name on the back of a check or a note, with or without further qualification.

Injunction: A writ or order issued under the seal of a court to restrain one or more parties to a suit or proceeding from doing an act which is deemed to be inequitable or unjust in regard to the rights of some other party or parties in the suit or proceeding.

Installment Note: A note which provides that payments of a certain sum be paid on the dates specified in the instrument.

Instrument: A written legal document created to effect the rights of the parties.

Interest Rate: The percentage of a sum of money charged for its use.

Intestate: A person who dies having made no will, or one defective in form, in which case, his estate descends to his heirs at law or next of kin.

Involuntary Lien: A lien imposed against property without consent of an owner; example: taxes, special assessments, and federal income tax.

Irrevocable: Incapable of being recalled or revoked; unchangeable.

Irrigation Districts: Quasi-political districts created under special laws to provide for water services to property owners in the district, an operation governed to a great extent by law.

Jalousie: A slatted blind or shutter, like a venetian blind, but used on the exterior to protect against rain as well as to control sunlight.

Jamb: The side post or lining of a doorway, window or other opening.

Joint: The space between the adjacent surfaces of two components joined and held together by nails, glue, cement, or mortar.

Joint Note: A note signed by two or more persons who have equal liability for payment.

Joint Tenancy: Joint ownership by two or more persons with right of survivorship; all joint tenants own equal interest and have equal rights in the property.

Joist: One of a series of parallel beams to which the boards of a floor and ceiling laths are nailed, and in turn supported by larger beams, girders, or bearing walls.

Judgment: The final determination of a court of competent jurisdiction of a matter presented to it; money judgments provide for the payment of claims presented to the court, or are awarded as damages, and so on.

Jurisdiction: The authority by which judicial officers take cognizance of and decide cases; the power to hear and determine a case; the right and power of a judicial officer to enter upon the inquiry.

Laches: Delay or negligence in asserting one's legal rights.

Land Contract: A contract ordinarily used in connection with the sale of property in cases when the seller does not wish to convey title until all or a certain part of the purchase price is paid by the buyer; often used when property is sold on small down payment.

Lateral Support: The support that the soil of an adjoining owner gives to his neighbors' land.

Lath: A building material of wood, metal, gypsum, or insulating board fastened to the frame of a building to act as a plaster base.

Lease: A contract between owner and tenant, setting forth conditions upon which tenant may occupy and use the property, and the term of the occupancy.

Legal Description: A description recognized by law: a description by which property can be definitely located by reference to government surveys or approved recorded maps.

Lessee: One who contracts to rent property under a lease contract.

Lessor: An owner who enters into a lease with a tenant.

Lien: A form of encumbrance that usually makes property security for the payment of a debt or discharge of an obligation. Examples: judgments, taxes, mortgages, and deeds of trust.

Life Estate: An estate measured by the natural life of a person.

Limited Partnership: A partnership with some partners whose contribution and liability are limited.

Lintel: A horizontal board that supports the load over an opening such as a door or window.

Lis Pendens: Suit pending, usually recorded to give constructive notice of pending litigation.

Listing: An employment contract between principal and agent authorizing the agent to perform services for the principal involving the latter's property; listing contracts are entered into for the purpose of securing persons to buy, lease or rent property. Employment of an agent by a prospective purchaser or lessee to locate property for purchase or lease may be considered a listing.

Louver: An opening with a series of horizontal slats set at an angle to permit ventilation without admitting rain, sunlight, or vision.

M.A.I.: Designates a person who is a member of the American Institute of Appraisers of the National Association of Real Estate Boards.

Margin of Security: The difference between the amount of the mortgage loan(s) and the appraised value of the property.

Marginal Land: Land that barely pays the cost of working or using.

Market Price: The price paid regardless of pressures, motives or intelligence.

Market Value: (1) The price at which a willing seller would sell and a willing buyer would buy, neither being under abnormal pressure; (2) As defined by the courts, is the highest price estimated in terms of money that a property will bring if exposed for sale in the open market allowing a reasonable time to find a purchaser with knowledge of property's use and capabilities for use.

Marketable Title: Merchantable title; title free and clear of objectionable liens or encumbrances.

Material Fact: A fact is material if the agent should realize it would be likely to affect the judgment of the principal in giving his consent to the agent to enter into the particular transaction on the specified terms.

Meridians: Imaginary north–south lines that intersect base lines to form a starting point for the measurement of land.

Metes and Bounds: A term used in describing the boundary lines of land, setting forth all the boundary lines, together with their terminal points and angles.

Minor: All persons under 21 years of age, except that any person lawfully married who is 18 or over is deemed an adult person for the purpose of entering into any engagement or transaction respecting property.

Molding: Usually patterned strips used to provide ornamental variation of outline or contour, such as cornices, bases, window and door jambs.

Monument: A fixed object and point established by surveyors to establish land locations.

Moratorium: The temporary suspension, usually by statute, of the enforcement of liability for debt.

Mortgage: An instrument recognized by law by which property is hypothecated to secure the payment of a debt or obligation; procedure for foreclosure in event of default is established by statute.

Mortgage Guaranty Insurance: Insurance against financial loss available to mortgage lenders from Mortgage Guaranty Insurance Corporation, a private company organized in 1956.

Mortgagee: One to whom a mortgagor gives a mortgage to secure a loan or performance of an obligation; a lender. (See definition of *Secured Party.*)

Mortgagor: One who gives a mortgage on his property to secure a loan or assure performance of an obligation; a borrower. (See definition of *Debtor.*)

Multiple Listing: A listing, usually an exclusive right to sell, taken by a member of an organization composed of real estate brokers, with the provisions that all members will have the opportunity to find an interested client; a cooperative listing.

Mutual Water Company: A water company organized by or for water users in a given district with the object of securing an ample water supply at a reasonable rate; stock is issued to users.

NAREB: National Association of Real Estate Boards.

Negotiable: Capable of being negotiated; assignable or transferable in the ordinary course of business.

Net Listing: A listing which provides that the agent may retain as compensation for his services all sums received over and above a net price to the owner.

Note: A signed written instrument acknowledging a debt and promising payment.

Notice of Nonresponsibility: A notice provided by law designed to relieve a property owner from responsibility for the cost of work done on the property or materials furnished therefor; notice must be verified, recorded and posted.

Notice to Quit: A notice to a tenant to vacate rented property.

Obsolescence: Loss in value due to reduced desirability and usefulness of a structure because its design and construction become obsolete; loss because of becoming old-fashioned and not in keeping with modern needs, with consequent loss of income.

Offset Statement: Statement by owner of property or owner of lien against property, setting forth the present status of liens against said property.

Open-end Mortgage: A mortgage containing a clause that permits the mortgagor to borrow additional money after the loan has been reduced, without rewriting the mortgage.

Open Listing: An authorization given by a property owner to a real estate agent wherein said agent is given the nonexclusive right to secure a purchaser; open listings may be given to any number of agents without liability to compensate any except the one who first secures a buyer ready, willing and able to meet the terms of the listing, or secures the acceptance by the seller of a satisfactory offer.

Option: A right given for a consideration to purchase or lease a property upon specified terms within a specified time.

Oral Contract: A verbal agreement; one which is not reduced to writing.

Orientation: Placing a house on its lot with regard to its exposure to the rays of the sun, prevailing winds, privacy from the street and protection from outside noises.

Overhang: The part of the roof extending beyond the walls, to shade buildings and cover walks.

Over-Improvement: An improvement which is not the highest and best use for the site on which it is placed, because of excess size or cost.

Par Value: Market value, nominal value.

Partition Action: Court proceedings by which co-owners seek to sever their joint ownership.

Partnership: A decision of the California Supreme Court has defined a partnership in the following terms: "A partnership between partners themselves may be defined to be a contract of two or more persons to unite their property, labor or skill, or some of them, in prosecution of some joint or lawful business, and to share the profits in certain proportions."

Party Wall: A wall erected on the line between two adjoining properties, which are under different ownership, for the use of both properties.

Parquet Floor: Hardwood laid in squares or patterns.

Patent: Conveyance of title to government land.

Penny: The term, as applied to nails, serves as a measure of nail length and is abbreviated by the letter "d".

Percentage Lease: Lease on property, the rental for which is determined by amount of business done by the lessee, usually a percentage of gross receipts from the business with provision for a minimum rental.

Perimeter Heating: Baseboard heating, or any system in which the heat registers are located along the outside walls of a room, especially under the windows.

Personal Property: Any property that is not real property.

Pier: A column of masonry, usually rectangular in horizontal cross section, used to support other structural members.

Pitch: The incline or rise of a roof.

Plate: A horizontal board placed on a wall or supported on posts or studs to carry the trusses of a roof or rafters directly; a shoe, or base member, as of a partition or other frame; a small flat board placed on or in a wall to support girders, or rafters.

Pledge: The depositing of personal property by a debtor with a creditor as security for a debt or engagement.

Pledgee: One who is given a pledge or a security. (See definition of *Secured Party*.)

Pledgor: One who offers a pledge or gives security. (See definition of *Debtor*.)

Plottage Increment: The appreciation in unit value created by joining smaller ownerships into one large single ownership.

Plywood: Laminated wood made up in panels; several thicknesses of wood glued together with grain at different angles for strength.

Police Power: The right of the state to enact laws and enforce them for the order, safety, health, morals and general welfare of the public.

Power of Attorney: An instrument authorizing a person to act as the agent of the person granting it, and a general power authorizing the agent to act generally in behalf of the principal. A special power limits the agent to a specific act: a landowner may grant an agent special power of attorney to convey a single and specific parcel of property. Under the provisions of a general power of attorney, the agent having the power may convey any or all property of the principal granting the general power of attorney.

Prefabricated House: A house manufactured, and sometimes partly assembled, before delivery to building site.

Prepayment Penalty: Penalty for the payment of a mortgage or trust deed note before it actually becomes due.

Prescription: The securing of title to property by adverse possession, by occupying it for the period determined by law barring action for recovery.

Prima Facie: Presumptive on its face.

Principal: The employer of an agent.

Privity: Mutual relationship to the same rights of property, contractural relationship.

Procuring Cause: That cause originating from series of events that, without break in continuity, results in the prime object of an agent's employment producing a final buyer.

Proration of Taxes: To divide or prorate the taxes equally or proportionately to time of use.

Purchase Money Mortgage or Trust Deed: A trust deed or mortgage given as part or all of the purchase consideration for property.

Quarter Round: A molding that presents a profile of a quarter circle.

Quiet Enjoyment: Right of an owner to the use of property without interference of possession.

Quiet Title: A court action brought to establish title; to remove a cloud on the title.

Quitclaim Deed: A deed to relinquish any interest in property that the grantor may have.

Radiant Heating: A method of heating, usually consisting of coils or pipes placed in the floor, wall, or ceiling.

Rafter: One of a series of boards of a roof designed to support roof loads. The rafters of a flat roof are sometimes called *roof joists.*

Range: A strip of land six miles wide determined by a government survey, running in a north–south direction.

Ratification: The adoption or approval of an act performed on behalf of a person without previous authorization.

Real Estate Board: An organization whose membership consists primarily of real estate brokers and salesmen.

Real Estate Trust: A special arrangement under federal and state law whereby investors may pool funds for investments in real estate and mortgages, yet escape corporation taxes.

Realtor: A real estate broker holding active membership in a real estate board affiliated with the National Association of Real Estate Boards.

Recapture: The rate of interest necessary to provide for the return of an investment, not to be confused with interest rate, which is a rate of interest on an investment.

Reconveyance: The transfer of the title of land from one person to the immediate preceding owner. This particular instrument or transfer is commonly used in California when the performance or debt is satisfied under the terms of a deed of trust, when the trustee conveys the title he has held on condition back to the owner.

Redemption: Buying back one's property after a judicial sale.

Reformation: An action to correct a mistake in a deed or other document.

Release Clause: A stipulation that upon the payment of a specific sum of money to the holder of a trust deed or mortgage, the lien of the instrument as to a specific described lot or area shall be removed from the blanket lien on the whole area involved.

Remainder: An estate which vests after the termination of the prior estate, such as a life estate.

Rescission of Contract: The abrogation or annulling of contract; the revocation or repealing of contract by mutual consent by parties to the contract, or for cause by either party to the contract.

Reservation: A right retained by a grantor in conveying property.

Restriction: The term as used in relating to real property means the owner of real property is restricted or prohibited from doing certain things relating to the property, or using the property for certain purposes. For instance, the requirement in a deed that a lot may be used for the construction of not more than a one-party dwelling, costing not less than ten thousand dollars ($10,000), is termed to be a restriction; also, a legislative ordinance affecting all properties in a given area, requiring that improvements on property shall not be constructed any closer than 25 feet to the street curb, is a restriction by operation of law.

Reversion: The right to future possession or enjoyment by the person, or his heirs, creating the preceding estate.

Reversionary Interest: The interest that a person has in lands or other property upon the termination of the preceding estate.

Ridge: The horizontal line at the junction of the top edges of two sloping roof surfaces. The rafters at both slopes are nailed at the ridge.

Ridge Board: The board placed on edge at the ridge of the roof to support the upper ends of the rafters; also called roof tree, ridge piece, ridge plate, or ridgepole.

Right of Survivorship: Right to acquire the interest of a deceased joint owner; distinguishing feature of a joint tenancy.

Right of Way: A privilege operating as an easement upon land, whereby the owner does by grant, or by agreement, give to another the right to pass over his land, to construct a roadway, or use as a roadway, a specific part of his land, or the right to construct through and over his land, telephone, telegraph, or electric power lines, or the right to place underground water mains, gas mains, or sewer mains.

Riparian Rights: The right of a landowner to water on, under, or adjacent to his land.

Riser: The upright board at the back of each step of a stairway. In heating, a riser is a duct slanted upward to carry hot air from the furnace to the room above.

Roman Brick: Thin brick of slimmer proportions than standard building brick.

Sales Contract: A contract by which buyer and seller agree to terms of a sale.

Sale-leaseback: A situation where the owner of a piece of property wishes to sell the property and retain occupancy by leasing it from the buyer.

Sandwich Lease: A leasehold interest which lies between the primary lease and the operating lease.

Sash: Wood or metal frames containing one or more window panes.

Satisfaction: Discharge of mortgage or trust deed lien from the records upon payment of the evidenced debt.

Scribing: Fitting woodwork to an irregular surface.

Seal: An impression made to attest the execution of an instrument.

Secondary Financing: A loan secured by a second mortgage or trust deed on real property.

Secured Party: The party having the security interest. Thus, the *mortgagee*, the *conditional seller*, or the *pledgee* are all now referred to as the secured party.

Security Agreement: An agreement between the secured party and the debtor that creates the security interest.

Security Interest: A term designating the interest of the creditor in the property of the debtor in all types of credit transactions. It thus replaces such terms as the following: *chattel mortgage; pledge; trust receipt; chattel trust; equipment trust; conditional sale; inventory lien.*

Section: Section of land is established by government survey and contains 640 acres.

Separate Property: Property owned by a husband or wife which is not community property; property acquired by either spouse prior to marriage or by gift or devise after marriage.

Septic Tank: An underground tank in which sewage from the house is reduced to liquid by bacterial action and drained off.

Set-back Ordinance: An ordinance prohibiting the erection of a building or structure between the curb and the set-back line.

Severalty Ownership: Owned by one person only. Sole ownership.

Shake: A hand-split shingle, usually edge grained.

Sheathing: Structural covering, usually boards, plywood, or wallboards, placed over exterior studding or rafters of a house.

Sheriff's Deed: Deed given by court order in connection with sale of property to satisfy a judgment.

Sill: The lowest part of the frame of a house, resting on the foundation and supporting the uprights of the frame. The board or metal forming the lower side of an opening, as a door sill, window sill, and so on.

Sinking Fund: Fund set aside from the income from property which, with accrued interest, will eventually pay for replacement of the improvements.

Soil Pipe: Pipe carrying waste out from the house to the main sewer line.

Sole or Sole Plate: A member, usually a 2 by 4, on which wall and partition studs rest.

Span: The distance between structural supports such as walls, columns, piers, beams, girders, and trusses.

Special Assessment: Legal charge against real estate by a public authority to pay cost of public improvements such as: street lights, sidewalks, street improvements, etc.

Specific Performance: An action to compel performance of an agreement, e.g., sale of land.

S.R.A.:   Designates a person who is a member of the Society of Real Estate Appraisers.

Statute of Frauds: State law which provides that certain contracts must be in writing in order to be enforceable at law. Examples: real property lease for more than one year; agent's authorization to sell real estate.

Straight Line Depreciation: Definite sum set aside annually from income to pay cost of replacing improvements, without reference to interest it earns.

String, Stringer: A timber or other support for cross members. In stairs, the support on which the stair treads rest.

Studs or Studding: Vertical supporting timbers in the walls and partitions.

Subject to Mortgage: When a grantee takes a title to real property subject to mortgage, he is not responsible to the holder of the promissory note for the payment of any portion of the amount due. The most that he can lose in the event of a foreclosure is his equity in the property. See also "assumption of mortgage" in this section. In neither case is the original maker of the note released from his responsibility.

Sublease: A lease given by a lessee.

Subordinate: To make subject to, or junior to.

Subordination Clause: Clause in a junior or a second lien permitting retention of priority for prior liens. A subordination clause may also be used in a first deed of trust permitting it to be subordinated to subsequent liens as, for example, the liens of construction loans.

Subpoena: A process to cause a witness to appear and give testimony.

Subrogation: The substitution of another person in place of the creditor, to whose rights he succeeds in relation to the debt. The doctrine is used very often when one person agrees to stand surety for the performance of a contract by another person.

Surety: One who guarantees the performance of another: Guarantor.

Survey: The process by which a parcel of land is measured and its area is ascertained.

Tax Sale: Sale of property after a period of nonpayment of taxes.

Tenancy in Common: Ownership by two or more persons who hold undivided interest, without right of survivorship; interests need not be equal.

Tentative Map: The Subdivision Map Act requires subdividers to submit initially a tentative map of their tract to the local planning commission for study. The approval or disapproval of the planning commission is noted on the map. Thereafter, a final map of the tract embodying any changes requested by the planning commission is required to be filed with the planning commission.

Tenure in Land: The mode or manner by which an estate in lands is held.

Termites: Ant-like insects which feed on wood.

Termite Shield: A shield, usually of noncorrodible metal, placed on top of the foundation wall or around pipes to prevent passage of termites.

Testator: One who leaves a will in force at his death.

Threshold: A strip of wood or metal beveled on each edge and used above the finished floor under outside walls.

Time Is the Essence: One of the essential requirements to forming of a binding contract; contemplates a punctual performance.

Title: Evidence that owner of land is in lawful possession thereof, an instrument evidencing such ownership.

Title Insurance: Insurance written by a title company to protect property owner against loss if title is imperfect.

Topography: Nature of the surface of land; topography may be level, rolling, mountainous.

Torrens Title: System of title records provided by state law (no longer used in California).

Tort: A wrongful act; wrong, injury; violation of a legal right.

Township: A territorial subdivision six miles long, six miles wide and containing 36 sections, each one mile square.

Trade Fixtures: Articles of personal property annexed to real property, but which are necessary to the carrying on of a trade and are removable by the owner.

Trade-in: An increasingly popular method of guaranteeing an owner a minimum amount of cash on sale of his present property to permit him to purchase another. If the property is not sold within a specified time at the listed price, the broker agrees to arrange financing to purchase the property at an agreed upon discount.

Treads: Horizontal boards of a stairway.

Trim: The finish materials in a building, such as moldings, applied around openings (window trim, door trim) or at the floor and ceiling (baseboard, cornice, picture molding).

Trust Deed: Deed given by borrower to trustee to be held pending fulfillment of an obligation, which is ordinarily repayment of a loan to a beneficiary.

Trustee: One who holds property in trust for another to secure the performance of an obligation.

Trustor: One who deeds his property to a trustee to be held as security until he has performed his obligation to a lender under terms of a deed of trust.

Undue Influence: Taking any fraudulent or unfair advantage of another's weakness of mind, or distress or necessity.

Unearned Increment: An increase in value of real estate due to no effort on the part of the owner; often due to increase in population.

Uniform Commercial Code: Effective January 1, 1965. Establishes a unified and comprehensive scheme for regulation of security transactions in personal property, superseding the existing statutes on chattel mortgages, conditional sales, trust receipts, assignment of accounts receivable, and others in this field.

Urban Property: City property; closely settled property.

Usury: On a loan, claiming a rate of interest greater than that permitted by law.

Valid: Having force, or binding force; legally sufficient and authorized by law.

Valley: The internal angle formed by the junction of two sloping sides of a roof.

Valuation: Estimated worth or price. Estimation. The act of valuing by appraisal.

Vendee: A purchaser; buyer.

Vendor: A seller; one who disposes of a thing in consideration of money.

Veneer: Thin sheets of wood.

Vent: A pipe installed to provide a flow of air to or from a drainage system or to provide a circulation of air within such system to protect trap seals from siphonage and back pressure.

Verification: Sworn statement before a duly qualified officer to correctness of contents of an instrument.

Vested: Bestowed upon someone; secured by someone, such as title to property.

Void: To have no force or effect; that which is unenforceable.

Voidable: That which is capable of being adjudged void, but is not void unless action is taken to make it so.

Voluntary Lien: Any lien placed on property with consent of, or as a result of, the voluntary act of the owner.

Wainscoting: Wood lining of an interior wall; lower section of a wall, when finished differently from the upper part.

Waive: To relinquish, or abandon; to forego a right to enforce or require anything.

Warranty Deed: A deed used to convey real property which contains warranties of title and quiet possession, and the grantor thus agrees to defend the premises against the lawful claims of third persons. It is commonly used in other states but not in California where the grant deed has supplanted it. The modern practice of securing title insurance policies has reduced the importance of express and implied warranty in deeds.

Waste: The destruction, material alteration of, or injury to premises by a tenant for life or years.

Water Table: Distance from surface of ground to a depth at which natural groundwater is found.

Zone: The area set off by the proper authorities for specific use; subject to certain restrictions or restraints.

Zoning: Act of city or county authorities specifying type of use to which property may be put in specific areas.

Index

295